W9-CSI-415

nal Bank for Reconstruction and Development / The World Bank

000
ank.org
rldbank.org

uct of the staff of the International Bank for Reconstruction and Devel-
Bank. The findings, interpretations, and conclusions expressed in this
arily reflect the views of the Executive Directors of The World Bank or
represent.

oes not guarantee the accuracy of the data included in this work. The
nominations, and other information shown on any map in this work do
ent on the part of The World Bank concerning the legal status of any ter-
ient or acceptance of such boundaries.

ons

ublication is copyrighted. Copying and/or transmitting portions or all of
mission may be a violation of applicable law. The International Bank for
evelopment / The World Bank encourages dissemination of its work
nt permission to reproduce portions of the work promptly.
photocopy or reprint any part of this work, please send a request with
to the Copyright Clearance Center Inc., 222 Rosewood Drive, Danvers,
hone: 978-750-8400; fax: 978-750-4470; Internet: www.copyright.com.
n rights and licenses, including subsidiary rights, should be addressed to
her, The World Bank, 1818 H Street, NW, Washington, DC 20433, USA;
mail: pubrights@worldbank.org.

2-6
-6882-4
33-4
3-6883-1
3213-6882-4

or Design.

Cataloging-in-Publication Data

n growth : opportunities, constraints, and strategic
ulu; with Lopamudra Chakraborti ... [et al.].

conditions—1960– 2. Africa—Politics and
I. Chakraborti, Lopamudra. II. Title.

2007002731

CHALLENGES OF

AFRICAN GROWTH

CH

AFRI

Opportuniti

©2007 The Internatio
1818 H Street NW
Washington DC 2043
Telephone: 202-473-1
Internet: www.worldb
E-mail: feedback@wo

All rights reserved

1 2 3 4 10 09 08 07

This volume is a prod
opment / The World
volume do not necess
the governments they
    The World Bank d
boundaries, colors, de
not imply any judgem
ritory or the endorsen

Rights and Permiss
The material in this pu
this work without per
Reconstruction and I
and will normally gra
    For permission to
complete information
MA 01923, USA; telep
    All other queries
the Office of the Publi
fax: 202-522-2422; e-

ISBN-10: 0-8213-688
ISBN-13: 978-0-8213
eISBN-10: 0-8213-68
eISBN-13: 978-0-821
DOI: 10.1596/978-0-8

Cover design by: Nayl

Library of Congress
Ndulu, B. J.
  Challenges of Africa
directions / Benno N
    p. cm.
    ISBN 0-8213-6882-
    1. Africa—Economi
government—1960–
    HC800.N427 2007
    338.96—dc22

THE WORLD BANK
Washington, D.C.

Contents

Tables

Foreword

Recent years have seen renewed international attention on Africa, which, despite recent successes in terms of increases in economic growth, reduced conflict, expanded political liberalization, and substantial improvements in governance, remains the continent where poverty is the deepest. It is now widely accepted that reduction in poverty and achievement of the Millennium Development Goals require further acceleration of economic growth, especially in those countries with large populations where growth had been elusive. The experiences of East and South Asia have demonstrated that sustained, poverty-reducing growth is possible, and these experiences have been echoed across a number of African countries as well over the past decade.

This study reviews the past half-century of economic growth in Africa and elsewhere in the world and distills that experience into a set of policy recommendations for economic practitioners in Africa. Of course, the geographic, institutional, and historical situations of each of Africa's 48 countries are very diverse, so the general principles provided here can only serve as a guideline for deeper, country-specific analysis of the opportunities for, and challenges to, accelerated shared growth. Nevertheless, I believe the analysis presented in this study can help establish the questions and areas of inquiry for practitioners examining this profound and critically important issue in their specific country setting. The African people deserve a future of increased prosperity that they have been denied by poor policy choices in the past.

Gobind Nankani
Vice President
Africa Region

Acknowledgments

This study is the second in a series of regional "Flagship" reports that the Africa Region is producing on a variety of economic issues to help clarify opportunities, constraints, and strategic directions for African development. It is the product of a team led by Benno J. Ndulu and assisted by Lopamudra Chakraborti, Lebohang Lijane, Vijaya Ramachandran, and Jerome Wolgin. Vijaya Ramachandran also prepared the background paper that became the basis for a major portion of the section on assessing constraints to growth at the firm level, and Abdoulaye Tall prepared a short paper for the sections on conflict and its costs to growth.

The team wishes to thank Gobind Nankani, vice president, Africa Region, who personally reviewed this book and provided some early guidance for the penultimate chapter on strategic options for growth. The team also wishes to thank John Page, chief economist, Africa Region, for substantive guidance and encouragement throughout the preparation of this work.

This study has benefited from numerous comments, suggestions, and recommendations at different stages of its preparation. The team would like to thank in particular the African Economic Research Consortium, the silent partner in this work, for allowing the team to draw from its very impressive and in-depth African growth research. Steve O'Connell has provided unwavering support for the study from its inception and is substantively present through the joint work on African growth he has done with the team leader, Benno Ndulu.

Very useful inputs were also received from Bank country economists involved in growth diagnostic work in Africa, who earlier on reviewed the concept note for this work and were of tremendous help in underpinning areas of critical importance to the challenge of African growth. In this regard, the team specifically thanks Victoria Kwakwa, Robert Johann Utz, Dino Leonardo Merotto, Robert Keyfitz, Mathurin Gbetibouo, Praveen Kumar, Wilfried Engelke, Douglas Addison, Preeti Arora, Lolette Kritzinger-van Niekerk, Jos Verbeek, Benu Bidani, Jeni Klugman, Karim El Aynaoui, Christina Wood, Peter Moll, Emmanuel Pinto Moreira, Jacques Morisset, Keiko Kubota, and Carlos Cavalcanti.

The team is particularly grateful to the peer reviewers, namely Sudhir Shetty (director, AFTPM), who also chaired the Bank-wide review meeting for the study; Alan Gelb (director, Development Policy, DECVP), Roberto Zhaga (chief economic adviser, PREM), Vivien Foster (lead economist, AFTPI), and Vikram Nehru (director, PRMED), who provided detailed comments and guidance for revising earlier drafts. Their inputs have helped hone the focus of the study. The advice and suggestions of those who attended the review meeting, particularly Demba Ba, Kathie Krumm, Yvonne Tsikata, and Mark Blackden, plus written comments from AFR staff, especially Louise Fox and Jorge Arbache, are also acknowledged with gratitude.

Earlier findings of the study were presented at various forums, in particular, at a DfID workshop on growth and at Chattam House, both in London, and at an AERC Special Senior Policy seminar in Kigali to discuss the results from the AERC Growth Research project. The constructive recommendations from these meetings have been invaluable.

On the production side, Richard Crabbe and his team have provided tremendous help for ensuring the efficient production of this book. He advised on practical issues such as editing, typesetting, printing, and publishing.

Finally, Yanick Brierre and Patricia Bunzigiye deserve special mention for the time and effort they have devoted in providing administrative support for the preparation and production of this book. Their efforts ensured that this work came to a successful conclusion.

Executive Summary

This report is one of a series of "Flagship Studies" intended to help clarify the opportunities, constraints, and strategic directions facing Africa and its partners as they attempt to accelerate economic growth to reduce poverty and put Africa on a path toward meeting the Millennium Development Goals. It is part of the analytic work promised in a plan titled "Meeting the Challenges of Africa's Development," also known as the African Action Plan (AAP), discussed at the World Bank Board in 2005. The AAP has a strong focus on increasing shared growth and recommends several actions by the World Bank that will support accelerating growth. Offering both a long-term approach and country-specific analysis, the report recommends learning from history and from diverse experiences to guide country-growth diagnostic work and strategies for scaling-up growth. The World Bank's Africa Region intends to provide further studies in this series that will examine in much greater depth several of the areas critical to growth. A study on financial markets has just been published. Another on infrastructure is being drafted.

Substantively, this report draws lessons from a half-century of growth experience in Africa and around the world, providing an important repository of lessons learned to shape growth strategies in Africa. It is influenced by, and builds upon, three major studies—*The Political Economy of Economic Growth in Africa, 1960–2000*, conducted under the African Economic Research Consortium; *Can Africa Claim the 21st Century?*, produced collaboratively by the

World Bank and African partner institutions; and the World Bank's study, *Economic Growth in the 1990s: Learning from a Decade of Reform,* which draws from in-depth reflection on growth experiences by respected practitioners.

The current report will seek to explain three key issues: (1) the opportunities and, hence, options for growth available to the diverse range of African countries; (2) the major constraints to exploiting these opportunities; and (3) the strategic choices to be made by African governments as well as by development partners, including the World Bank, in supporting actions taken by African countries.

The distinguishing characteristic of this study is its long-term perspective, together with its analysis and description of the African growth experience from 1960 (the time when most African countries became independent) to the present. Although there are some commonalities among countries, the growth experiences are also quite diverse, with a few countries experiencing consistent long-term growth, a few experiencing long-term stagnation and decline, and the majority experiencing growth between 1960 and 1973, decline between 1974 and 1994, and renewed growth since 1995. This long-term perspective explains the current situation in which African countries, for the most part, find themselves—low levels of per capita income and high levels of poverty.

Six countries have more than tripled their per capita incomes between 1960 and 2005; nine countries have per capita incomes equal to or less than where they started in 1960; and the rest have seen some net improvement, but not enough to make a real dent in poverty levels. Many countries seen as fast growers in 1970, such as Côte d'Ivoire, flamed out and have found themselves stagnating or declining during the past 30 years. The critical point is that frequently, over the long term, the tortoise beats the hare. Steady progress and consistent performance, in good times as in bad, are the watchwords. Many African countries made policy choices in 1974 that continue to haunt them today, whereas a few are experiencing the blessings of different choices made at the same time.

The report draws six key lessons to inform the growth strategies in Sub-Saharan Africa:

- *African countries' growth experience is extremely varied and episodic.* From a regional strategic perspective, addressing two challenges peculiar to the region is the key to success—the slow growth of large countries and the extreme instability of growth across a large number of African countries. Countries with large populations, such as the Democratic Republic of Congo, Ethiopia, Nigeria, and Sudan, will have to grow more rapidly and on a more sustained basis to improve the livelihood of a "typical" African and to generate regional traction through positive spillover effects, similar to the experiences in Southern Africa and East Asia. Another cross-cutting challenge for the region is how to best manage responses to shocks, particularly in the resource-rich countries, in which their fortunes are currently closely tied to the fortunes of key minerals in the world market.

- *Although lower levels of investment are important for explaining Africa's slower growth, it is the slower productivity growth that more sharply distinguishes African growth performance from that of the rest of the world.* Investment in Africa yields less than half the return measured in growth terms than in other developing regions. This situation clearly calls for looking beyond the creation of conditions that would attract new investors to more explicitly pursuing measures that help to raise productivity of existing and new investment. These include reducing transaction costs for private enterprise, particularly indirect costs; supporting innovation to take advantage of new technological opportunities; and improving skills and institutional capacity to support productivity growth and competitiveness. African countries and populations are still highly dependent on agriculture for food, exports, and earning of income in general. Productivity in this sector lags far behind the phenomenal progress made in Asia and Latin America, and it should be a key target for raising overall productivity of African economies.

- *Consistent with much of the cross-country growth analysis, evidence from the research reviewed earlier suggests that policy and governance matter a great deal for growth.* Taking a half-century of African growth experience as a whole and controlling for differences in the composition of opportunities, the impacts of poor policy have been shown to typically account for between one-quarter and one-half of the difference in predicted growth between African and non-African developing countries. However, the evidence also suggests that the importance of policy in explaining the growth differential between African countries and others may have waned since the 1990s as a result of major reforms implemented in the region, which have moved policy performance in African countries much closer to the global average. Thus, whereas it is imperative for countries to identify and address other binding constraints, sustaining these gains in the improvement of the policy environment will have to be a permanent feature of any growth strategy adopted by a country. In particular, it means maintaining durable macroeconomic stability and continued propping up of efficient market functioning.

- *Overcoming disadvantages arising from geographic isolation and fragmentation, as well as natural resource dependence, will be necessary if Africa is to close the growth gap with other regions.* Estimates show that taking actions to compensate for these disadvantages may facilitate closing up to one-third of the growth gap with other developing countries. With much higher proportions of countries and populations in Africa being landlocked and resource rich, it is necessary to compensate for these disadvantages, primarily by closing the infrastructure gap and better managing and using resource rents.

- *Growth of trading partners' economies has a very powerful influence.* The key transmission mechanisms are trade and capital flows: these require greater openness, strengthening capabilities for taking advantage of the rapid growth in the global markets, and improving the investment climate to make African countries better destinations for global capital than in the past. On the side of trade, evidence shows that integration with global markets is associated with higher growth, underpinning the need for growth strategies to emphasize scaling up and diversifying exports. Enhanced competitiveness and reduced barriers to trade are the two critical areas of action. It is important to note that although concerns with border trade policies and facilities (for example, port capacity and efficiency) are still crucial, increasingly, constraints such as infrastructure, standards, and access to information have become much more binding. A core part of any growth strategy, therefore, will need to target reducing the costs of transacting trade—particularly reducing supply chain costs—as well as the cost of trade processes.

- *The analysis points to a very large role played by the delayed demographic transition in Africa in explaining its relatively slower growth performance.* In all the empirical studies of the sources of growth differences, the demographic variables consistently predict two-thirds of the observed difference between average growth in Sub-Saharan Africa and other developing regions. Two types of consequences from this delayed transition are particularly important. The first, and probably the biggest, challenge is the uncharacteristically high level of age dependency, with its implications on fiscal and household/parental pressure for taking care of the overwhelming number of the young. The second relates to the rapid growth of the labor force, potentially a positive driver of growth but also possibly a negative force if employment opportunities do not keep pace. The latter concern relates to the growing potential instability from rapidly rising youth unemployment. Whereas the strategy needs to address the fundamentals of the slow demographic transition, such as how to speed up a reduction in fertility, appropriate actions are also needed to increase employability of youth and expand opportunities to engage in a growing private sector at home.

This analysis then leads to a set of four specific pillars—areas in which action is needed to accelerate growth. These four pillars are critical but not comprehensive. They are as follows.

The first pillar, **the investment climate**, mainly focuses on reducing indirect costs to firms (which are generally infrastructure related), with energy and transportation topping the list of major impediments, and reducing and mitigating risk, particularly those risks relating to security of property, such as poor adjudication of disputes, crime, political instability, and macroeconomic instability. Although effort in individual countries is the focal point of action, we also suggest pooling efforts to develop cohesive investment areas by coordinating investment promotion, coordinating policy, improving security, and increasing connectivity.

The second pillar is **infrastructure,** mainly targeting transactions costs in the production of goods and services. Transportation and energy make up the largest proportion of indirect costs for businesses, weighing heavily on the competitiveness of firms in most African countries in which investment climate surveys were conducted. Particular focus would be on how to reduce the high costs associated with the remoteness of landlocked countries to facilitate trade with neighbors, as well as with the rest of the world. It is clear that countries will need to look beyond individual country borders and adopt a regional approach to coordinate cross-border infrastructure investment, maintenance, operational management, and use (for example, power pooling) to lower costs.

The third pillar is **innovation,** primarily emphasizing investment in information technology and skill formation (higher education) for enhanced productivity and competitiveness. The potential comparative advantage of low wages in Africa can be nullified by low productivity. Surveys of investors show that labor is not cheap where productivity is low. Information and communications technology (ICT) is now the main driver for productivity growth. Strong empirical evidence shows that investment in ICT and in higher education boosts competitiveness, making both key parts of the growth agenda. As late starters, African countries can make a huge leap forward and beyond antiquated technology by exploiting the ICT technological advantages.

The fourth pillar is **institutional capacity**. The results from the investment climate assessment surveys and analysis for the 2005 *World Development Report* identify costs associated with contract enforcement difficulties, crime, corruption, and regulation as being among those weighing most heavily on the profitability of enterprises. The main focus of action here would be partly to strengthen the capacity of relevant public institutions for protecting property rights and partly to strengthen scrutiny of, and accountability for, public actions. Building institutional capacity entails strengthening individual competencies, organizational effectiveness, and rules of the game. Under this pillar, particular attention would be paid to capacity and space for scrutiny of public action, mainly within a framework of a strong domestic accountability system, and capacity to clarify and protect property rights to spur private enterprise. The key strategic areas of action, therefore, include enforcement of contracts (for example, commercial courts); exercise of voice as an agency of restraint, with enhanced involvement of civil society, media, and parliament; enhanced revenue transparency in resource-rich countries; and prevention of corruption as a country-driven agenda, including checks and balances.

Applying these strategies in a specific country context is beyond the scope of this study. Each country faces its own challenges and opportunities. Each country has to work within its own historical and geographical resources and constraints. Dealing with these specific situations is a subject of specific analysis and beyond the scope of a generalized study such as this one. Nevertheless, we hope that the ideas and approaches raised here will enable analysts and policy makers at the country level to approach their particular challenges with a more informed sense of what may be important and of what has worked in the past in other situations.

Abbreviations

AERC	African Economic Research Consortium
DRC	Democratic Republic of Congo
ECOSOC	United Nations Economic and Social Council
EITI	Extractive Industries Transparency Initiative
FDI	foreign direct investment
FOB	free on board
ICT	Information and communications technologies
IFC	International Finance Corporation (of the World Bank Group)
LDCs	less developed countries
MDGs	Millennium Development Goals
MFI	microfinance institutions
NEPAD	New Partnership for Africa's Development
ODA	official development assistance
OECD	Organisation for Economic Co-operation and Development
PPP	purchasing power parity
RTS	remote transactions system (*smart cards*)
SADC	Southern African Development Community
TFR	total fertility rate
WAPP	West Africa Power Market Development Project

Facing the Challenges of African Growth: Opportunities, Constraints, and Strategic Directions

This report is one of a series of "Flagship Studies" intended to help clarify the opportunities, constraints, and strategic directions facing Africa and its partners as they attempt to accelerate economic growth in order to reduce poverty and put Africa on a path toward meeting the Millennium Development Goals (MDGs). The report is part of the analytic work promised in the plan titled "Meeting the Challenges of Africa's Development" (World Bank 2005e), also known as the African Action Plan (AAP). The AAP has a strong focus on increasing shared growth. By undertaking a long-term approach and country-specific analysis, this report combines learning from history and from diverse experiences to guide country growth diagnostic work and strategies for scaling up growth. It is the intention of the World Bank's Africa Region to provide further studies in this series that will examine in much greater depth several of the areas critical for growth. A study on financial markets was recently published. Another on infrastructure is currently being drafted.

Substantively, this report draws lessons from a half-century of growth experience in Africa and around the world, providing an important repository of lessons learned to shape growth strategies in Africa. It is influenced by, and builds upon, three major studies—*The Political Economy of Economic Growth in Africa, 1960–2000* (Ndulu et al., eds. forthcoming), conducted under the African Economic Research Consortium (AERC); *Can Africa Claim the 21st Century?* (World Bank 2000a), produced collaboratively by the World Bank and African partner institutions; and *Economic Growth in the 1990s: Learning from a Decade of Reform* (World Bank 2005d), which draws from an in-depth reflection on growth experiences by respected practitioners.

The AERC anchored a major African growth project, which is just concluding with a two-volume series to be published by Cambridge University Press. With 26 country studies covering more than 75 percent of the region's population, this project is by far the most comprehensive country-based assessment of Africa's growth experience to date. A number of country teams had access to excellent recent country studies from the USAID-supported project Equity and Growth through Economic Research (EAGER) or the Emerging Africa project or both (Berthelemy and Soderling 2001, 2002). Both sets of studies contain sustained treatments of growth experiences at the country level and make in-depth use of cross-country literature.

Country case studies focused on two questions. First, how did policies and shocks combine to produce the observed growth outcomes? Researchers developed microeconomic evidence linking policies and shocks to the resource allocation decisions of households and firms, and particularly to the scale and ex ante efficiency of investment in human and physical capital. Second, why were these policies chosen? Researchers gathered information on the beliefs of the political elite, the interests to which they responded, and the institutions through which political competition was mediated (Ndulu and O'Connell 2006a).

The two major World Bank studies of growth, *Can Africa Claim the 21st Century?* (World Bank 2000a) and *Economic Growth in the 1990s* (World Bank 2005d), present a good mix of analytical and policy experience insights about what matters most for growth. *Can Africa Claim the 21st Century?* focused on four pillars: (1) improving governance and resolving conflict, (2) investing in people, (3) increasing competitiveness and diversifying economies, and (4) reducing aid dependency and strengthening partnerships. In addition to building upon the many points emphasized in the study, the current report emphasizes strategies that are largely part of the second and third pillars, such as investing in tertiary education, harnessing skills for innovation, and reducing behind-the-border barriers to scaling up and diversifying exports.

The messages emerging from *Economic Growth in the 1990s* emphasize the importance of country-specific growth diagnostics in identifying binding constraints and what is needed to relieve them. This approach can best be summarized by the following quote from the foreword of the report:

The central message is that there is no unique universal set of rules. Sustained growth depends on key functions that need to be fulfilled over time: Accumulation of physical and human capital, efficiency in the allocation of resources, adoption of technology, and the sharing of the benefits of growth. Which of these functions is the most critical at any given point in time, and hence which policies will need to be introduced, which institutions will need to be created for these functions to be fulfilled, and in which sequence, varies depending on initial conditions and the legacy of history. (World Bank 2005d, xiii)

That spirit infuses this current report, particularly in its discussion of the options and a country's process of making strategic choices.

The current report will seek to answer three key questions: (1) What are the opportunities and, hence, options for growth available to the diverse range of African countries? (2) What are the major constraints to exploiting these opportunities? (3) What are the strategic choices to be made by African governments, as well as by development partners, including the Bank, in supporting actions taken by African countries?

It is important to emphasize up front the diverse history, opportunities, and current growth conditions in different African countries, and how these make any growth strategy, first and foremost, a country-specific task. This has become much more pertinent as Africa's income and policy landscape has become significantly more diverse in the past decade and a half. There are now 13 middle-income countries in Sub-Saharan Africa, which although they host only 13 percent of total Sub-Saharan Africa population, account for 66 percent of all incomes earned in the region. Seven of these middle-income countries are in the lower-middle-income country group[1] (per capita incomes between $826 and $3,255), and the other six are in the upper-middle-income country group.[2] With the exception of South Africa and Mauritius, none of the others were in this category in 1960. Out of the 13 middle-income countries, 7 have acquired their current status largely on account of their mineral wealth, including oil. Not all oil or other mineral producers, however, have progressed to this group. For example, Nigeria, Sudan, and Zambia remain low-income countries.

The rest of the countries (35), which host 87 percent of all Sub-Saharan Africans, are in the low-income country category and account for one-third of all income generated in the region. The diversity of growth performance among these is also striking, as we will elaborate later.

Poverty in Africa: Largely a Growth Challenge

Poverty is increasingly assuming an African face, and eradicating it has become a predominantly African challenge. Although the region currently accounts for only 10 percent of the world's population, it now accommodates 30 percent of the world's poor. The world as a whole has made remarkable progress in reducing extreme poverty over the past three decades, cutting it by nearly two-thirds between 1970 and 2000. In contrast, the trend in Sub-Saharan Africa has been in the opposite direction, increasing from 36 percent of the population in 1970 to 50 percent in 2000. As a result, one in two Africans (or 300 million people) is poor, spending less than $1 a day on basic necessities of life. This proportion is twice as high as the world average, and the number of poor is twice as high as it was in 1970.

Africa's slow and erratic growth performance, particularly when compared with the other developing regions, has been identified as the single most important reason it is lagging in eradicating poverty. Already by the 1950s, African incomes, which had gained considerable ground in relative terms since 1913, had begun to diverge markedly from incomes elsewhere in the developing world (Maddison 2001). This divergence increased sharply when African populations completely missed out on the economic transformation that took place in the developing world—particularly in Asia—in the second half of the 20th century (Ndulu and O'Connell 2006a).

For the 45 years since 1960, Africa's per capita income grew at about one-fifth of the average rate for other developing countries (0.5 percent versus 2.5 percent). Although in 1960, per capita incomes for Africa and East Asia were virtually the same, as a result of this growth difference, by 2004 the gross domestic product (GDP) per capita in East Asia was five times higher than that in Africa (figure 1.1). This is similar to Ndulu and O'Connell's (2006a) observation: when measured in purchasing power parity (PPP)–adjusted terms, in 1960 African incomes per capita were more than two-thirds of those of the East Asia and Pacific; by the end of the 20th century, African incomes were less than one-fourth. Data also suggest a sharper divergence of incomes between African and non-African populations than between African and non-African countries. The larger divergence is mainly because of the relatively rapid growth of very populous countries such as China, India, and Indonesia in Asia. In contrast, the large countries in Africa, including the Democratic Republic of Congo, Ethiopia, Sudan, and Nigeria, have on average grown more slowly than smaller ones.

FIGURE 1.1

Comparative Per Capita Income Growth Paths: Sub-Saharan Africa versus Other Regions

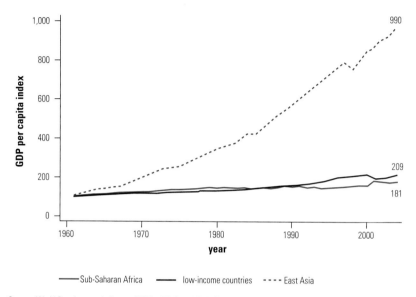

Sources: World Development Indicators (WDI) 2006, Penn World Tables (PWT) 6.1 (Heston, Summers, and Aten 2002), and Global Development Network (GDN) 1998.

Note: PPP = purchasing power parity. Index for 1960 = 100 (1996 PPP $).

The growth experience is also quite diverse within Africa. A look at long-term trends shows how countries have distinguished themselves in terms of how much their income per capita has grown over the 45-year period. Figure 1.2 depicts the wide variation in the progress made by 40 African countries for which we have complete data. Each country's progress in per capita income since 1960 is measured by the ratio of per capita income in 2004 to that in 1960 (in 1996 international dollars). One group's (nine countries) income per capita has actually regressed relative to the levels in 1960.[3] Surprisingly, only three among these are countries that have suffered from prolonged conflict (Angola, Sierra Leone, and the Democratic Republic of Congo). The rest appear to have had long periods of very slow growth or to have suffered prolonged crises as they struggled to climb out of the shocks suffered during the late 1970s.

Several of the middle income countries experienced rapid growth through a large part of the 45-year period, ending up with per capita incomes several times the initial 1960 levels. The rest of the countries are

FIGURE 1.2
Per Capita Incomes in 2004 Relative to 1960
1996 international $

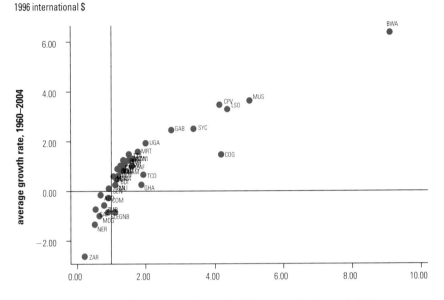

ratio of per capita income in 2004 to per capita income in 1960

Sources: World Bank WDI 2006; PWT 6.1 (Heston, Summers, and Aten 2002); and GDN 1998.

Note: AGO = Angola; BEN = Benin; BDI = Burundi; BFA = Burkina Faso; BWA = Botswana; CAF = Central African Republic; CIV = Côte d'Ivoire; CMR = Cameroon; COG = Congo, Rep. of; COM = Comoros; CPV = Cape Verde; ERI = Eritrea; ETH = Ethiopia; GAB = Gabon; GHA = Ghana; GIN = Guinea; GMB = Gambia, The; GNB = Guinea-Bissau; GNQ = Equatorial Guinea; KEN = Kenya; LSO = Lesotho; MDG = Madagascar; MLI = Mali; MOZ = Mozambique; MRT = Mauritania; MUS = Mauritius; MWI = Malawi; NAM = Namibia; NER = Niger; NGA = Nigeria; RWA = Rwanda; SDN = Sudan; SEN = Senegal; SLE = Sierra Leone; STP = São Tomé and Principe; SWZ = Swaziland; SYC = Seychelles; TCD = Chad; TGO = Togo; TZA = Tanzania; UGA = Uganda; ZAF= South Africa; ZAR = Congo, Dem. Rep. of; ZMB = Zambia; ZWE = Zimbabwe.

bunched in a narrow range between stagnation (ratio of 1) and a doubling of income per capita over a 45-year period—a relatively low achievement by global standards. Most of these experienced economic stagnation for two decades between the mid-1970s and mid-1990s, usually after respectable growth performance in the previous decade and a half. For countries like Uganda and Ghana, rapid growth during the past 15 years have enabled them to more than recoup the severe losses in income suffered during the previous two decades. As expected, differences in average growth rates match the differences in the progress made in terms of per capita incomes.

What is also striking is that countries with very similar opportunities also have very different growth experience and outcomes, depending on the strategies pursued and the policy disposition adopted. Figure 1.3 presents

FIGURE 1.3

Similar Opportunities, Different Strategies, Different Results

a. Côte d'Ivoire and Mauritius

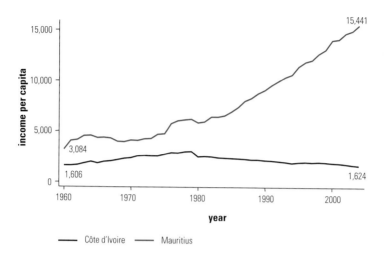

b. Botswana and Zambia

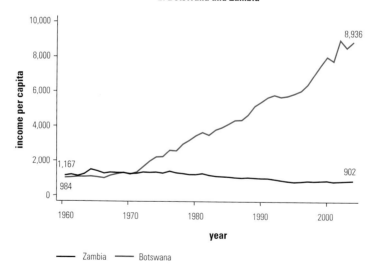

Source: WDI 2006, PWT 6.1 (Heston, Summers, and Aten 2002); and GDN 1998.

Note: Income per capita is in 1996 international dollars, PPP adjusted.

two examples of very striking contrasts of growth paths between Botswana and Zambia, both landlocked, resource-rich countries, and between Mauritius and Côte d'Ivoire, both coastal, resource-poor countries and initially both primarily commodity dependent. The two stories are elaborated in chapter 2, but we mention it at this stage to show how differences in the long-term strategies resulted in the countries exploiting similar opportunities in different ways; thus, Botswana and Mauritius ended up being upper-middle-income countries, whereas Zambia's and Côte d'Ivoire's per capita incomes have hardly progressed relative to their 1960 levels.

The past decade and a half has seen a particularly sharp increase in the diversity of growth performance and indeed in the way countries have positioned themselves for the future. Thirteen African countries, though still in the low-income group, have sustained annual growth rates exceeding 5 percent for more than a decade now, and they have set the groundwork for faster and more diversified growth in the future. The challenge for this group of countries is to harness opportunities for increasing growth rates to the 7 percent or higher needed for achieving the Millennium Development Goals (MDGs). Other countries, such as Somalia and Liberia, are in conflicts or are just emerging from them, and typically have lost significant ground in terms of income levels relative to the early 1960s. For the countries that have experienced limited success, the challenge is to learn from the experiences of higher-growth countries about what works and what does not, and to implement the changes needed to get growth started.

These growth differentials are also reflected in the differences in the status of human development. For example, Ndulu and O'Connell (2006a) show that within Sub-Saharan Africa, a 1 percent increase in the long-term growth rate of real GDP per capita was associated with an increase in an index of cumulative human development of nearly one-half percent. Table 1.1, at the end of this chapter, provides a snapshot comparison of human development, first at the outset of the 1960–2004 period and then at the end. With the exception of the primary enrollment rate, which was already high outside of Africa in the early 1960s, Africa has fallen further behind the rest of the developing world.

However, the shortfall was not as severe for nonincome measures as it was for income poverty, partly reflecting the relatively greater focus of national strategies and development assistance on human development in the 1970s and again in the 1990s. The latter phase followed the steep erosion of the gains in social development during the 1980s, due primarily to the failure to raise and maintain the growth of per capita incomes necessary for sustaining the earlier achievements. By 2004, Africa exceeded the level of primary enrollment rate that had prevailed in other developing regions in 1960. However, the other human development indicator, life expectancy at birth, was less than the level prevailing in other developing regions in 1962 (the beginning year), primarily due to the massive AIDS problem crippling African countries in recent times.

There is also a close link between income and another dimension of poverty preponderant in Africa—undernutrition. A recent International Food Policy Research Institute study on the causal relationship between income and undernutrition concludes that sustained income growth can produce a sizable reduction in undernutrition (Haddad et al. 2002). The study estimates, for example, that a sustained 2.5 percent growth in per capita income maintained over the next decade would reduce undernutrition by a range of 27 percent to 34 percent by 2015, depending on what happens to community and household infrastructure.

A growing body of evidence confirms that it is not simply higher growth, but higher shared growth, that is more effective in accelerating poverty reduction. While there is wide variation across countries in this relationship, there is undeniable evidence that inequality has a major influence on the efficacy of growth in reducing poverty. For example, a typical (median) country that experienced both growth in the average living standards and falling inequality was able to reduce poverty seven times faster than one that experienced growth with rising inequality (Ravallion 2001). This relationship also holds for countries suffering declines in living standards.

Although this report will not focus on the distributional consequences of growth, there is a need to pay greater attention to this dimension of poverty reduction to complement the impact of accelerating growth, particularly by enhancing the income-earning opportunities for the poor more than for other income-earning segments, or by enabling their greater participation in the growth process.[4]

Breaking Out of the Low-Growth Syndrome—A Daunting Task but a Real Possibility

There is no doubt that the growth challenges faced by African countries are daunting. However, they are not insurmountable. The experience of

Asian countries over the past three and a half decades, in particular, shows that countries can break out of the poverty trap, embark on sustained growth, and experience rapid gains in living standards. More recently, Asian countries have also been able to overcome a financial crisis and resume robust growth.

Africa's own record provides similar examples. Mauritius, Botswana, and the Seychelles have maintained per capita income growth rates above 3 percent for nearly four decades, allowing them to make major strides in improving living standards and placing them in the group of middle-income countries. Sub-Saharan Africa as a whole experienced quite robust growth between 1960 and 1973, when its per capita income grew at an annual average rate of nearly 3 percent, and it is capable of regaining that pace of economic progress, as the recent resumption of rapid growth in the region has shown. In 2005, 17 countries in Sub-Saharan Africa were growing at average rates exceeding 5 percent annually. Several others have shown themselves to be capable of short spurts of high growth. The challenge for them is to sustain such a pace for longer periods.

As late starters, African countries have a possibility of accelerating the pace of economic progress, provided they can create the right conditions to exploit the advantages information-based technology offers to enhance productivity and competitiveness and learn lessons from successful growth experiences. The *Global Competitiveness Report, 2005–2006* (WEF 2006) presents striking evidence to conclude that investment in higher education and in information and communications technology (ICT) boosts competitiveness. Countries across the world seem to have sharply distinguished themselves in these terms.

Starting late also has its disadvantages. In particular, Asia's recent success presents a huge challenge to the competitiveness of Africa. Countries in the region will have to learn in the face of intense competition. As we will see in greater detail later in this report, several African firms already have shop-floor costs that are comparable to or competitive with those in China, but they quickly lose that advantage to huge differences in indirect costs, largely infrastructure related. With appropriate investments and improvement in infrastructure services, such a gap can be closed. Indeed, a reduction in indirect costs and improvement in skills, combined with lower-cost labor, would enable African countries to compete more effectively in the global market.

The difficulty most countries will face in getting started on a high-growth path partly relates to the wide range of constraints they face, given their limited fiscal space and institutional capacity. The challenge is made more daunting by the need for a big push to offset or mitigate the disadvantages of Africa's unfavorable endowments or to break out of apparent poverty traps. As more countries attain prosperity, however, the power of example and emulation will naturally spread, underscoring the importance of positive regional spillover effects and the need to exploit cross-country strategic complementarities in the development agenda.

Leadership, too, is crucial for success. Recent research demonstrates the importance of leadership in achieving and sustaining growth. Glaeser et al. (2004) find that in an initially poor economy, economic growth since the 1960s has, to a significant extent, been a consequence of having the right leader. The authors establish that in the post-1960 growth record, the impact of leaders has been huge and widely dispersed, implying that some leaders have been associated with rapid growth, while others have not. They show that good leaders accumulate capital, avoid wars, and are rewarded with longer tenure, particularly in countries with higher educational achievements. Using the Indian post-1980 growth experience, Rodrik and Subramanian (2004) demonstrate the importance of the leadership's attitudinal disposition toward markets and business in influencing growth in a country context. Jones and Olken (2004), citing Easterly et al. (1993), find robust empirical evidence that national leaders, particularly in autocratic settings, matter in explaining shifts in growth. They do so either directly, by influencing the policy environment, or indirectly, by shaping institutions (Ndulu 2006a). Though the occurrence of good leadership is still widely shown to be a matter of chance, increasingly, analytic work is pointing toward the importance of political competition, transparency, and strong domestic accountability, not only in raising the chances of having good leadership emerge, but also in sustaining it.

The Report: An Overview

Africa's slow growth over the second half of the 20th century is accounted for by two primary factors: a relatively low rate of capital accumulation, and a low productivity growth rate for the investments that are made. Slightly less than half of Africa's growth difference with the other developing regions is due to slower accumulation of physical capital; slightly more than half is accounted for by the slower growth in productivity. Investment levels since the 1960s have remained relatively low in Africa, with their share of GDP averaging only half that in the rest of the developing world. Furthermore, for similar levels of investment, African economies have on average achieved only one-third to one-half of the growth achieved in other developing regions.

The analysis of the sources of growth, discussed in greater detail in chapter 3, points to the central role of poor investment incentives, including low returns. A substantial part of the report will therefore explore three sets of constraints that are behind poor incentives for accumulation and relatively slow productivity growth in the region: geography, demography, and policy and institutions.

The first set are constraints that are part of Africa's endowments—long distances from markets, tropical climates and soils, small markets, few navigable rivers, and so forth. More than 90 percent of Sub-Saharan Africa lies within the tropics, where the burden of disease is high and negatively affects life expectancy, human capital formation, and labor force participation (Artadi and Sala-i-Martin 2003). This compares to 3 percent of Organisation for Economic Co-operation and Development (OECD) countries and 60 percent of East Asia. Sub-Saharan Africa is highly fragmented—48 small economies with a median GDP of $3 billion (Wormser 2004). On average, each country shares borders with four countries, often with different trade and macroeconomic policy regimes (table 1.1). Forty percent of the population lives in landlocked countries with high transportation costs and poor trade facilitation. These constraints cannot be changed, but they can be compensated for through public and private actions, such as improving infrastructure to effectively reduce distances or integrate markets, and introducing antimalaria programs to contain the tropical disease that wreaks havoc on life expectancy and saps strength from the labor force.

The second set of constraints relates to Africa's slow demographic transition, which has put considerable pressure on public and private investable resources. Demographic transition began late in Africa and is proceeding at a slower pace than that experienced in other regions of the world. Fertility rates began declining in Africa around the mid-1980s, compared to the 1950s for Latin America and 1960s for Asia, and rates appear to be proceeding more slowly than in the other regions (Lucas 2003). Uncharacteristically high levels of age dependency have created fiscal and household pressure to care for the overwhelming number of the young (as well as achievement of the MDGs). The rapid increase in the labor force, although potentially a positive contributor to growth, can turn negative if employment opportunities do not keep pace, leading to instability from agitation by the rapidly rising numbers of unemployed youth. Although measures can be taken to help accelerate the demographic transition, the changes in basic demographics are likely to remain slow relative to the medium-term frame of growth outcomes considered here. Therefore, efforts to accelerate reductions in fertility will work only with complementary, carefully considered measures to compensate for some of the consequences of the delayed demographic transition, such as paying particular attention to enhancing employability of youth through vocational training and job creation. This is an area where much more analytical and policy attention is needed.

The third set of constraints is largely historical, institutional, or policy related and can be acted upon in the context of public policy. These constraints affect investment incentives by reducing risk-adjusted returns to investment and hence raising the hurdle rates for those seeking to invest in the region; by raising transaction costs affecting profitability of enterprises and competitiveness of products; and by limiting absorption and constraining productivity growth due to capacity shortfalls.

The scope of action is largely in the policy sphere. We emphasize in this report two dimensions of policy action: avoiding policy distortions ("sins of commission") and addressing the issue of underprovision of public goods to support the growth process ("sins of omission"). The first dimension includes actions needed for sustained macroeconomic stability, maintenance of a prudent exchange rate policy to support export-led growth, and improved market efficiency to spur private sector initiatives and enterprise. The second dimension includes ensuring good governance and bureaucratic efficiency and the effective provision of those goods and services that the private sector alone would not adequately provide, such as infrastructure or protection of the commons.

The ideas proposed in this report for country growth strategies relate largely, though not entirely, to the third set of constraints. The following includes a proposed set of actions that are likely to help reduce risk and transaction costs while increasing institutional capacity:

- *Improving the investment climate* by reducing and underwriting risk, as well as by increasing the security of property

- *Embarking on a "big push" in infrastructure investment,* with a particular emphasis on transportation and energy to partly compensate for disad-

vantages arising from Africa's unfavorable geography, to reduce transaction costs, and to improve firm-level profitability

- *Promoting innovation* by investing in ICT and higher education to increase
  competitiveness in the global knowledge-based economy

- *Increasing institutional capacity* by targeting a few priority areas: enforcement of contracts, greater exercise of voice, enhanced revenue transparency in resource-rich countries, and reduction of corruption through
  a country-driven agenda

The rest of this report elaborates on how these areas of strategic action
have been identified and offers ideas that individual countries can use in
developing growth strategies. The diversity of conditions and history pre-
cludes a strategy that fits all African countries, because the above-
mentioned constraints do not apply equally to all. Rather, the lessons
drawn from the growth experiences analyzed in this report would be helpful in narrowing down the scope and process of searching for the most
binding constraints and deciding what to do about them.

As stated earlier, the 48 countries of Sub-Saharan Africa range from
sophisticated, middle-income countries such as South Africa, to failed
states such as Somalia; from large, oil-rich countries such as Nigeria, to
small, resource-poor countries such as Niger; from countries that have
come out of conflict and have experienced tremendous recent success,
such as Mozambique and Rwanda, to countries that seem trapped in conflict, poverty, and poor governance, such as Somalia. Each country situation is unique and requires specific analysis of constraints and
opportunities. However, the experiences that we distill in this study can
provide some information on strategic directions that have proved profitable to other developing countries, and that should be examined by analysts and practitioners seeking to accelerate growth in specific situations.

It is also true that a report of this type can neither be comprehensive nor
contain detailed policy prescriptions for each setting. We have chosen to
emphasize those strategic choices that are most closely associated with
energizing private investment in the short to medium term, and with fostering efficiency and competitiveness as preconditions for export-led
growth. Despite their importance, we will touch only lightly on a number
of sectoral issues such as human resource development, agriculture, and
gender, and encourage more in-depth work in the context of the "flotilla"
of regional flagships mentioned at the outset.

For many African countries and for the foreseeable future, agriculture will be the centerpiece of the development trilogy of rapid economic growth, poverty reduction, and food security (Timmer 2003). It looms large in typical African economies, in terms of both overall economic growth and the livelihoods of the majority of the poor. Agriculture is a major domestic supplier of food and a source of income earning. A key strategic challenge is to make efforts in agriculture worthwhile by raising the sector's profitability. A three-pronged approach is recommended: (1) ensure better prices and policy environment; (2) reduce transaction costs—in investment, production, and marketing; and (3) raise labor and land productivity through technological innovation.

The latter challenge is particularly critical if the region is to embark on a successful "green revolution" to raise the productivity of agriculture. This will require a combination of actions to increase the area under irrigation, increase the use of high-yielding varieties, improve crop husbandry through extension services (increase knowledge), integrate markets, and rejuvenate Africa's farmlands. Roy (2006) presents some striking facts about how far Africa has been left behind in agricultural productivity and how denuded African farmlands are of key nutrients. Some 75 to 80 percent of Africa's farmland is degraded at the annual rate of 30 to 60 kilograms of nutrients per hectare. Yet fertilizer use in Africa is the lowest of any region in the world. In 2002/03, Sub-Saharan Africa used 8 kilograms (kg) of fertilizer per hectare, compared to 80 kg for Latin America, 98 kg for North America, 175 kg for Western Europe, and 202 kg for East Asia. Sub-Saharan Africa's consumption of fertilizer, at 2 million tons, is less than what Bangladesh alone consumes, at 3.4 million tons a year (Roy 2006; Versi 2006). This gap in fertilizer use exists notwithstanding the fact that Africa (including North Africa) has the highest endowment of principal ingredients for making fertilizer, including phosphate deposits, nitrates, and crude oil. Import costs of fertilizer are also very high: $600 per ton in some landlocked African countries in contrast to $150 per ton in the United States. Transport cost is a dominant proportion of the cost difference. With respect to these factors, a major institutional challenge is creating space for greater private sector (particularly smallholder sector) and community participation.

Chapter 2 benchmarks African long-term growth performance in a global perspective and elaborates on the key features and patterns of this growth experience. Our particular interest is to highlight cross-country and temporal diversity, emphasizing demographic and other features that differentiate African growth patterns from those of other developing regions. Two broad features of the African growth record stand out. Growth in most African countries has been more episodic than in other developing regions. A distinct characteristic of the African long-term growth experience is its historical U-shape path, featuring a deep and prolonged contraction of growth during 1974 to 1994, a period sandwiched between moderately high growth rates of the 1960s and late 1990s. Most of the African countries experienced this pattern, with many of them beginning their postindependence years with about a decade of fairly robust growth before experiencing its collapse, largely beginning in the second half of the 1970s and lasting until 1995, followed by a subsequent recovery (Pritchett 1998). The clear exceptions are Botswana and Mauritius, which maintained fairly high rates of growth even by global standards throughout the 45-year history reviewed here. It is noteworthy that during the past decade and a half, there has been much greater diversity of growth performance across African countries.

Another distinct feature of Africa's growth record highlighted in this chapter is its juxtaposition with a population explosion. In contrast to other developing regions, Africa embarked on a slow demographic transition only in the mid-1980s. Total fertility rates fell sharply outside of Africa, while rates remained virtually unchanged within Africa for two and a half decades after independence. Population growth rates therefore diverged sharply, and from the early 1970s through the remainder of the century, African populations grew more rapidly than the non-African developing world had grown *at its peak,* and age dependency across most African countries continued to rise sharply. It is therefore not surprising that differences in per capita incomes diverged more sharply with other regions than the gaps in economic growth. Indeed, the more intense demographic pressure from higher levels of age dependency ratios may partly explain the lower savings rates in the region, as well as fiscal pressures in catering to a larger dependent-age population, a point we will return to later. Furthermore, unlike other regions, large countries in Africa have experienced much slower economic growth, bringing the population-weighted average per capita income growth rates even lower.

Chapter 3 examines the influential factors behind this growth record and assesses the relative importance of these factors in the context of the growth experience in African countries. This is done using three approaches. First, at an aggregate level, using the conventional decomposition of sources of growth, we assess the relative importance of capital accumulation, labor, and productivity to growth. This is done for the region as a whole and for 19 African countries for which complete and consistent data are available. We rely in particular on the work of Collins and Bosworth (1998, 2003) and Ndulu and O'Connell (2003), with the latter covering a larger set of African countries. The results confirm the importance of low levels of capital accumulation and also highlight the importance of the productivity residual in African growth performance. Globally, Bosworth and Collins (2003) estimate that total factor productivity growth accounts for 41 percent of growth in the 84 countries they study. This is certainly true for the 19 African countries included in the sample, notwithstanding the significant diversity among them. This feature holds true through all three phases of the region's growth path. It dominates the period of growth contraction between the mid-1970s and mid-1990s, and leads the growth recovery phase of the past decade.

The central role of investment incentives in dealing with both slow capital accumulation and productivity growth suggests a focus on improving the investment climate, which, in addition to identifying actionable policy areas, would also target reducing transactions costs and relieving capacity limitations. The importance of productivity growth also points us to the role of innovation (technical progress) in raising productivity and competitiveness. Productivity, in turn, is influenced not only by the quantity and quality of capital stock, but also the quality and quantity of knowledge (Lindbaek 1997).

Second, and partly to confirm the above conclusions, we use firm-level data from investment climate surveys to assess the relative importance of different factors on the attractiveness of African countries to investors, as influenced by the cost of doing business. The assessment uses the benchmarks of other developing countries to compare the state of institutional, policy, and regulatory frameworks; business regulations and their enforcement; adequacy and quality of infrastructure; stability of the macro economy; protection of property rights; and functioning of the financial system.

Costs of contract enforcement difficulties, inadequate infrastructure, crime, corruption, and regulation can amount to over 25 percent of sales— or more than three times what firms typically pay in taxes (World Bank 2005f). Akin to these findings, the investment climate assessment work reviewed for this report and previous papers focusing on Africa conclude that while shop-floor-level unit costs in Africa tend to be comparable to those in other developing regions, indirect costs—primarily the cost of infrastructure services (transportation and energy), weak contractual enforcement, corruption, and skill deficiency—are significantly higher in the African countries surveyed. The impact from these constraints varies across countries and sectors, demanding that countries make their own assessments. But these appear to be strong candidates based on the evidence reviewed.

Finally, we use results from cross-country empirical research to compare the extent of the deviation of the growth conditions in African countries from those in other regions and to establish where the gaps are widest. It is a benchmarking exercise for African growth conditions. We make these assessments relative to three comparators: global average, South Asia, and East Asia and Pacific. Noting that the region has seriously lagged behind in growth, we include East Asia and Pacific among the comparators to provide African countries with a target for their efforts to close the gap. We also track the changes in the individual components of these growth conditions (the drivers for growth) over the three phases of the U-shaped path of the African growth experience, to identify those areas in which Africa is closing the gap with other developing regions and those areas that require much more effort. This analysis is done at the regional level and for 36 individual countries that have adequate data over the entire 45-year period.

We judiciously use findings from cross-country growth studies, and from empirical work done for this report, to help identify factors that tend to have the highest likelihood of influencing growth performance in Africa[5] and globally, without drawing causality conclusions. We appreciate the fundamental questions of exogeneity and identification (Temple 1999) plaguing cross-country growth regression.[6] Hence, we limit the use of this empirical work mainly to description and comparison of growth conditions in Africa and comparator regions. More detailed econometric discussion and results from empirical work done specifically for this report are presented in the appendix.

Three broad conclusions stand out from this analysis. First, consistent with much of the cross-country growth analysis, evidence reviewed here suggests that policy and governance matter a great deal for growth. Taking 45 years of African growth experience as a whole and controlling for differences in the composition of opportunities, we find that the impact of poor policy typically accounted for between one-quarter and one-half of the difference in predicted growth between African and non-African developing countries (Collier and O'Connell 2006; Ndulu and O'Connell 2006a; and empirical work for this report). The benchmarking analysis also shows that the relative importance of macroeconomic policy in explaining the growth differential between African countries and others may have waned since the 1990s, as a result of major reforms implemented in the region, which have moved policy performance in African countries much closer to the global average. Second, overcoming disadvantages from differences in the opportunity structures (locational and natural resource dependence) between Africa and other regions may facilitate closing up an additional one-third of the growth gap with other developing countries (Collier and O'Connell 2006). Finally, our analysis points to a very large role played by the delayed demographic transition in Africa. In all estimations undertaken for this study, differences in the demographic variables consistently predict two-thirds of the observed difference between average growth in Sub-Saharan Africa and in other developing regions (see tables 3.4 and 3.5 in chapter 3, the appendix, and Ndulu and O'Connell 2006a).

Chapter 4 undertakes a more in-depth analysis of a selective list of constraints emerging from the analysis in chapter 3 and lays the groundwork for a more prioritized discussion of strategic ideas and options. Chapter 4 draws extensively from African and global experience. It also tries to highlight the extent to which the levels and impacts of these constraints are different in African countries than in other regions. The chapter includes an assessment of their past and potential impacts on the region's and individual African countries' growth performance, using empirical analysis done for this report and from other sources. The chapter begins with the identification of a set of unfavorable endowments that have constrained African growth. It then looks at three other groups of constraints: risks, transaction costs, and capacity.

Although they are not predicaments, challenges from unfavorable geography, the curse of misgoverning rents from substantial mineral resources, demographic pressures, and ethnic and regional polarization have typically made development activities much more costly to carry out in Africa than in other regions. The challenges are manifested in the form of location in the disease-prone tropics, geographic isolation and fragmentation, a history that is fraught with conflict-motivating ethnic polarization, as well as a delayed demographic transition. The tropical location affects the prevalence of disease, work stamina, and pests, and the landlocked feature negatively affects the cost of production and trade, primarily because of higher transportation and transit costs. Together with the consequences of sovereign fragmentation and ethnolinguistic fractionalization (Easterly and Levine 1997), development under these conditions is relatively more expensive and slower. Easterly and Levine (2003) and Acemoglu and Robinson (2001) also find that many of these effects are mediated through the quality of institutions. Although we recognize that slow growth may be influenced by these constraints, they can be mitigated through appropriate investments and policy actions.

In addition to the risks associated with an unfavorable policy environment, the investment climate in Africa is adversely affected by frequency of conflict, corruption, and insufficient local scrutiny. Investors are discouraged by not being reasonably sure of the safety of their assets due to the perceived high risk of conflict, not being able to make a reasonable projection of profitability because of high price instability, and facing the risk of being unable to repatriate profits because of exchange controls when a country is unable to earn enough foreign exchange. These risks are valid for both foreign and domestic investors. Flight of financial wealth from Africa is symptomatic of the absence of both attractive opportunities and conditions to invest at home. It is estimated that in 1990, Africans held up to $360 billion, or 40 percent, of their wealth outside the region, in search of safer havens and higher returns (Collier, Hoeffler, and Pattillo 1999). This compares with just 6 percent of East Asian wealth and 10 percent of Latin American wealth being held outside of their respective regions. More broadly, action at the individual country level to improve the investment climate may require complementary regional efforts to improve the collective reputation of the region as an attractive destination for investment.

Relatively high transaction costs in the region make capital accumulation, production, and trade relatively expensive in Africa. For example, dollar-for-dollar investment in African countries yields significantly less expansion of productive capacity because prices of capital goods are 70 percent higher than in OECD and Southeast Asian countries (Sala-i-Martin, Doppelhofer, and Miller 2004). Using this information, Artadi and Sala-i-Martin (2003) estimate that the average growth rate in African countries would have been 0.44 percentage points higher each year if the relative price of investment goods was the same as in OECD countries or

East Asia.[7] Amjadi and Yeats (1995) demonstrate that relatively high transportation costs, especially for processed products, often place African exporters at a serious competitive disadvantage. In 1970, for example, net freight payments to foreign nationals absorbed 11 percent of Africa's export earnings. That ratio had increased to 15 percent by 1990. And for landlocked African countries, the freight cost ratio exceeds 30 percent, as exports must transit neighboring territories. In a similar vein, a more recent study by the African Development Bank (AfDB 1999) on exports to the United States found that freight charges as a proportion of cost, insurance, and freight value are on average approximately 20 percent higher for African exports than for comparative goods from other low-income countries.

These transaction costs arise mainly because of the higher costs of infrastructure services (particularly transportation and energy), which make up a disproportionately large part of production and trade costs; barriers to trade, which raise the cross-border transaction costs; and bureaucratic red tape and inefficiencies, which exacerbate these costs. The remoteness of population concentrations, accentuated by high internal transportation costs, resulted in estimated median transportation costs for intra-Africa trade (including transshipments) that are 65 percent higher than in Latin America and twice that of East and South Asia (Limao and Venables 2001).

Capacity encompasses human competencies, organizational effectiveness, and institutional effectiveness in enforcing the rules of the game. Improvement of workers' skills is a fundamental source of economic progress and increasing human welfare (Adam Smith, cited in Eatwell 1996). These improvements are achieved not only through education and formal training, but also through learning by doing. Although basic education is widely considered to be critical for poverty reduction, there is emerging evidence from a large number of studies that secondary and higher education are more significant in raising long-term growth rates and income levels (Barro 1999; Barro and Lee 1993; Hanushek and Kim 1995). This impact is evidenced primarily through improved capabilities to absorb technological advances. Furthermore, studies have also found that foreign direct investment (FDI) has had a larger impact on growth than domestic investment, due to its higher productivity. This impact, however, is reached only when there is sufficient capability in the host country to absorb the complex technologies that come with FDI (Borensztein, De Gregorio, and Lee 1998; Lumbila 2005).

Progress in overcoming shortages of skilled and trained manpower in African countries seems to be disappointingly slow despite substantial resources devoted by both governments and donors to this effort during the past three decades. Moreover, African countries have struggled to retain the few skilled professionals they produce. The region has lost more highly skilled professionals. It has been estimated that for a number of African countries, more than 30 percent of their highly skilled professionals have been lost to the OECD countries (Carrington and Detragiache 1999; Haque and Aziz 1998). Nearly 88 percent of adults who emigrate from Africa to the United States have a high school education or higher (Speer, cited by Zeleza, 1998). Apraku (1991), in a survey of African immigrants in the United States, found that 58 percent of the respondents had either PhDs or MDs, and an additional 19 percent had master's degrees. The HIV/AIDS pandemic has exacerbated the loss of skilled manpower in the region.

Likewise, a lack of state capacity to carry out basic public management functions constrains delivery of basic services to its citizens and raises the cost of doing business, discouraging the private investment that is essential for growth. The problems here are linked to bureaucratic inefficiency, low levels of incentives, and meritocracy, leading to underutilization of the human capacity in the public sector.

Chapter 5 identifies a set of cross-cutting growth strategies. Six lessons are drawn from the preceding analysis of 45 years of Africa's growth experience to inform growth strategies:

- *African countries' growth experiences are extremely varied and episodic.* However, two challenges are peculiar to the region—the slow growth of large countries and the extreme instability of growth across a large number of African countries, making growth in large countries and prudent management of the impact of shocks key themes of growth strategies in the regional.

- W*hile lower levels of investment are important for explaining Africa's slower growth, it is the slower productivity growth that more sharply distinguishes African performance from the rest of the world.* This situation clearly calls for looking beyond the creation of conditions for attracting new investors to more explicitly pursuing measures that help raise productivity of existing and new investments.

- *Consistent with much of the cross-country growth analysis, evidence from the research reviewed in this report suggests that policy and governance matter a great deal for growth.* Thus, while it is imperative that countries identify and address other binding constraints, sustaining recent gains in the improvement of the policy environment would be a desirable permanent feature of any growth strategy a country adopts.

- *The evidence also suggests that overcoming disadvantages arising from geographic isolation and fragmentation, as well as natural resource dependence, will be necessary if Africa is to close the growth gap with other regions.*

- *The results from the empirical analysis suggest a very powerful influence from the growth of trading partners' economies,* underscoring the importance of enhanced competitiveness and reduced barriers to trade in order to take advantage of opportunities offered by the global market.

- *Analysis points to the very large role played by the delayed demographic transition in Africa in explaining its relatively slower growth performance.* This is an area that will need much more work to determine what would be helpful for accelerating demographic transition in Africa.

The experiences of countries that have sustained rapid growth in Asia, Latin America, and even Africa have tended to be almost all export led. However, a wide range of options is available from the strategies that these countries have followed to scale up and diversify exports. Some African economies can realistically hope to follow the main Asian model or the route Mauritius has taken, in which a central component of growth is manufactured exports. For African countries that have sufficiently abundant valuable natural resources, like Botswana, their most likely route to prosperity may be through the equitable exploitation of their resource base—mineral exports. Some countries may be able to follow the emerging Latin American model of modern agriculture, such as agribusiness in Chile, Costa Rica, or Colombia, or natural resource–based, export-oriented industrialization, as in Indonesia or Malaysia. Other countries may be so disadvantaged that prosperity for their populations will depend on employment opportunities in more fortunate neighboring economies (for example, Swaziland and Lesotho vis-à-vis South Africa, or Burkina Faso vis-à-vis Côte d'Ivoire) or, like India, on the pursuit of the high-value service sector—the office economy. In any case, the paths to prosperity are many and varied.

The stage for scaling up growth in the region is set by documenting the revival of growth that got under way in the mid-1990s, partly due to a response to the economic and political reforms of the late 1980s and early

1990s. We argue that Africa now faces a window of opportunity, with a growing number of politically stable countries facing the prospect of mutually reinforcing declines in fertility rates and increases in capital formation and productivity growth.

The strategic agenda rests on four pillars, which primarily target resolution of the constraints that are identified in chapter 4 and discussed in greater detail in chapter 5. The first pillar involves *improving the investment climate* by reducing indirect costs to firms and reducing and mitigating risks. Indirect costs are generally infrastructure related, with energy and transportation topping the list of major impediments; risks to be mitigated are particularly those relating to security of property, such as poor adjudication of disputes, crime, political instability, and macroeconomic instability. While effort in individual countries is the focal point of action, we also suggest pooling efforts to develop cohesive investment areas by, for example, coordinating investment promotion, coordinating policy, improving security, and increasing connectivity

In focusing on improving the business environment it is important to make the distinction that Rodrik and Subramanian (2004) make based on their analysis of India's growth revival since the 1980 pro-market and pro-business reforms. The role of leadership in spearheading the needed reforms and public action is critical for success. The former is concerned with removing impediments to the market, favoring entrants and consumers, and the latter is focused on raising the profitability of established enterprises—favoring incumbents and producers. Both orientations are important, but the sequence adopted by countries has varied, with differential impacts. India began with pro-business reforms in the 1980s before embarking on market liberalization in the 1990s.

The second pillar is *infrastructure*, which mainly targets transaction costs in production of goods and services. As the foregoing summary suggests, transportation and energy make up the largest proportion of indirect costs, weighing heavily on the competitiveness of firms in most African countries where investment climate surveys were conducted. Particular focus would be on how to reduce the high costs associated with the remoteness of landlocked countries in order to facilitate trade with neighbors as well as with the rest of the world. It is clear that there will be a need to look beyond individual country borders and adopt a regional approach to coordinate crossborder infrastructure investment, maintenance, operational management, and use (for example, power pooling) in order to lower costs.

Mindful of the need for more effective use of infrastructure assets, the chapter also emphasizes the importance of enhancing capacity for nonforbearing regulation of use and maintenance of these assets. Private-public partnerships would help ensure that these essentially public services not be underfunded and consequently require greater involvement of the public sector than in the previous two decades. At the same time, delivery of services would benefit from the operational efficiency of private management.

The third pillar is *innovation*, primarily emphasizing investment in information technology and skill formation (higher education) for enhanced productivity and competitiveness. The potential comparative advantage of low wages in Africa can be nullified by low productivity. Surveys of investors show that labor is not cheap where productivity is low (Lindbaek 1997). ICT is now the main driver for productivity growth. There is strong empirical evidence that shows that investment in ICT and in higher education boosts competitiveness, making both key parts of the growth agenda. As late starters, African countries can make a huge leap forward and beyond antiquated technology by exploiting the technological advantages of ICT.

The fourth pillar is *institutional capacity*. Again, the results from the investment climate assessment surveys and analysis for the *World Development Report* (World Bank 2005f) identify costs associated with contract enforcement difficulties, crime, corruption, and forbearing regulation as being among those weighing most heavily on the profitability of enterprises. The main focus of action here would be partly to strengthen the capacity of relevant public institutions for protecting property rights and partly to strengthen scrutiny of, and accountability for, public actions. Building institutional capacity entails strengthening individual competencies, organizational effectiveness, and rules of the game. Under this pillar, particular attention would be paid to capacity and space for scrutiny of public action—mainly within a framework of a strong domestic accountability system and capacity to clarify and protect property rights to spur private enterprise. The key strategic areas of action, therefore, would include enforcement of contracts (for example, commercial courts); exercise of voice as an agency of restraint, with enhanced involvement of civil society, media, and parliament; enhanced revenue transparency in resource-rich countries; and prevention of corruption as a country-driven agenda, including checks and balances.

Chapter 5 concludes with emphasis on the need to address the huge financing gap for scaling up growth. Several attempts to estimate the financing needs of African nations have been made, mainly on the basis of achieving the MDGs. To achieve annual growth rate of 7 percent, United Nations Conference on Trade and Development (UNCTAD 2000) estimated that Africa requires investment ratios averaging 25 percent of GDP over the next decade. Against Africa's saving rate of around 9 percent of GDP, this represents a major financing gap. For the short- to medium-term financing, it is clear that African countries are not in a position to generate any meaningful part of this requirement, making foreign savings (FDI and official development assistance, or ODA) and reversal of capital flight critical for achieving these targets. Over the longer term, however, African countries have to focus on measures to raise domestic resources as well as to retain its wealth on the continent. The gap appears to be particularly acute in the financing of public sector programs (shares of ODA financing of government budgets exceed 40 percent in a number of strong growth performers, such as Mozambique, Uganda, and Tanzania). Raising revenue efforts is therefore also important for domestic resource mobilization and ultimate reduction of dependence on aid.

Figure 1.4 is a schematic of the growth process discussed in this report. It describes the interactions among opportunities, the political environment significant to growth, and the critical constraints to exploiting the opportunities for growth. In a sense, the figure presents a snapshot of the key elements of the growth strategies outlined in the discussions of the earlier chapters and subsequently elaborated. We owe the schematic to Professor Ishikawa (2006), who developed it in the context of offering comments on the report to illustrate the complex interactions among economic variables in the process of determining growth outcomes.

The underlying growth model of the figure identifies the key channels through which output can be increased, either through accumulation of physical or human capital, or through rises in productivity growth spurred by improved efficiency and innovation. Three sets of factors are highlighted (in boxes 1, 2, and 3 in the schematic) that would influence the outcomes of sustained growth and, eventually, poverty reduction. First is the set of the initial conditions (box 1) that define the scope of opportunities prevailing in the region and constrain the policy and strategic choices (box 2) for accelerating growth. In addition, this set of factors directly influences the incentives and pace of capital accumulation and productivity growth. A set of political economy variables (box 3) are influential in shaping both strategic and policy choices. Leadership and how it is selected, the quality of public scrutiny, and accountability are among the most crucial aspects of political processes that have a bearing on the country's economic governance and, hence, on the quality of decisions. The outcome of the growth process is not confined simply to raising the nation's income, because the ultimate goal is poverty reduction and improved livelihoods. For the latter outcome, broad sharing of benefits from economic growth is imperative.

Though not a blueprint, the pillars of the growth strategies discussed earlier form the centerpiece of any attempt to increase competitiveness, diversify production, and accelerate growth in the medium term. The broad strategic approaches presented here need to be tailored to the specific situation of each country, which, in turn, means specific analysis of each country setting to reflect the political, social, and economic environments. Lessons can be learned from the experiences of East and South Asia, as well as from successful countries on the continent. What does Botswana have to teach African countries about managing mineral wealth and prudent public investment scrutiny? What lessons can be derived from Mauritius on export diversification? What lessons can Liberia and Burundi, for example, learn from Mozambique's and Rwanda's transformation from conflict to being among the fastest growing countries in the world? It is the hope of the authors that this report will strengthen the desire for such learning.

TABLE 1.1
Regional Growth Comparisons

			Initial values				
Region	Number of countries	Real GDP per capita (1996 PPP$)	Gross primary enrollment rate, 1960	Life expectancy at birth (years), 1962	Road density, 1969 (km road/ km² land)ᵃ	Real GDP per capita	
SSA	40	1,423.2	37.1	41.1	0.098 (23)	2,588.9	
Other developing	55	2,953.5	79.9	55.9	0.251 (25)	8,568.6	
LAC	24	3,103.0	86.6	56.5	0.057 (6)	6,039.2	
SAR	5	934.4	48.6	46.7	0.290 (1)	2,506.4	
EAP	13	3,508.3	90.5	58.5	0.538 (7)	14,929.4	
MENAT	13	2,899.3	68.4	55.6	0.171 (11)	9,209.2	
Industrialized	18	8,656.1	108.6	71.0	1.039 (16)	27,328.8	

Sources: WDI 2006, PWT 6.1 (Heston, Summers, and Aten 2002), GDN 1998, Ndulu 2006b, and Collier and O'Connell 2006.

Note: SSA = Sub-Saharan Africa; LAC = Latin America and the Caribbean; SAR = South Asia; EAP = East Asia and Pacific; MENAT = Middle East and North Africa, including Turkey; — = not available; km = kilometer; km² = square kilometer.

a. Number of countries in regional sample is given in parentheses.

b. An economy is classified as resource-rich if it generates more than 10% of its GDP from primary commodity rents (the excess of world prices over production costs). The category of primary commodities included is energy resources, other minerals and forests. They are also referred to as "natural resources". This is calculated as a share of the total number of countries in each region.

c. The Democratic Republic of Congo, Sudan, and Ethiopia have been treated as landlocked countries.

d. Only one country was sampled, Turkey. The average in Middle East and North Africa is zero.

	Ending values			Endowments		
	Gross primary enrollment rate, 2004	Life expectancy at birth (years), 2004	Road density (km road/ km^2 land), 1999	Fragmentation, (average number of borders	Share of population in landlocked countries (%)	Share of natural resource economy[b]
	95.8	47.9	0.130	4.00	40.2[c]	30
	107.5	71.3	0.411	2.91	7.51	29
	111.5	70.5	0.122	2.34	2.77	20
	103.8	65.1	0.850	2.75	3.78	0
	107.0	73.3	0.719	2.09	0.42	19
	103.3	73.0	0.334	4.44	23.06[d]	60
	102.5	78.9	1.447	—	—	—

FIGURE 1.4

Analytical Framework of the Growth Model

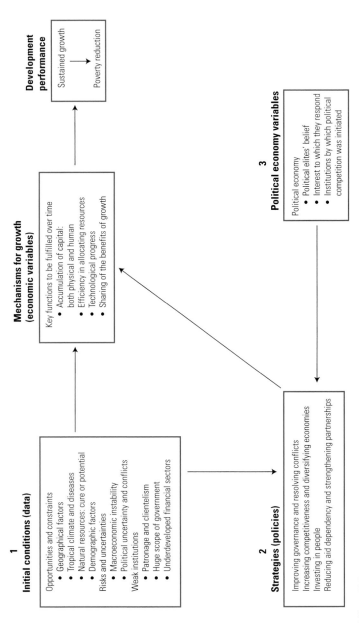

Source: Ishikawa 2006.

Notes

1. Angola, Cameroon, Cape Verde, Democratic Republic of Congo, Lesotho, Namibia, and Swaziland.
2. Botswana, Equatorial Guinea, Gabon, Mauritius, Seychelles, and South Africa.
3. These include Angola, Central African Republic, Comoros, Democratic Republic of Congo, Madagascar, Niger, Senegal, Sierra Leone, and Zambia.
4. For a comprehensive analysis of this issue see World Bank (2006d).
5. A short list of noteworthy contributions that draw on global data to make Africa-relevant contributions include Sachs and Warner (1995) on outward orientation; the same authors (1997, 2001) on the natural resource curse; Bloom and Sachs (1998) on geographic and demographic constraints; Masters and McMillan (2001) on tropical location and the disease environment; Easterly and Levine (1997) on ethnic fractionalization and policy; the same authors (1998) on neighborhood (spillover) effects; Collier (1999) and Collier and Hoeffler (2004) on civil wars; Mauro (1995) on corruption; Knack and Keefer (1995) on the rule of law; Acemoglu, Johnson, and Robinson (2001) on institutional legacies of the colonial period; Guillaumont, Guillaumont Jeanneney, and Brun (1999), Dehn (2000), and Blattman, Hwang, and Williamson (2004) on vulnerability to external shocks; Burnside and Dollar (2000) on aid; and Glaeser et al. (2004) on political leaders.
6. Researchers have attempted to reduce the dimensionality problem by isolating determinants that are robust to the inclusion or noninclusion of other variables (for example, Levine and Renelt 1993, Artadi and Sala-i-Martin 2003) and by constructing portmanteau variables that aggregate a variety of related proxies (for example, the celebrated Sachs and Warner "openness" variable, or the "diversion" variable constructed by Hall and Jones (1999).
7. This cost differential is also reflected in the wide divergence between the average share of investment in GDP for Sub-Saharan Africa measured in domestic and international prices. In domestic prices, this ratio for the period 1960 to 1994 (weighted by average GDP at 1985 international prices) was 19 percent, compared to only 9.5 percent at 1985 international prices.

CHAPTER 2

Africa's Long-Term Growth Experience in a Global Perspective

A central concern of this chapter is to highlight and characterize the relative stagnation of African economic growth in the past 45 years. For the entire four and a half decades (1960–2004), per capita income grew at a yearly average of 0.5 percent in the 41 Sub-Saharan Africa countries, compared to 3 percent in the 57 countries in the rest of the world's developing regions for which data for the full period are available. Sub-Saharan Africa missed out on the economic transformation that took place in the developing world—particularly in Asia—in the second half of the 20th century.

Two broad features differentiate the African growth record from the records of other developing regions. First, growth in most African countries has been more episodic than in other developing regions. For the region as a whole, a distinct long-term growth feature is its historical U-shaped path, featuring a deep and prolonged contraction of growth during 1974 to 1994, a period sandwiched between the moderately high growth rates of the 1960s and late 1990s. Most African countries experienced this pattern, with many of them beginning their postindependence years with a decade or so of fairly robust growth before that growth collapsed, beginning in the mid-1970s and lasting until 1995. This was followed by a subsequent recovery (Pritchett 1998), with much greater diversity emerging across countries in the region.

Second is the juxtaposition of this poor record with a population explosion that has served to further depress individual African incomes in comparison with those of citizens of other regions. In contrast to other developing regions, Africa embarked on a slow demographic transition only in the mid-1980s. Total fertility rates fell sharply outside Africa, while remaining virtually unchanged within Africa for two and a half decades after independence. Population growth rates therefore diverged sharply, and from the early 1970s through the remainder of the century, African populations grew more rapidly than the non-African developing world had grown *at its peak*. It is therefore not surprising that compared with other regions, differences in per capita incomes diverged more sharply than the gaps in economic growth. The difference in the population-weighted average growth rates, compared with other regions, is more pronounced, as figure 2.1 shows.

At the regional level, the four largest countries (Democratic Republic of Congo, Ethiopia, Nigeria, and South Africa), which account for 43 percent of total African population, posted a weighted-average per capita income growth rate of 0.26 percent—well below the regional average for the four and a half decades. As we will discuss further, resumption of sustained growth in these four African giants (particularly in Democratic Republic of

FIGURE 2.1

Smoothed Average Growth in Real GDP Per Capita: Sub-Saharan Africa and Other Regions

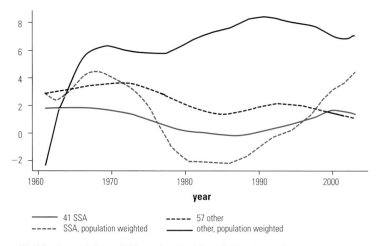

Sources: World Development Indicators (WDI) 2006, Penn World Tables (PWT) 6.1 (Heston, Summers, and Aten 2002), and Global Development Network (GDN) 1998.

Note: GDP = gross domestic product; SSA = Sub-Saharan Africa.

Congo, Ethiopia, and Nigeria) will go a long way toward bridging the individual income gaps between Sub-Saharan Africa and other developing regions. In the rest of this chapter we will focus on four main dimensions of the African growth experience: its evolution over the past four and a half decades, comparison with developing countries in Asia, diversity of experience and impact on individual incomes within Africa, and its sectoral composition.

Evolution

A distinct characteristic of Africa's long-term growth experience is its historical U-shaped path. Average, per capita growth rates of around 2 percent in the early 1960s rose to nearly 5 percent by the end of that decade, fell steadily through the early 1970s, turned negative during the mid-1980s, and then climbed back to around 2 percent since the mid-1990s.

As seen in figure 2.1, of the 41 African countries for which consistent growth data are available, African economies grew fairly rapidly during the first decade and a half after gaining independence. The average growth rate of the population-weighted per capita income for these 41 SSA countries in the early 1960s exceeded those of the other 57 developing countries. Between 1960 and 1994, nearly half of African countries for which comparable data existed, suffered per capita income losses exceeding 20 percent in constant 1985 US dollars (O'Connell and Ndulu 2000). The great bulk of these losses occurred between 1974 and 1994 (Rodrik 1998). The global deceleration of the 1970s took substantial portions of the continent into outright contraction. This period began with a set of shocks to energy and tropical commodity markets (1974–79), and ended with a concentrated wave of African democratic reforms (1989–94). By 2005, African growth had rebounded to the levels of the 1960s, comprised of much larger and more diversified economies than the 1960s decade.

Growth stagnation set in much earlier and lasted longest for the group of 34 African countries currently classified as low-income countries, compared to the 13 lower and upper, middle-income countries in the region (figure 2.2). The group of 34 low-income countries hosts 87 percent of Africa's population.

As noted earlier, for the entire four and a half decades (1960–2004), per capita income grew at a yearly average of 0.5 percent in the 41 SSA coun-

FIGURE 2.2

Average Growth Rates in Sub-Saharan Africa, by Income Categories

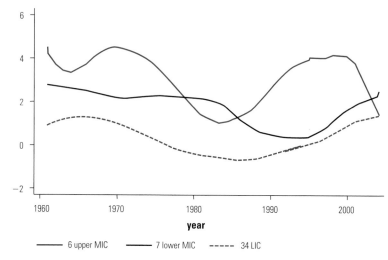

Source: WDI 2006.

Note: MIC indicates middle-income countries and LIC indicates lower-income countries. Growth rates refer to smoothed average growth rates in real GDP per capita.

tries compared to 3 percent in the 57 countries in the rest of the developing regions, for which data for the full period are available. Specifically, for the first decade and a half (1960–73), 13 African countries exceeded the global average growth rate (figure 2.3). These were Botswana, Côte d'Ivoire, Gabon, Kenya, Lesotho, Malawi, Mauritania, Namibia, Nigeria, Seychelles, South Africa, Tanzania, and Togo. Indeed, many development observers then were more optimistic about progress in Africa compared to Asian countries, particularly because countries such as Côte d'Ivoire, Ghana, and Zambia already had per capita incomes that exceeded those of East Asian countries, including the Republic of Korea.

A prolonged period of economic contraction occurred in Africa between 1974 and 1994, while other regions sustained or increased their growth. As a result, only seven African countries exceeded the global average growth rate during this period. These were Botswana, Burkina Faso, Cape Verde, Democratic Republic of Congo, Lesotho, Mauritius, and Seychelles. The trough for the growth contraction was reached in the 1980s, when there was the greatest divergence of the levels of incomes per head in Africa compared to other developing countries.

FIGURE 2.3
Average Per Capita Growth Rates: Global Distribution

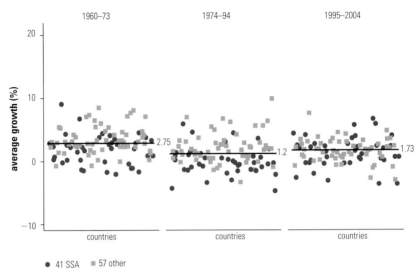

Sources: WDI 2006, PWT 6.1 (Heston, Summers, and Aten 2002), and GDN 1998.

Note: The horizontal line in each panel indicates the global average for the relevant time period. SSA = Sub-Saharan Africa.

During the last decade (1995–2004), there was a rapid revival of growth in Africa, resulting in 20 countries' per capita income growing at a pace exceeding the global average. The new entrants into this growth club were predominantly either countries with new discoveries or revived exploitation of natural resources (Angola, Chad, Equatorial Guinea, and Sudan) or strong reformers (Benin, Ethiopia, Ghana, Malawi, Mali, Mozambique, Senegal, and Tanzania). The revival of African growth since the mid-1990s lends the distinctive U shape to the region's overall growth record for 1960–2004.

Benchmarking against Asian Economies

African growth performance diverged significantly from that of other regions. Figure 2.4 compares average growth rates in Africa with those of East Asia and Pacific (EAP) and South Asia (SAR) from 1960 to 2004. The first point of difference is the significantly higher levels of growth observed in the Asian economies, on average, over the entire period in comparison

FIGURE 2.4

Smoothed Average Growth in Real GDP Per Capita: Sub-Saharan Africa, South Asia, and East Asia and Pacific

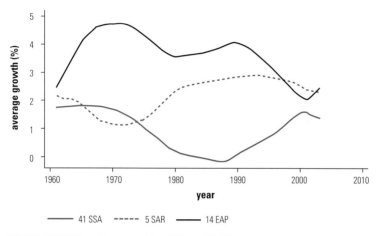

Sources: WDI 2006, PWT 6.1 (Heston, Summers, and Aten 2002), and GDN 1998.

Note: SSA = Sub-Saharan Africa; SAR = South Asia; EAP = East Asia and Pacific.

to Africa, except in the early 1960s. The East Asian growth path lies completely above Africa's regional average growth rate throughout the four decades, whereas the South Asian countries start out with growth rates similar to Africa's, only to diverge from it for the rest of the time period. The divergence of growth performance is particularly sharp between the mid-1970s and mid-1980s, during which a combination of Asia's accelerating growth and the collapse of growth in Africa quickly widened the gap. More than half of this growth gap was accounted for by the sharp contraction of growth in Africa, rather than by the acceleration of Asian growth rates. The more recent convergence of the two sets of growth rates, likewise, is more a result of the brisk recovery of growth in African countries since the mid-1990s, while Asian countries have maintained fairly high average growth rates.

Second, unlike Africa's U-shaped evolution of growth rates, Asian countries have followed a sustained growth path. In the initial phase from 1960 to 1973, East Asia and Pacific's growth rates rose very steeply, attaining a peak average around the early 1970s, and beginning a slow decline along with the rest of the world about the same time as African economies began a sharp decline. South Asia began its steep rise in growth late in the 1970s and sustained the pace to reach the EAP average rates in the late 1990s. Since 1995, African-country average growth rates appear to be converging with those of East Asia and Pacific and South Asia.

As observed earlier, the gap in terms of population-weighted average growth rates was much wider during the entire period. The resultant divergence of African incomes relative to those of Asian incomes, measured in terms of real gross domestic product (GDP) per capita, is phenomenal and mirrors the comparative time trends of the growth performance as discussed (see figure 2.5).

Diversity across Africa

Although the evolution of the average growth performance described above fits most African countries' experiences, it masks a wide variation of growth performance across individual African countries within each of the three phases. For example, roughly half of the 21 economies studied by Pritchett (1998)—a group accounting for nearly 80 percent of Sub-

FIGURE 2.5

GDP Per Capita Index—Sub-Saharan Africa and Other Regions, 1960–2004

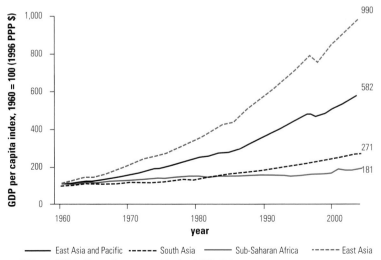

Source: WDI 2006, PWT 6.1 (Heston, Summeres, and Aten), and GDN 1998.

Note: GDP per capita index 1960 = 100.

Saharan Africa's GDP and population—exhibited reasonably robust growth before the long period of stagnation; the other half tended to show persistent stagnation at growth rates below 1.5 percent throughout.

As a further illustration of the differences, figure 2.6 shows the diametrically opposite patterns of growth rates observed in four African countries. Nigeria and Democratic Republic of Congo, for instance, exhibit the typical U-shaped pattern of growth discussed earlier. In contrast, Botswana and Mauritius follow an inverted U-shaped growth path, reaching their peaks of 8 percent to 10 percent in the 1970s and 1980s, respectively, before leveling off to around 4 percent to 5 percent in the more recent years, more or less similar to the experience of Asian countries.

What is more striking is how rapidly country growth performance has diversified since the mid-1990s. Between 1995 and 2004, 12 African countries have seen GDP growth rates in excess of 5 percent, alongside others that are experiencing negative growth rates. This differentiation is becoming wider over time, as exemplified by the comparative performance dur-

FIGURE 2.6
Smoothed Average Growth in Real GDP Per Capita: Nigeria, Democratic Republic of Congo, Botswana, and Mauritius

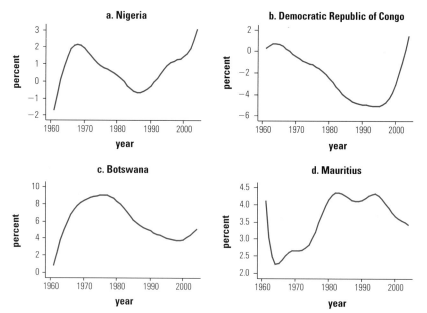

Sources: WDI 2006, PWT 6.1 (Heston, Summers, and Aten 2002), and GDN 1998.

ing the most recent five-year period (1999–2004). Excluding the oil countries, median per capita growth rates in the fastest-growing, middle, and slowest-growing thirds of the African countries we have studied—each comprising 13 countries—were 3.3 percent, 1.2 percent, and –1.0 percent, respectively.[1] Outside of the mineral-exporting group, rapid growth during this period has also been associated with substantial diversification of production and exports.

The other major contrast is between large and small countries' growth rates (figure 2.7a). African countries with large populations exceeding 35 million (Nigeria, Democratic Republic of Congo, Ethiopia, and South Africa) have grown much more slowly than small and medium-size countries, pulling down population-weighted average growth rates of the region. An extreme example is the case of the Democratic Republic of Congo, which hosts nearly 8 percent of Sub-Saharan Africa's population, with a negative average growth rate of per capita income for the 45-year period of –2.7 percent. The average growth rate for the group fell behind the others particularly sharply during the growth contraction phase. The gap closed rapidly after the late 1990s, partly reflecting revival of growth in Nigeria, helped along by the oil price boom, reduction of hostilities in the Democratic Republic of Congo, and strong growth performance in Ethiopia after the fall of the Derg regime.

As can be seen in figure 2.7b, population growth rates from 1960 to 2004 within Africa were higher for countries with large- and medium-size populations than for those with small ones. At the same time, GDP per capita growth rates of all three categories, as seen in figure 2.7a, started improving around 1995, following the downward trends in population growth rates of all three categories of countries from 1985 to 1990. The figure shows that these large countries have grown on average about 1.5 percent to 3 percent slower than the small countries over the period from 1960 to 1990. It is only from the 1990s until 2004 that there seems to be a convergence pattern among all three types of countries based on their total population sizes. The evidence also points to the age dependency ratios of the small countries being about 7 percent to 10 percent lower than both the medium-size and the large countries. However, the potential labor force growth rates for these three categories do not seem to be significantly different from one another, as can be seen in figure 2.7d.

We also distinguish growth performance across countries in four opportunity groups, determined by location and resource endowment. Table 2.1

FIGURE 2.7
Growth Rates and Demographic Indicators, by Size

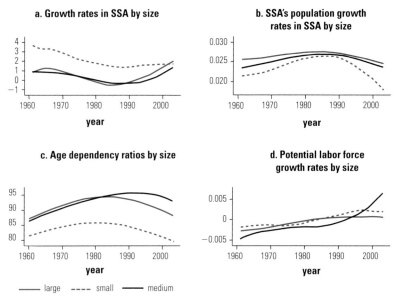

Sources: WDI 2006, PWT 6.1 (Heston, Summers, and Aten 2002), and GDN 1998.

includes the list of countries classified by opportunity sets, along with their GDP and population shares in Sub-Saharan Africa, as well as other key indicators of economic and social progress at the beginning and end of the period of analysis (1961–2004). About one-third of African economies are landlocked, compared to the global average of 11 percent. About 30 percent of the countries in Sub-Saharan Africa are resource rich, compared to 19 percent in EAP and 0 percent in SAR. These criteria are important in terms of distinguishing growth performance (Collier and O'Connell 2006). Globally, while coastal economies have invariably done better than their landlocked counterparts, resource-rich coastal countries have underperformed compared with the coastal resource-poor economies over the entire period from 1970 to 2004.

Figure 2.8 confirms broadly that SSA coastal economies outperform landlocked economies, but being resource rich under both categories confers a growth performance advantage over their poorer cousins, particularly during times of resource price booms. What is even more striking is that the landlocked, resource-rich economies trump all other categories, most likely driven by Botswana's stellar sustained growth performance. The other resource-rich, landlocked country included in the sample is Zambia, which, as we saw earlier, posted reasonably rapid growth until the mid-1970s.

The impact of the diverse growth experience is also reflected in the impact it has had on individual incomes and welfare. Taking a long-term trend look, countries have distinguished themselves in terms of how much their incomes per capita have grown over the 45-year period. Figure 2.9 depicts the wide variation in the progress made by the 40 African countries for which we have complete data. Table 2.1 also presents the population and income weights of each of these countries. Each country's progress in per capita income since 1960 is measured by the ratio of per capita income in 2004 to that in 1960 (in 1996 international dollars). In nine countries income per capita has actually regressed relative to the levels in 1960.[2] Surprisingly, only three among these are countries that have suffered from prolonged conflict (Angola, Sierra Leone, and Democratic Republic of Congo). The rest appear to have had long periods of very slow growth or to have suffered prolonged crises as they struggled to climb out of the shocks suffered during the late 1970s.

As expected, African middle-income countries generally grew more rapidly than their counterpart low-income ones. Of the 13 middle-income countries, 7 have acquired their current status largely on account of their mineral wealth, including oil. Not all African middle-income countries, however, experienced rapid growth or grew throughout the 45-year period. South Africa's 2004 GDP per capita at 1996 international prices, for example, was only 20 percent above that of 1960. Equatorial Guinea's newfound oil wealth suddenly catapulted it into the club of upper-middle-income countries. Given that more than half of the African middle-income countries are resource rich, volatility of growth has also been a characteristic of their growth experience.

The rest of the Sub-Saharan Africa countries are bunched in a narrow range between stagnation (ratio of 1) and a doubling of income per capita over a 45-year period—a relatively low achievement by global standards. Most of these experienced economic stagnation for two decades between the mid-1970s and mid-1990s, usually after respectable growth performance in the previous decade and a half. For countries such as Uganda, Mozambique, and Ghana, rapid growth during the past 15 years has enabled them to more than recoup the severe losses in income suffered during the previous two decades. As expected, differences in average

TABLE 2.1

Growth and Selected Indicators in African Countries, Categorized by Opportunity Groups

Country	Average growth in real GDP per capita, 1961–2004 (%)	Ratio of income in 2004 to 1960 (per capita)	Proportion of GDP in SSA, 1960 (%)	Proportion of population in SSA, 1960 (%)	Gross primary enrollment rate, 1960 (%)
Coastal, Resource Rich					
Gabon	2.44	2.73	4.86	0.22	—
Mauritania	1.59	1.75	1.80	0.44	8
Congo, Rep. of	1.47	4.17	0.73	0.44	78
Cameroon	1.01	1.28	2.76	2.37	65
Nigeria	0.86	1.18	1.69	18.26	36
Namibia	0.83	1.34	5.33	0.28	—
Guinea	0.23	1.05	4.48	1.40	30
Angola	−0.16	0.69	4.01	2.15	21
Sierra Leone	−0.83	0.88	1.75	1.00	23
Coastal, Resource Poor					
Mauritius	3.61	5.01	5.03	0.30	98
Cape Verde	3.45	4.16	1.62	0.09	—
Tanzania	1.43	1.52	0.62	4.56	25
Kenya	1.23	1.49	1.27	3.73	47
Gambia	1.09	1.41	1.55	0.16	12
South Africa	1.00	1.60	8.01	7.78	89
Togo	0.89	1.21	1.46	0.68	44
Benin	0.70	1.20	1.75	0.92	27
Mozambique	0.60	1.05	2.55	3.34	48
Côte d'Ivoire	0.55	1.01	2.62	1.69	46
Ghana	0.22	1.85	1.36	3.03	38
Senegal	0.10	0.95	2.99	1.43	27
Comoros	−0.24	0.91	3.15		14
Guinea–Bissau	−0.85	1.11	0.69	0.24	25
Madagascar	−0.99	0.64	2.01	2.40	52
Landlocked, Resource Rich					
Botswana	6.37	9.08	1.60	0.21	42
Zambia	−0.59	0.77	1.90	1.41	42
Landlocked, Resource Poor					
Lesotho	3.31	4.38	1.17	0.39	83
Seychelles	2.48	3.4	5.01	0.02	—
Uganda	1.93	1.98	0.91	2.94	49
Malawi	1.32	1.64	0.69	1.58	—
Sudan	1.31	1.61	1.65	4.99	25
Burkina Faso	1.22	1.42	1.25	2.07	8
Ethiopia*	0.82	1.27	0.86	10.19	7
Chad	0.69	1.93	1.91	1.37	17
Rwanda	0.56	1.13	1.53	1.23	49
Burundi	0.44	1.16	0.84	1.32	18
Mali	0.23	1.11	1.62	1.95	10
Central African Rep.	−0.76	0.54	3.52	0.69	32
Niger	−1.31	0.49	2.63	1.35	5
Congo, Dem. Rep. of	−2.66	0.24	1.57	6.86	60

Sources: Author calculations based on WDI 2006, PWT 6.1 (Heston, Summers, and Aten 2002), and GDN 1998.

Note: Ethiopia became landlocked in 1994, with the independence of Eritrea. Seven out of the 47 countries are not included because they did not have complete data for 1960. — = not available; km = kilometer; km² = square kilometer.

Life expectancy at birth, 1962 (years)	Road density, 1969 (km road/ km² land)	Proportion of GDP in SSA, 2004 (%)	Proportion of population in SSA, 2004 (%)	Gross primary enrollment rate, 2004 (%)	Life expectancy at birth, 2004 (years)	Road density 1999 (km road/ km² land)
41.48	0.020	7.29	0.18	130	54.08	0.032
39.46	0.007	1.73	0.39	94	53.26	0.007
42.64	—	1.68	0.53	89	52.48	0.037
40.46	0.095	1.93	2.25	117	45.98	0.074
40.46	0.096	1.10	19.71	99	43.65	0.213
43.72	—	3.92	0.28	—	47.46	0.080
34.29	—	2.58	1.11	79	53.90	0.124
33.96	0.060	1.51	1.97	—	41.18	0.041
32.01	—	0.85	0.75	145	41.11	0.158
60.26	0.970	13.82	0.17	103	72.67	0.941
52.96	—	3.70	0.07	111	70.42	0.273
41.66	0.018	0.52	5.07	101	46.19	0.100
45.95	0.070	1.04	4.50	111	48.35	0.112
32.96	—	1.20	0.20	81	56.34	0.270
49.95	—	7.03	6.48	—	44.64	0.298
40.51	—	0.97	0.69	101	54.80	0.138
40.03	0.060	1.16	0.94	99	54.57	0.061
38.51	0.047	1.47	2.67	95	41.83	0.039
40.46	0.109	1.45	2.39	—	46.12	0.158
46.05	—	1.38	2.96	81	57.20	0.173
38.21	0.078	1.55	1.41	76	56.14	0.076
43.49	—	1.58	0.08	85	62.87	0.395
34.93	—	0.42	0.21	—	44.95	0.156
41.67	—	0.71	2.39	134	55.65	0.086
47.51	—	8.00	0.24	105	35.49	0.018
42.76	0.046	0.81	1.41	99	38.08	0.090
44.44	—	2.83	0.25	131	35.60	0.196
—	—	9.36	0.01	110	—	—
45.46	0.130	0.99	3.52	125	48.89	—
38.43	0.113	0.62	1.55	125	40.22	0.302
39.67	—	1.45	4.79	60	56.55	0.005
36.97	0.060	0.97	1.69	53	48.10	0.046
36.91	0.006	0.60	9.71	77	42.48	0.029
35.46	0.020	2.03	1.21	71	43.88	0.027
42.96	0.250	0.95	1.18	119	43.92	0.486
41.96	—	0.54	1.01	80	44.23	0.564
36.78	0.009	0.99	1.69	64	48.31	0.012
39.49	0.034	1.05	0.55	64	39.41	0.038
35.96	0.005	0.72	1.69	45	44.70	0.008
41.96	0.060	0.21	7.46	—	43.71	0.069

FIGURE 2.8

Sub-Saharan Africa's Smoothed Average Growth in Real GDP Per Capita by Opportunity Groups

Countries with full set of growth observations

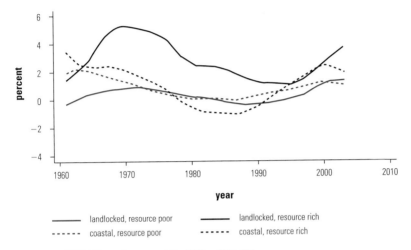

Sources: WDI 2006, PWT 6.1 (Heston, Summers, and Aten 2002), and GDN 1998.

FIGURE 2.9

Growth Experience of Countries in Sub-Saharan Africa

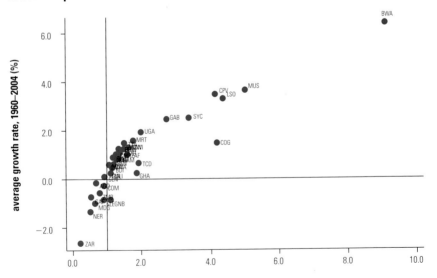

Sources: WDI 2006, PWT 6.1 (Heston, Summers, and Aten 2002), and GDN 1998.

growth rates match the differences in the progress made in terms of per capita incomes.

What is also striking is that countries with very similar opportunities also have very different growth experience and outcomes, depending on the strategies pursued and the policy disposition adopted. To illustrate this, boxes 2.1 and 2.2 present contrasting outcomes from different strategic approaches adopted by pairs of countries with similar resource bases or geographic situations. These pairs can have widely differing experiences because of different strategic approaches. The two boxes compare the experiences of Botswana and Zambia, both landlocked and resource rich, and Mauritius and Côte d'Ivoire, both coastal and (initially) agriculturally based. Differences in the long-term strategies adopted in exploiting similar opportunities ended up with Botswana and Mauritius being in the upper-middle-income countries; however, Zambia's and Côte d'Ivoire's per capita incomes have hardly progressed relative to their levels in 1960.

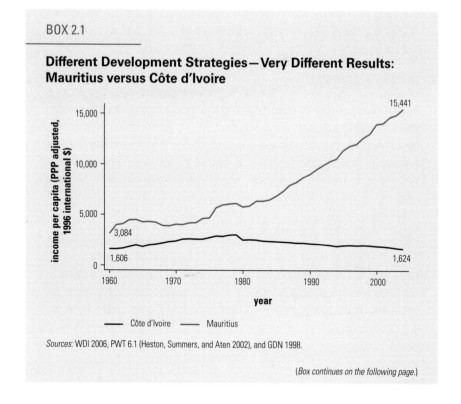

BOX 2.1

Different Development Strategies — Very Different Results: Mauritius versus Côte d'Ivoire

Sources: WDI 2006, PWT 6.1 (Heston, Summers, and Aten 2002), and GDN 1998.

(Box continues on the following page.)

BOX 2.1 *continued*

Côte d'Ivoire and Mauritius are both coastal, resource-poor countries that chose to pursue very different development paths with very different outcomes. Côte d'Ivoire chose the import substitution approach to structural transformation after initial and successful agricultural export–led growth. Mauritius opted for export diversification and export-led structural transformation after initial attempts to follow an import substitution strategy. By 2004, Côte d'Ivoire's GDP per capita of $1,624 (in 1996 international dollars) was more or less the same as it was in 1960 ($1,606). In contrast, with a GDP per capita of $15,441 (in 1996 international dollars) in 2004, Mauritius' income per capita is five times its 1960 level of $3,084.

Mauritius did have a head start in human development—much higher life expectancies and educational attainment. Mauritius consolidated this position and is now among the world's upper-middle-income countries. From a largely monoculture economy—sugar, with initial intent to take the path of import substitution—Mauritius changed strategies in the early 1970s toward a private sector–led, diversified export economy and has stayed the course at a phenomenal average growth rate of 5.4 percent for nearly four decades now.

This pivotal strategy involved a combination of export-promotion policies, channeling of rents from preferential sugar export agreements with Europe (guaranteed volume of exports at a price on average about 90 percent above market price) to finance domestic private sector investment for export diversification, and export-oriented foreign direct investment from economies like Hong Kong (China). In successfully exploiting the global opportunities for growth, the role of government was emphasized in creating political, social, and economic institutions for the better functioning of markets.

Policies aimed at securing manufactured export–led growth proved crucial for the sustained growth performance of this isolated island economy. Since the mid-1980s, the volume of goods imported and exported by Mauritius has grown rapidly, at annual rates of 8.7 percent and 5.4 percent, respectively. The openness ratio has correspondingly increased from about

70 percent to 100 percent, while Africa's average stagnated at around 45 percent (Subramanian 2001). Preferential access provided by Mauritius' trading partners for sugar and for textile and clothing, which together accounted for about 90 percent of Mauritius' total exports, implicitly subsidized the export sector growth.

Côte d'Ivoire, however, locked in primary commodity export dependence, presents a contrasting growth experience. For the 45 years since 1960 the average growth rate of Côte d'Ivoire's per capita income has been approximately zero. The significant growth in the first 15 years since 1960, under Houphet Boigny was virtually offset by the decline in income per capita since the late 1970s. Agriculture provided about 75 percent of export earnings in 1965, with coffee and cocoa as the country's major exports. By 2004, this situation had hardly changed—agriculture provided 60 percent of export earnings, with the coffee and cocoa sector, bringing in about 40 percent of export revenue (AfDB/OECD 2005).

In contrast to the Mauritian strategy of export diversification and export-led growth (and like many other African countries), Côte d'Ivoire implemented a vigorous but unsuccessful import substitution strategy for manufacturing and agricultural processing. The strategy was financed by a combination of taxing the agricultural sector and attracting foreign direct investment into capital-intensive industrial activities. Foreign direct investment was attracted through incentives that offered attractive returns to investors and reduced infrastructural transaction costs. Between 1960 and 1980, light manufacturing grew at the rate of 13 percent per year, and its contribution to GDP increased from 4 percent in 1960 to 17 percent in 1984. In 2002–03, this contribution remained more or less unchanged at 18 to 19 percent. It is argued, however, that the bulk of earnings from the capital invested in industry flowed out of the country in the forms of tax-free profits, salary remittances, and repatriated capital.

A key contrast with Mauritius on the policy front is the overvaluation of the CFA franc, which became most severe during 1980 to 1994, ushering in the growth collapse and the Côte d'Ivoire debt crisis, which Mauritius did not have. By the time these problems were resolved in the mid-1990s, nearly two decades after Mauritius embarked on its reforms, instability had set in, exacerbating stagnation.

BOX. 2.2

Contrasting Growth Paths of Two Landlocked, Resource-Rich Countries: Botswana and Zambia

Sources: World Development Indicators (WDI) 2006, Penn World Tables (PWT) 6.1 (Heston, Summers, and Aten 2002), and Global Development Network (GDN) 1998.

Botswana and Zambia are two landlocked, resource-rich African countries that have followed two very different approaches in managing and using the rents from their resource wealth to achieve very different outcomes. Botswana's remarkable per capita income growth performance, averaging 6.4 percent over the period from 1960 to 2004, enabled it to move from a low-income poor country in 1960 to an upper-middle-income country ($8,936 in 1996 international dollars) since 1998. Zambia's per capita income, however, on average retrogressed at (0.6 percent per annum over the past 45 years, and as a result, its 2004 level of $902 in 1996 international prices is 23 percent below the 1960 level of $1,167. It is striking that Botswana's 1960 per capita income was 20 percent below that of Zambia. The two countries' income paths crossed each other around 1970, moving in opposite directions.

Botswana, the fastest-growing economy in Africa (and among the fastest globally) is landlocked, natural resource dependent, and lacking a history as a settler colony; hence, it is not a beneficiary of institutions evolving where colonists settled. Arguably, four major reasons are behind this success story: the strength of its state capacity; its being part of Southern Africa's relatively effective infrastructure system, which helped offset the negative effects of remoteness; its belonging to the Southern African customs union and monetary area (for a long period), which served as a commitment instrument against rent seeking; and, most important, its incessant following of the self-disciplinary rule called the Sustainable Budget Index, for the use of mineral rents and managing of reserves, combined with stringent application of public scrutiny to the government's expenditure and investment program (Maipose and Matsheka 2006; Rodrik 2003).

About 40 percent of Botswana's growth rate, on average, was accounted for by the growth in the mining sector, although recent economic diversification has reduced this contribution (Iimi 2006). Minerals accounted for 80 percent of its exports. The government share of mineral revenue averaged around 50 percent, and this source of revenue amounts to 35 percent of GDP.

Botswana managed and used rents from its mineral wealth prudently and equitably. Part of its strategy was to channel the returns from the abundant mineral endowment into improving human capital and the social well-being of its citizens. The government avoided Dutch disease mainly because the government had taken care not to spend more than the economy could absorb. Reserve accumulation during boom periods and rapid responses to adverse terms-of-trade shocks are two crucial facets of Botswana's super-prudent macroeconomic policy. For example, three funds were established to provide for stabilization reserves, public debt service, and local development opportunities (Faber 1997).

A secure political elite (with electoral support since independence) had pursued growth-promoting policies, which it developed or modified, and maintained viable traditional and modern institutions of political, economic, and legal restraint, thereby minimizing the adverse consequences of resource wealth. Sustainable development was underlined by development planning and pragmatism—not ideological dogma. Under this approach, all mineral revenues were supposed to finance investment expenditure, defined as development expenditure and recurrent spending on education and health.

Zambia chose a very different approach to managing and using its natural resource wealth. Following the Fabian socialist principle—the state has

(Box continues on the following page.)

BOX 2.2 *continued*

responsibility for collecting and redistributing rents from capital, natural resources, and labor to achieve egalitarian goals—Zambia's first leader decided
to have strong state involvement in the copper industry. Overall, policy environment and weaknesses in governance in Zambia combined to create a
capital-hostile environment, limiting accumulation and undermining productivity growth by diverting investable resources to unproductive uses.

Mwanawina and Mukungushi (2006) present three sad stories of the copper industry in Zambia. First, around the time of independence, Zambia,
along with other key producers, adopted a monopolistic strategy in the
global mining market by cutting down production with the hopes of affecting the world supply of copper and exerting upward pressure on the world
price of copper. Consequently, the country lost out on potential mineral revenues at the same time it was diverting financial resources toward maintenance of stocks, away from investment.

Second, government discouraged private investment in the industry, notwithstanding stagnation of production following nationalization. This exacerbated
the pressure on local borrowing and deterioration of the balance-of-payments
position. The decline in production continued even after the privatization of
the major mining assets, including the development of the Konkola Deep
Mining Project and the Mufurila and Nkana divisions in 2000; fiscal pressures
mounted largely because of huge tax concessions given to the new owners
of the mines. This denied the government much-needed tax revenue, not to
mention the huge liabilities that the government assumed concurrently.

Third, notwithstanding sustained declines in copper prices in the world
market, the government stance was to treat this as a reversible shock that
needed to be financed, rather than viewing this as a longer-term change requiring serious adjustment and diversification efforts away from copper.
Combined with the effects of a failed import substitution strategy, the collapse in Zambia's revenue base from copper led to a long-trend decline in
per capita income and social development.

Whereas a much narrower difference in the average investment rates between the two countries is much less (investment-GDP ratios of 20 percent for Zambia and 26 percent for Botswana), the wide differences in GDP
growth are quite striking. This gap most likely illustrates how the difference
in policy environment and in the quality of scrutiny of public investment can
have huge effects on the ex ante productivity of investment.

Sectoral Composition

Globally, structural transformation of economies has provided the bedrock of accelerated and sustained growth. Rural and agriculture-dominated economies in Asia, for example, have undergone significant diversification away from agriculture even as they underwent phenomenal productivity growth in that sector through the green revolution. The rapidly growing Asian countries, for example, have either diversified toward manufactures or agro-industries. Africa remains the region most dependent on agriculture for livelihood, exports, and employment although, as in the case of the growth experience, there is some diversity across countries within Africa.

Slow growth has gone hand in hand with limited structural diversification. Traditional agriculture continues to absorb the majority of the labor force in many African countries, a feature no longer observed in any other region of the world. At the close of the 20th century, nearly three-quarters of African livelihoods were still being earned in the agricultural sector—fully a standard deviation above the level characteristic of other developing countries *in the late 1960s* (Ndulu and O'Connell 2006a). As will be seen later, the relative size of the agricultural sector is in line with the low level of per capita income in most African countries. On average, agriculture by the end of the 20th century still contributed roughly one-third of total GDP in African countries, a share nearly two standard deviations above the non-African developing-country mean[3] (O'Connell and Ndulu 2000). Irrigation is expensive and extremely limited, with the result that African agriculture remains largely rain fed and subject to periodic drought.

However, Africa's share of GDP in industry and within its manufacturing subsector (accounting for about 60 percent of industry) has risen slowly since the early 1970s, mirroring the trend of the overall developing-country mean. The African share, however, diverges strongly from that of the East Asia and Pacific, which increased substantially over the period, and more recently, Sub-Saharan Africa is also slipping behind South Asian countries. The services sector share of GDP has averaged 43 percent in Sub-Saharan Africa. This average showed a pattern of increase until the early 1980s, and then decreased thereafter.

Following the approach used by Syrquin and Chenery (1989; see table 2.2), O'Connell and Ndulu (2000) assess whether the patterns of sectoral transformation in African countries depart systematically from what

TABLE 2.2
Predicted Shares of Economic Structure at Selected Levels of Income Per Capita
Percent

Component of economic structure	Actual average share for $y < 300$	Share predicted for per capita income level (at official exchange rates)		
		$y = 300$	$y = 500$	$y = 1,000$
	(1)	(2)	(3)	(4)
Final demand				
Private consumption	79	73.3	70.2	66.4
Government consumption	12	13.6	13.5	13.7
Investment	14	18.4	20.8	23.3
Exports	16	19.3	20.7	22.6
Imports	21	24.6	25.2	26.0
Food consumption	39	0.15	34.5	29.1
Trade				
Merchandise exports	14	15.2	16.9	18.8
Primary	13	13.9	14.9	15.2
Manufacturing	1	1.3	2.0	3.7
Production (value added)				
Agriculture	48	39.4	31.7	22.8
Mining	1	5.0	6.6	7.7
Manufacturing	10	12.1	14.8	18.1
Construction	4	4.4	4.9	5.5
Utilities	6	6.7	7.4	8.1
Services	31	32.4	34.6	37.8
Labor force				
Agriculture	81	74.9	65.1	51.7
Industry	7	9.2	13.2	19.2
Services	12	15.9	21.7	29.1

Source: Syrquin and Chenery 1989, cited in O'Connell and Ndulu 2000.

would be expected given the continent's overall income levels and cross-country norms.

The authors conclude that given the levels of income and population, the size of the service sector is markedly smaller in Sub-Saharan Africa, and that of industry and its manufacturing subsector is markedly larger than would be predicted on the basis of cross-country norms. Agricultural output shares are just slightly higher in Sub-Saharan Africa than predicted on the basis of income and population. The share of the labor force in agriculture, in contrast, is notably larger. Consistent with these findings, the labor productivity differential in favor of nonagricultural activities tends to be much higher in Sub-Saharan Africa than in other regions.

In fact, despite the large relative size of agriculture in GDP, African countries have been diversifying into manufacturing more rapidly than would be expected given their levels of per capita income (O'Connell and Ndulu 2000). The movement into services is somewhat slower than predicted.

Finally, the structure of exports has also remained fairly undiversified, with continued concentration in a narrow band of primary commodities (Berthelemy and Soderling 2001, 2002), including minerals. Collier and O'Connell (2006), using global data on rents from primary commodity exports, specifically from energy, mineral, and forest resources, classify a country as a "natural resource economy" or "resource rich" if it generates more than 10 percent of its GDP in primary commodities rents. Using this criterion comparing Sub-Saharan Africa with other developing regions excluding Middle East and North Africa, they find that a stark contrast already existed in 1960, with 12.5 percent of the SSA sample classified as resource rich, compared to only 7 percent of the non-Sub-Saharan Africa sample. With new mineral deposit discoveries, over time this difference expanded as 16.7 percent of the African sample acquired resource-rich status, compared to only 10.5 percent of the non-African.

One consequence of Africa's delayed structural transformation and uncharacteristically high dependence on primary commodities has been high growth volatility, with some stemming from erratic world commodity prices. Furthermore, for nearly three decades since the late 1960s, world commodity prices have tended to decline, resulting in declining export revenues, sometimes even in the face of expanding quantities of exports. More recently, however, with China's phenomenal increase in demand for base metals and oil, this trend appears to have reversed, leading to a rise in growth in oil exporting countries and other mineral exporters, such as Zambia.

Conclusions

There are three important conclusions we can draw from the analysis of the growth record in this chapter. First, unlike their Asian counterparts, African countries, though capable of spurts of high growth, have been unable to sustain these over longer periods. It is therefore imperative to understand the reasons behind episodic growth that characterizes many of these countries, and to place greater emphasis on prudent management of responses to shocks. Second, not only has the past decade and a half seen more countries with higher growth, but there has been a significant upward shift in the growth trajectory for the 15 fast growers, as well as a sustaining of the faster pace. This may point to concurrent scaling up of growth, diversification of its sources, and fundamental changes in the growth process. In any case, this change challenges the report to explain this shift and draw lessons for the future. Third, there is far greater diversity in growth performance during the past decade and a half than during the period of growth collapse in the previous two decades. It is therefore important to better understand what characteristics distinguish these countries and hence are critical drivers of growth. Furthermore, since there are also significant differences in the growth performance across opportunity groups, country context is important to the success of growth strategies, and any strategic direction offered at the level of this report has to provide options that accommodate the different contextual needs. It is also for this reason that the report not only looks at regional trends, but also presents assessments of the relative importance of the key drivers for individual countries.

Notes

1. Oil-exporting countries grew at a median per capita rate of 3.5 percent. The upper, middle, and lower thirds of the growth distribution comprise 17 percent, 29 percent, and 25 percent of Africa's population, respectively.
2. These include Angola, Central African Republic, Comoros, Democratic Republic of Congo, Madagascar, Niger, Senegal, Sierra Leone, and Zambia.
3. For these sectoral GDP shares, we use value added in constant 1995 dollars in order to abstract from relative price movements.

CHAPTER 3

Explaining the African Growth Record: What Appears to Matter Most

In this chapter, we examine the influential factors behind the African growth record and assess their relative importance in the growth experience in African countries. This is done using three approaches: First, at an aggregate level we employ the conventional decomposition of sources of growth to assess the relative importance of capital accumulation, labor, and productivity to growth. This is done for the region as a whole and for the 19 African countries for which complete and consistent data are available. We rely in particular on the work by Collins and Bosworth (1996, 2003) and Ndulu and O'Connell (2003), with the latter covering a larger set of African countries. A key conclusion from this analysis is that we have to look beyond differences in the rate of factor accumulation to understand Africa's lagging growth performance compared with that of other regions. We have to unpack the large productivity residual by employing meso- and microanalysis.

Second (and partly to confirm the aforementioned conclusions), we use firm-level data from investment climate surveys to assess the relative importance of different factors on the attractiveness of African countries to investors and the cost of doing business. The assessment uses the benchmarks of other developing countries to assess the state of institutional, policy, and regulatory frameworks; business regulations and their enforcement; adequacy and quality of infrastructure; macroeconomic stability; protection of property rights; and functioning of the financial system. A separate study assessing constraints to private sector growth, prepared as a background paper for this report (Ramachandran, Tata, and Shah 2006), provides more details of this assessment.

Third, we compare the extent of the deviation of the growth conditions in African countries from those obtaining in other regions, to establish where the gaps are widest. First, using the vast cross-country empirical work on growth and employing global data assembled for this study, we identify the globally important factors for explaining growth and assess how these are important in the African countries' growth experience. Then we undertake a benchmarking exercise for African growth conditions relative to three comparators—global average of developing countries, South Asia, and East Asia and Pacific. Noting that the region has lagged seriously behind in growth, we include East Asia and Pacific among the comparators to emphasize the magnitude of the effort needed to close the gap. We also track the changes in the individual components of these growth conditions (that is, the factors influencing growth) over the three phases of the U-shaped path of the African growth experience, in order to identify the areas in which Africa is closing the gap with other developing regions and those areas requiring much more effort toward such closure. This analysis is done at the regional level and for 36 individual countries that have adequate data over the entire period of 45 years.

We judiciously use findings from cross-country studies, which have helped to identify factors that tend to have the highest likelihood of influencing growth performance, without drawing causality conclusions from them. We appreciate the wide range of econometric and conceptual problems plaguing cross-country growth regression. The appendix has a more detailed econometric discussion and empirical analysis behind this assessment. We use the results from the empirical work presented in the appendix to more explicitly assess the relative contribution of each factor of growth to the gap between African growth and that of other regions.

Sources of Economic Growth: Lessons from Growth Accounting

Long-term growth is a product of both the rate of capital accumulation (physical and human) and returns to investment. The results from growth decompositions point to the importance of both factors in Africa's growth experience, as is the case in all other regions. In a global study, Bosworth and Collins (2003) estimate that total factor productivity (TFP) growth accounts for 41 percent of growth in 84 countries they study. For Sub-Saharan Africa as a whole, slightly less than half of the growth difference with the other developing regions is due to slower accumulation of physical capital per worker, and slightly more than half is accounted for by the slower growth in the productivity residual. As noted earlier, not only are investment levels lower in the region but the returns are also much lower. At international prices, the level of investment in Sub-Saharan Africa (SSA) averaged about half that in other developing regions and yielded about half of the average investment returns.

The results of the decompositions are presented in tables 3.1 and 3.2 (Bosworth and Collins 2003), whereby gross domestic product (GDP) growth per worker is broken down into the contribution of physical and human capital and a productivity growth residual. The U-shaped path of Africa's average growth rate resurfaces. In the 1960–73 phase, the average growth rate of output per worker was 2.7, of which 1.6 percentage points represented the contribution by TFP and 0.9 percentage points was capital accumulation. During this period, both capital accumulation and TFP were on a rising trend, while the contribution of education per worker was minimal, at 0.16 percentage points.

The period spanning 1973 to 1990 marked a serious collapse in growth as output per worker fell precipitously at an average rate of –0.48 percent annually. The contribution of the productivity residual in this period turned sharply negative, at –1.16 percentage points, more than offsetting the marginally positive contributions of physical capital accumulation (at 0.41 percent) and education per worker (at 0.27 percent).

In the past decade and a half (1990–2003), some improvements in the growth of output per worker for SSA were registered, moving the regional average into the non-negative levels. Again, the contribution of TFP dominated this growth recovery. This is consistent with the findings of other studies (for example, Berthelemy and Soderling 2001), which found that Africa's recovery in the second half of the 1990s was entirely accounted for by rapid increases in the productivity residual. The contribution of human capital also increased sharply during this period to 0.40 percentage points.

The standard interpretation of a low residual is slow technological progress (O'Connell and Ndulu 2000). The traditional approach has been to break down technical change into three branches—*invention*, the cre-

TABLE 3.1
Sources of Growth, by Regions, 1960–2003

Region/period	Output	Contribution of			
		Output per worker	Physical capital	Education	Factor productivity
World (84)					
1960–2003	3.82	2.26	1.00	0.33	0.91
1960–73	5.10	3.42	1.22	0.31	1.85
1973–90	3.41	1.68	0.89	0.40	0.38
1990–2003	3.09	1.88	0.93	0.27	0.67
Industrial countries (22)					
1960–2003	3.36	2.23	0.95	0.31	0.95
1960–73	5.16	3.86	1.34	0.32	2.16
1973–90	2.79	1.53	0.75	0.38	0.39
1990–2003	2.31	1.55	0.84	0.22	0.49
China (1)					
1960–2003	6.91	4.97	1.86	0.36	2.68
1960–73	3.40	1.21	0.30	0.37	0.53
1973–90	7.55	5.24	1.95	0.41	2.80
1990–2003	9.70	8.51	3.32	0.29	4.72
East Asia less China (7)					
1960–2003	6.52	3.81	2.23	0.53	1.02
1960–73	6.92	3.94	1.86	0.48	1.55
1973–90	7.20	4.26	2.65	0.61	0.95
1990–2003	5.24	3.12	2.05	0.47	0.58
Latin America (23)					
1960–2003	3.70	0.95	0.54	0.36	0.05
1960–73	5.97	3.09	0.90	0.29	1.88
1973–90	2.83	−0.18	0.56	0.44	−1.17
1990–2003	2.61	0.33	0.14	0.34	−0.16
South Asia (4)					
1960–2003	4.63	2.44	1.02	0.35	1.05
1960–73	3.41	1.31	1.00	0.29	0.02
1973–90	5.02	2.82	0.84	0.37	1.58
1990–2003	5.34	3.10	1.29	0.40	1.38
Africa (19)					
1960–2003	3.20	0.60	0.43	0.28	−0.11
1960–73	5.14	2.73	0.93	0.16	1.62
1973–90	2.28	−0.48	0.41	0.27	−1.16
1990–2003	2.48	−0.09	−0.05	0.40	−0.44
Middle East (9)					
1960–2003	4.56	1.92	1.02	0.45	0.43
1960–73	6.37	4.28	1.51	0.33	2.39
1973–90	3.89	1.15	1.28	0.50	−0.63
1990–2003	3.64	0.61	0.20	0.51	−0.11

Source: Bosworth and Collins 2003.

TABLE 3.2

Sources of Growth, Africa, 1960–2003

Region/period	Output	Contribution of			
		Output per worker	Physical capital	Education	Factor productivity
Cameroon					
1960–2003	3.40	1.13	0.88	0.27	−0.03
1960–73	2.46	0.79	0.67	0.19	−0.07
1973–90	5.10	2.77	2.31	0.36	0.09
1990–2003	2.14	−0.64	−0.74	0.23	−0.13
Côte d'Ivoire					
1960–2003	3.82	0.42	0.28	0.31	−0.17
1960–73	8.20	4.56	1.55	0.19	2.77
1973–90	2.36	−1.02	0.52	0.41	−1.94
1990–2003	1.46	−1.71	−1.28	0.30	−0.72
Ethiopia					
1960–2003	3.05	0.64	1.02	0.20	−0.56
1960–73	4.47	2.17	2.20	0.06	−0.09
1973–90	2.09	−0.64	0.62	0.23	−1.48
1990–2003	2.90	0.82	0.36	0.28	0.17
Ghana					
1960–2003	2.59	−0.13	0.10	0.33	−0.56
1960–73	2.71	0.39	0.75	0.67	−1.03
1973–90	1.15	−1.69	−0.81	0.19	−1.07
1990–2003	4.38	1.43	0.67	0.16	0.60
Kenya					
1960–2003	4.31	1.04	−0.02	0.37	0.69
1960–73	6.78	3.78	0.66	0.32	2.78
1973–90	4.53	0.95	−0.18	0.44	0.68
1990–2003	1.61	−1.50	−0.47	0.32	−1.35
Madagascar					
1960–2003	1.49	−1.04	−0.05	0.24	−1.23
1960–73	2.30	−0.09	0.09	0.09	−0.27
1973–90	0.90	−1.56	−0.24	0.32	−1.64
1990–2003	1.45	−1.30	0.05	0.30	−1.64
Mali					
1960–2003	3.24	1.17	0.31	0.08	0.77
1960–73	2.94	1.10	0.61	0.06	0.43
1973–90	2.28	0.08	0.07	0.10	−0.09
1990–2003	4.82	2.67	0.33	0.09	2.24
Malawi					
1960–2003	3.84	1.44	1.35	0.20	−0.11
1960–73	5.46	3.17	4.66	0.08	−1.51
1973–90	3.49	0.50	0.59	0.19	−0.28
1990–2003	2.71	0.94	−0.90	0.32	1.54

(Table continues on the following page.)

TABLE 3.2 (continued)
Sources of Growth, Africa, 1960–2003

Region/period	Output	Output per worker	Physical capital	Education	Factor productivity
Mauritius					
1960–2003	4.97	2.53	0.56	0.38	1.58
1960–73	4.07	1.38	−0.17	0.45	1.10
1973–90	5.57	2.83	0.56	0.44	1.81
1990–2003	5.09	3.32	1.29	0.25	1.75
Mozambique					
1960–2003	2.86	0.92	0.34	0.14	0.44
1960–73	5.08	3.05	0.33	0.09	2.62
1973–90	−1.37	−3.11	−0.42	0.18	−2.88
1990–2003	6.38	4.23	1.35	0.12	2.72
Nigeria					
1960–2003	3.34	0.71	1.28	0.32	−0.88
1960–73	5.14	2.73	1.96	0.09	0.66
1973–90	2.08	−0.55	1.18	0.34	−2.04
1990–2003	3.20	0.38	0.76	0.53	−0.90
Rwanda					
1960–2003	2.80	0.22	0.82	0.19	−0.78
1960–73	2.40	−0.25	0.18	0.16	−0.59
1973–90	4.06	0.88	1.93	0.20	−1.23
1990–2003	1.57	−0.17	0.01	0.20	−0.39
Senegal					
1960–2003	2.65	0.10	−0.06	0.16	0.00
1960–73	1.49	−0.98	−0.54	0.11	−0.56
1973–90	2.81	0.27	−0.14	0.17	0.23
1990–2003	3.61	0.98	0.53	0.20	0.25
Sierra Leone					
1960–2003	2.07	0.40	−0.18	0.24	0.34
1960–73	3.76	2.62	0.52	0.19	1.89
1973–90	2.03	0.29	−0.32	0.30	0.31
1990–2003	0.47	−1.62	−0.69	0.22	−1.15
South Africa					
1960–2003	3.18	0.55	0.27	0.26	0.02
1960–73	5.73	3.46	0.76	0.13	2.54
1973–90	2.11	−0.63	0.36	0.21	−1.20
1990–2003	1.97	−0.60	−0.39	0.50	−0.71
Tanzania					
1960–2003	3.76	0.88	0.12	0.04	0.73
1960–73	5.74	3.02	0.04	−0.13	3.12
1973–90	2.75	−0.25	0.24	0.12	−0.60
1990–2003	3.82	1.06	0.09	0.12	0.85

TABLE 3.2 (continued)
Sources of Growth, Africa, 1960–2003

Region/period	Output	Contribution of			
		Output per worker	Physical capital	Education	Factor productivity
Uganda					
1960–2003	3.69	0.77	0.67	0.24	−0.14
1960–73	4.23	0.70	1.38	0.16	−0.82
1973–90	1.16	−1.50	−0.05	0.33	−1.78
1990–2003	6.54	3.90	0.92	0.22	2.73
Zambia					
1960–2003	1.69	−0.93	−0.85	0.33	−0.41
1960–73	3.45	0.92	0.39	0.27	0.27
1973–90	0.95	−2.01	−1.44	0.30	−0.87
1990–2003	1.53	−0.55	−1.19	0.45	0.20
Zimbabwe					
1960–2003	3.83	0.93	−0.22	0.45	0.69
1960–73	6.34	3.45	−0.47	0.24	3.69
1973–90	3.28	−0.19	−0.43	0.70	−0.46
1990–2003	−0.70	−2.52	0.12	0.33	−2.95

Source: Bosworth and Collins 2003.

ation of new products and processes; *innovation*, the transfer of invention to commercial application; and *diffusion*, the spread of innovation into the economic environment (Freeman 1991). Notwithstanding the interdependence and feedback among these branches, the first two branches typically entail production of new knowledge, which is costly and risky to produce but cheap to imitate at the diffusion stage. The public-good nature of knowledge and the difficulties of establishing and protecting property rights are partly behind these features. Most African countries (except South Africa) are technological followers and are more likely to engage in the third branch of technical change, diffusion.

Singapore's case presents an interesting contrast to slow technological progress in Africa. It is an example of a successful technological follower whose major source of long-term growth was technical change, initially via diffusion and some innovation. Ho and Hoon (2006) develop an approach to accounting for sources of Singapore's economic growth by explicitly identifying channels through which Singapore, as a technological follower, benefited from international research and development (R&D) spillovers. They show that 57.5 percent of Singapore's real GDP-per-worker growth rate (1970–2002) is due to multifactor productivity and, more specifically, 52 percent of the growth is explained by an increase in capacity to absorb new technology by improving educational quality and by forging effective links to the world's technological leaders through trade (particularly machinery imports) and foreign direct investment. They also conclude that these two were the most influential factors behind Singapore's fast pace of multifactor productivity catch-up with technological leaders. These findings are consistent with findings from other empirical research. For example Coe, Helpman, and Hoffmaister (1997) and Hejazi and Safarian (1999) show empirically that how much any single follower-economy benefits from international R&D spillovers depends on its distance from the frontier and its stock of human capital, as well as its integration with technology leaders through trade and foreign direct investment.

Apart from slow technological progress, there are several other candidates that could explain the slow multifactor productivity growth in African countries. These include falling capacity utilization, particularly during times when shortage of foreign exchange constrained raw materials imports;[1] high rates of depreciation of physical capital, associated, for example, with poor maintenance of public infrastructure, climate shocks that undermine total factor productivity in agriculture, and pervasiveness of civil strife that destroys physical capital or suspends its use. At shorter frequencies, the residual may also reflect fluctuations in aggregate demand, which would affect output via capacity utilization and some degree of underemployment.

The weak empirical link between physical capital accumulation and growth is a distinct feature of the SSA growth experience, particularly during the two decades of economic stagnation between 1970 and 1995. Table 3.3 shows the ex post returns to investment in the developing regions. Clearly there is some variation in the average economywide returns to aggregate investment across the regions. Africa does not compare well with the fast-growing regions of the developing world, including East Asia and Pacific (EAP), Europe and Central Asia (ECA), and South Asia (SAR).

Interestingly, growth collapse occurred without a corresponding collapse of investment. In spite of the relatively high ex ante rates of returns to investment in the region during the 1980s, for example, three sets of reasons may be behind this striking feature. Capital accumulation may not be taking place at the same rate as recorded investment. As noted earlier, the average relative price of investment goods for Sub-Saharan Africa was 70 percent higher than for the Organisation for Economic Co-operation and Development (OECD)

TABLE 3.3
Productivity of Investment—Returns
Ratio of growth rate to investment rate

Years	AFR	EAP	ECA	LAC	MNA	SAR
1960–69	0.326	0.301	0.263	0.259	0.540	0.314
1970–79	0.243	0.316	0.215	0.247	0.239	0.225
1980–89	0.151	0.146	0.109	0.085	0.106	0.235
1990–99	0.074	0.191	−0.229	0.143	0.214	0.220
2000–02	0.109	0.237	0.258	0.048	−0.022	0.175

Source: Ndulu 2006b.

Note: AFR = Africa; LAC = Latin America and the Caribbean; MNA = Middle East and North Africa.

countries, or East Asia (Sala-i-Martin, Doppelhofer, and Miller 2004). Using this information, Artadi and Sala-i-Martin (2003) estimate that the average growth rate in African countries would have been 0.44 percentage points higher each year if the relative price of investment goods was the same as in OECD countries or East Asia.[2] In Africa, physical capital accumulation is import intensive, but in most of these countries capital goods attract very low tariff rates or are preferentially exempted. The relatively higher investment prices most likely result from high transport costs caused by shipping cartels, port inefficiencies (reflecting poor quality of infrastructure or management), or simple lack of scale economies (Collier 2002; Yeats and Ng 1997).

In addition, failures in governance might have contributed through distortions that gradually undermine the quality of the capital stock and generate a negative residual. The governance failures could arise out of the dominance of inefficient public sector investment during the period of growth collapse, the prevalence of tax avoidance and self-insurance by firms and households, and the diversion of resources into rent seeking and corruption (Vishny and Shleifer 1993). These may all have contributed to generating an inefficient composition of aggregate investment in Africa that eroded the quality of the capital stock. A general bias against private sector accumulation, emphasized by Mkandawire and Soludo (1999), would produce the same effect unless justified by an unusually high marginal product of public capital (Ndulu and O'Connell 2006b).

A third possibility that is somewhat speculative is based on increasing returns and threshold effects and argues that investment yields would have been much higher if investment rates had been high enough (Sachs et al. 2004). Structural features that impede the flow of information and trade, even if unchanged over time, can lower the residual by limiting the

scope for agglomeration economies and the diffusion of existing technological knowledge (Barro and Sala-i-Martin 1995).

Two important conclusions emerge from analysis of the sources of
growth. First, whereas the results confirm the importance of low levels of
capital accumulation in explaining the slow growth in a large number of
African countries, they also highlight the importance of the productivity
residual in African growth performance. Globally, Bosworth and Collins
(2003) estimate that total factor productivity growth accounts for 41 percent of growth in the 84 countries they studied. This is certainly true for
African countries included in the sample, notwithstanding the significant
diversity across those countries. This feature holds true through all three
phases of the region's growth path. It dominates the period of growth contraction and leads the growth recovery phase of the past decade.

Second, the central role of investment incentives in both capital accumulation and productivity growth leads us to focus on improving the
investment climate, which in addition to identifying actionable policy
areas also targets reducing transaction costs and relieving capacity limitations. The importance of productivity growth further points us to the role
of innovation (technical progress) in raising productivity and competitiveness. The potential comparative advantage of low wages in developing
countries, including Africa, can be nullified by low productivity, in part
because of the scarcity of complementary professional skills. Surveys of
investors show that labor is not cheap where productivity is low. Productivity in turn is influenced not only by the quantity and quality of capital
stock, but also by the quality and quantity of knowledge (Lindbaek 1997).

Doing Business in Africa: The Investment Climate—
Transaction Costs, Risk, Capacity

It is generally accepted that the private sector is the cornerstone for growth.
Markets have proved effective in creating opportunities for increasing
incomes through productivity growth. Functioning markets are thus a critical mechanism for poverty alleviation. The challenge is, therefore, to harness private initiative delivered through markets for sustained growth and
development. The key requirement in this regard is the overall quality of
the investment climate, and Africa has fallen short in this respect. The state
of the investment climate has presented major impediments to economic
growth. While the deficiencies in African economies are to some extent

influenced by geographic aspects, they are largely the outcomes of ill-advised government policies. A weak investment climate inhibits the effectiveness of the private sector and also results in prohibitive costs of doing business.

The *investment climate* is an all-encompassing phrase that captures a broad array of concerns, including institutional, policy, and regulatory frameworks; business regulations and their enforcement to ensure that sound rules not only exist but are observed and respected by both the markets and the states; adequacy and quality of infrastructure; and general conditions in which markets operate. A sound investment climate will also include a stable macroeconomy that facilitates decision making, well-defined property rights, an effective judicial and contracting system, and a functioning financial system.

This section therefore discusses the different elements of the investment climate as they pertain to African countries. Of particular interest is the state of individual components in Africa, highlighted with benchmarking against other developing regions.

The Cost of Doing Business in Africa: The Role of Transaction Costs

Investment in Africa is relatively expensive, with the highest cost of doing business in the world. The costs of infrastructure services make up a disproportionately large part of production and trade costs, barriers to trade raise the cross-border transaction costs, and bureaucratic red tape and inefficiencies exacerbate these costs. The analysis described in this section is drawn from Eifert, Gelb, and Ramachandran (2005). It is based on a selected group of six African countries, which are benchmarked against India and China. The latter two countries have been chosen for comparative analysis because of their strong performance in the area of traditional manufactured exports. Further, it has been observed that the severity of the impact of a weak investment climate is not uniform across market participants. In particular, firm size and ownership determine how much of a burden falls on the firm. Thus, this analysis also includes an intraregional comparison based only on size and ownership of firms.

Infrastructure

Sub-Saharan Africa has weaker infrastructure than other developing regions. This is equivalent to saying that the costs of power, transport, telecommunications, and security are higher than other regions, as described later.

Electricity

While infrastructure presents problems across the entire spectrum, access to reliable and affordable energy has been without doubt the most problematic in Africa. The problems in this sector originate from government failures and prevalence of state-owned monopolies, which have generated a host of inefficiencies. For example, it takes an average of 174 days to get connected to a power grid in Zambia, compared to 18 days in China. In the 2004 Investment Climate Assessment for Tanzania, 59 percent of surveyed firms considered electricity to be the most serious impediment to enterprise activity, and this pattern is similar in most comparator countries.

The poor quality of infrastructure causes power outages of a frequency not experienced in any other region. The performance deficiencies in this sector impose different kinds of costs on firms. The first and most obvious cost associated with power is output loss, which was about 9 percent in Kenya compared to 2 percent in China. As figure 3.1 shows, this cost is also high in the other African countries.

The second cost is due to the need for backup facilities. In Tanzania, 55 percent of firms had generators, compared to 27 percent for China

FIGURE 3.1
Energy Costs and Power Outages

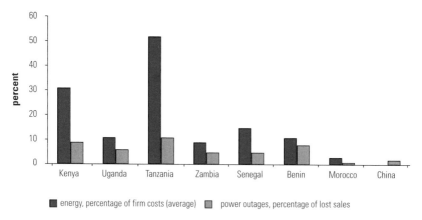

Source: World Bank Enterprise Surveys (2001–05).

FIGURE 3.2
Types of Firms Owning Generators

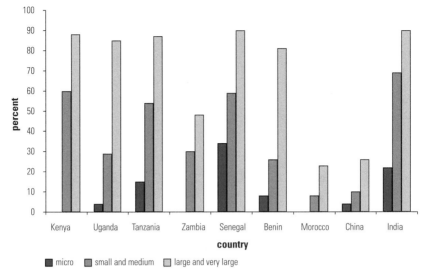

Source: World Bank Enterprise Surveys (2001–05).

Note: A missing bar indicates that the data are not available.

(Tanzania ICA). Not only are generators expensive to obtain but they are also less efficient in providing power, especially for small and medium enterprises. The burden of power outages is not distributed uniformly across firms. The cost of generators can be prohibitively high for small firms. This burden falls disproportionately on small firms as they are unable to compensate for fluctuations in the power supply. Figure 3.2 shows that in all countries, large enterprises were considerably more likely to own generators than their small counterparts.

Rules, Regulations, and Procedures

Complexity of regulations and procedures imposes yet another burden to some classes of enterprises. In particular, customs and trade regulations have been found to present a major constraint on firms in Africa (figure 3.3). For the selected countries, Tanzania has the highest lag time for clearance of both exports and imports, at 14 days and 7 days, respectively. Delays in clearing goods can have a substantial impact on competitiveness. In fact, cumbersome customs and trade regulations, and poor customs administration, have been found to discourage firms from seeking export markets.

FIGURE 3.3
Days to Clear Imports and Exports

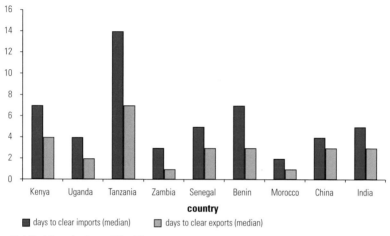

Source: World Bank Enterprise Surveys (2001–05).

The negative impact of complex regulations is also evident in the number of inspections that firms are subjected to each year, as well as the fraction of management time devoted to dealing with regulations (figure 3.4). While the scores for most of the African countries are high, it is interesting

FIGURE 3.4
Inspections and Management Time Spent Dealing with Regulations

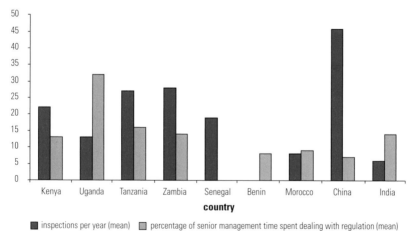

Source: World Bank Enterprise Surveys (2001–05).

Note: A missing bar indicates that the data are not available.

that China has a considerably higher number of inspections, but the amount of time China's management spends dealing with regulations is the lowest of all comparators. This high burden of inspections and regulations also encourages firms to remain in the informal sector. Survey results also show that regulations and inspections are arduous for exporting enterprises and as such may be a disincentive to pursuing export-oriented activity.

Cost of Security

Figure 3.5 indicates the high level of insecurity in the operating environment. The cost of crime and cost of security as a percentage of sales is high in Sub-Saharan Africa, relative to other parts of the world. Data also indicate that unofficial payments to get things done can be significant and are as high as 4 percent in Kenya. Informal payment required to secure a contract is also high in many countries, indicating the weakness of the judicial system.

FIGURE 3.5

Crime, Unofficial Payments, and Securing of Contracts

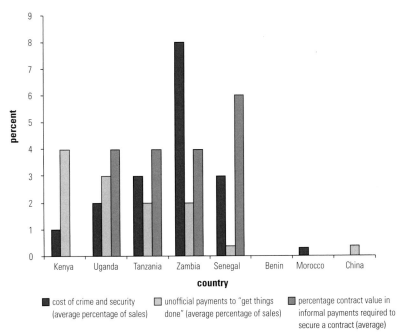

Source: World Bank Enterprise Surveys (2001–05).

Note: A missing bar indicates that the data are not available.

Estimates of Gross and Net Total Factor Productivity: Africa in Comparative Perspective

Comparing net and gross total factor productivity provides another view of how debilitating these costs are to firm performance. In previous work carried out using the same investment climate data set, a comparison has been made of the performance of African firms with those in the other countries. In particular, Eifert, Gelb, and Ramachandran (2005) consider the cost of energy as well as a range of indirect costs such as transport, telecommunication, security, land, bribes, marketing, and so on, which are not often considered in the analysis of TFP. These costs are netted out from value added to yield a net value added from which a corresponding measure of net total factor productivity is derived. This broader view of firm performance, which extends beyond the traditional emphasis on factory-floor productivity and labor costs, is important in order to understand economic outcomes in Africa. Together with the losses that depress (gross) productivity, indirect costs associated with operating expenses—energy, transport, telecom, security, land, bribes, marketing, and so on—represent a heavy drag on net productivity and profitability in most African countries in our sample and serve as a brake on competitiveness. Without going into too much technical detail, we present the key results of the analysis here.

The cost breakdown shows the relatively large burden of infrastructure and public services—energy, transport, telecom, water, and security costs—that together account for more than half of all indirect costs to firms.

Figure 3.6 provides a cross-country comparison of firms' cost structures, including labor (wages, benefits); capital (interest, finance charges, machine depreciation); raw materials; and other indirect costs. In strong performers such as China, India, Nicaragua, Bangladesh, Morocco, and Senegal, the combination of energy and indirect costs are 13 to 15 percent of total costs, around half the level of labor costs. In contrast, this combination in most African countries accounts for 20 to 30 percent of total costs, often dwarfing labor costs. It is worth noting that capital costs—also tightly related to the business environment—appear to be a major component of costs in Ethiopia, Nigeria, and Zambia.

The gap between African and other firms widens when gross and net TFP are compared, as indirect costs interact with other firm characteristics

FIGURE 3.6
Cost Structures, Firm-Level Average by Country

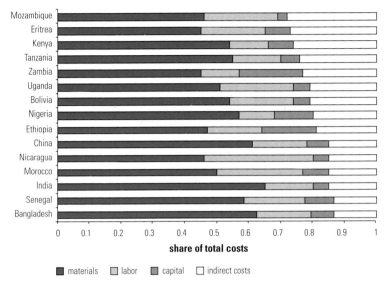

Source: Eifert, Gelb, and Ramachandran 2005.

(figure 3.7).[3] African countries in the mid-range of 40 to 60 percent of Chinese *gross* TFP fall to 20 to 40 percent when *net* TFP is compared. Kenya, which appears relatively strong on gross TFP, falls dramatically on net TFP as a result of very high indirect costs. Zambia, the most extreme case, falls from 30 percent to 10 percent. Only in Senegal—the strongest African performer on both gross and net TFP—is the effect of indirect costs relatively low. African countries have shortfalls in factory-floor productivity, but high indirect costs further weaken their relative performance.

Existing research also highlights the enormous importance of exporting in the context of African firms (Bigsten and Söderbom 2006). While we now increasingly acknowledge the wide diversity in performance across African countries, enterprise survey data show a similar pattern across firms within countries in Africa—pushing us to go beyond country characteristics in order to understand better what matters for performance. It is striking, for example, that the likelihood of an African firm *with* export experience exporting at the time of the survey is more than three times as high as an identical firm that has never exported, signaling significant fixed entry costs into the exporting business beyond general country conditions.

FIGURE 3.7

Net and Gross Total Factor Productivity, Adjusted Prices

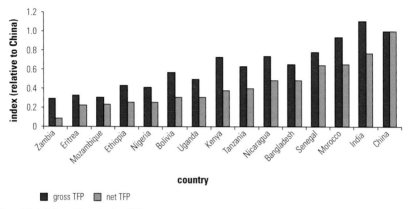

Source: Eifert, Gelb, and Ramachandran 2005.

Many of these costs are described in the previous figures. What is interesting in the African context is that they tend to vary at the firm level as well as at the country level. New research on firm perceptions also indicates that there is enormous variance at the firm level as opposed to the sector or country level; these perceptions are well correlated with actual firm experience with regard to the investment climate (Gelb 2007). What is also interesting is that variables such as the supply of electricity—which one typically does not expect to vary at the firm level—in fact vary quite a lot across different types of firms. There is also very strong evidence that participating in the export market has a relatively strong impact on raising productivity, and hence competitiveness, of the firm through learning by exporting. The estimated productivity gains from learning in Africa range from 20 to 25 percent in the short run to 50 percent in the long run. This learning effect appears to be larger in Africa than elsewhere, perhaps given past high trade restrictions and the larger technological gap with developed countries, which translate into a wider scope for learning. Mengistae and Pattillo (2004), among several others, show a strong positive correlation between productivity and exporting among African firms. This conclusion remains robust even after careful accounting for the possibility of causality going in the opposite direction—that is, efficient firms self-select to export (Bigsten et al. 2004; Van Biesebroeck 2005). Panel data, which will be forthcoming for several countries in Sub-Saharan Africa over the next few years, will enable us to better understand exactly how this learning takes place in practice and what learning infrastructure is needed to absorb and adapt technology to local circumstances.

Indigenous Entrepreneurs and Minority-Owned Firms

A variety of interesting differences are revealed when we disaggregate the investment climate survey data to look at domestic, entrepreneur-owned firms. Data show the average firm size of an indigenously owned firm versus a firm owned by an entrepreneur from a minority ethnic group (that is, of Asian, Middle Eastern, or Caucasian descent). We see that indigenously owned firms are the smallest—most are well below 50 workers. European-, Asian-, and Middle Eastern–owned firms are substantially larger in all the countries reported. From here on, we group European, Asian, and Middle Eastern entrepreneurs into one category, of *non-indigenous*.

Our data also show that indigenously owned firms enter the market at a significantly smaller size than minority ethnic–owned firms. While the average firm size at startup of minority-owned firms in Tanzania is about 100 employees, that number is just under 40 employees for an indigenously owned firm. For most countries where we have these data, the difference in startup size is close to 50 percent. We also find that the difference in startup size persists over time, that the difference in size at time of survey is not much different than the difference in size at startup, and that, in many cases, a large gap emerges over time between indigenous and minority entrepreneurs.

On the other hand, minority-owned firms start operations at a significantly larger size than indigenous African–owned firms. But the data also show that not all African entrepreneurs start small. Further disaggregation of indigenously owned firms shows that for African entrepreneurs, education is very important in determining the size at which they start operations. African entrepreneurs with a university education start much larger enterprises compared to those that do not have a university degree in all countries surveyed.[4]

Figure 3.8 shows that the difference in size persists over time in most countries. Size at the time of the survey is also higher for indigenous entrepreneurs with access to a university education than for those without such an education. There are two possible interpretations of this result—the

FIGURE 3.8
Average Current Size of African Firms by University Education

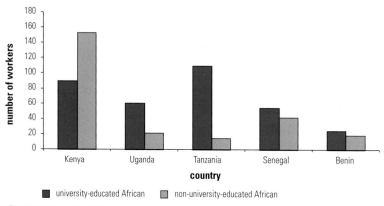

Source: Ramachandran and Shah 2006.

completion of a university degree reflects a higher ability that is also responsible for entrepreneurial success and/or the university degree enables access to a network of other business professionals that is useful for the success of the business. While minority ethnic firms have access to these networks via family ties, indigenous firms may have to build these networks in alternative ways.

Access to trade credit may help to explain some of these numbers. Figure 3.9 shows that in four African countries, a larger percentage of minority-owned firms use trade credit compared to indigenous African enterprises.

Data collected in the 1990s show that the indigenous firms receiving trade credit have had a much longer relationship with their suppliers than have minority-owned firms in East Africa. A detailed exploration of the issue of trade credit shows that repeated transactions are necessary to establish trade credit for indigenous African enterprises (Biggs and Shah 2006).[5] But for minority-owned firms, the length of the relationship with the supplier does not make much difference. The number of years dealing with suppliers has no bearing on access to credit relative to using cash for transactions, in sharp contrast to the situation for indigenous firms.

Econometric analysis shows that for small and medium enterprises owned by minorities, the only variable affecting access to trade credit is firm size, and the magnitude of its importance is much smaller than for

FIGURE 3.9
Percentage of Firms Receiving Credit

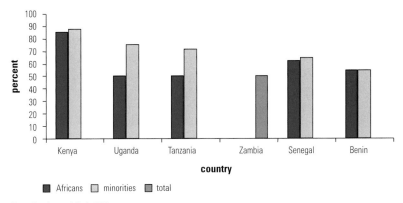

Source: Ramachandran and Shah 2006.

indigenous African firms (Biggs and Shah 2006). The authors argue that members of ethnic networks do not have to rely on establishing long-term relationships with suppliers to get credit, as their reputation in the network provides enough information to lenders. The authors also indicate that even smaller firms in the business network have access to credit.

For indigenous firms, firm size is very important in determining trade credit access, as is the length of relationship with supplier. In the absence of good information on indigenous African firms, suppliers use size as a proxy for information. Thus, only larger firms get credit. Smaller indigenous African firms have to establish long-term relationships with each supplier to get credit. There is coordination failure in the indigenous African business community that prevents firms from developing an informal credit information system analogous to the ethnic minority business community.

The aforementioned results are in large part due to the absence of networks in the indigenous community. This leads to a paucity of information, thereby preventing small, indigenously owned firms from accessing capital or knowledge that would enable them to grow and prosper. This problem is compounded by the lack of enforceability of contracts and the weakness of the judicial system. It is not necessarily a lack of capital per se, but more the *lack of availability of information* that is slowing the growth of indigenous firms in the African private sector.[6]

Benchmarking of Growth Conditions in African Countries

In this section, we use the results from Africa-related cross-country analysis to more explicitly assess the relative importance of various constraints to growth in explaining the gap between African growth and that of other regions. It is essentially a benchmarking exercise for African growth conditions. The main objective of the benchmarking assessments carried out here is *not* to establish causality but to infer the significance of the different constraints on growth by isolating predetermined variation in the determinants of growth. Furthermore, we track the evolution of these growth conditions over time and the changes in their relative importance, taking into account the results of reform programs pursued in various African countries. This tracking helps to identify the areas in which Africa is closing the gap with other developing regions and those requiring much more effort toward such closure.

A large amount of work has been done to identify key factors influencing growth and channels through which these factors operated. A short list of noteworthy contributions that draw on global data to make Africa-relevant contributions includes Sachs and Warner (1995) on outward orientation; the same authors (1997, 2001) on the natural resource curse; Bloom and Sachs (1998) on geographical and demographic constraints; Masters and McMillan (2001) on tropical location and the disease environment; Easterly and Levine (1997) on ethnic fractionalization and policy; the same authors (1998) on neighborhood (spillover) effects; Collier (1999) and Collier and Hoeffler (2004) on civil wars; Mauro (1995) on corruption; Knack and Keefer (1995) on the rule of law; Acemoglu, Johnson, and Robinson (2001) on institutional legacies of the colonial period; Guillaumont, Guillaumont Jeanneney, and Brun (1999), Dehn (2000), and Blattman, Hwang, and Williamson (2004) on vulnerability to external shocks; Burnside and Dollar (2000) on aid; and Glaeser et al. (2004) on political leaders.

The appendix presents an update of the analysis done under the African Economic Research Consortium growth research to identify systematic features of the growth process and assess the importance of different drivers of growth (see O'Connell and Ndulu 2000; Ndulu and O'Connell 2006a; and Hoeffler 1999/2000). Given the estimated influence of each determinant on growth, this analysis assesses the extent to which the differences in the growth environment (levels of the growth conditions and factors) explain the deviation of the predicted growth rate of Africa from the global sample mean, East Asia and Pacific mean, and South Asia mean over the entire period from 1960 to 2004. This is akin to undertaking the regression-based growth decomposition discussed in Ndulu and O'Connell (2006a).[7] These assessments are made relative to three comparators— global average, East Asia, and East Asia and Pacific. Given that the region has seriously lagged behind in growth, including East Asia among the comparators allows us to target ambition in an effort to close the gap. Applied this way, results from cross-country growth analysis can also help to inform and direct country-level analysis into its most productive areas (Collier and Gunning 1999).

How Do African Countries Compare with the Other Regions?

Table 3.4 shows the actual growth deviations and the contributions of various factors of growth in explaining this deviation. Average growth rates observed in Africa for the entire time period were 1.12 percentage points lower than the global sample mean, and the deviations were even higher relative to the growth paths for both EAP at 2.78 percentage points and South Asia at 1.72 percentage points, respectively.

Based on this assessment, demographic factors explained the largest part of the deviation of Africa's predicted growth. The difference in the levels of the cluster of demographic factors accounts for 0.86 percentage points out of the total growth gap of 1.12 percentage points relative to the global mean. The cluster has similar dominance in explaining the growth gap with EAP and SAR. Differences in age dependency ratios and potential labor force growth rates accounted for 1.49 percentage points of the 2.78-percentage-point growth gap with EAP and by 0.96 percentage points of the 1.72-percentage-point gap with South Asia. Africa's delayed demographic transition compared to other developing regions is a key factor in understanding its lagging position in growth.

Differences in the initial conditions also explain a significant part of the deviation. These include differences in initial income and life expectancy at birth. For the SSA region, the adverse impact of the much lower life expectancy at birth significantly reduces the positive convergence impact of lower initial income, leaving a net impact on growth of only 0.39 percentage points relative to the global sample mean growth, instead of 1.18 percentage points. With more or less similar levels of initial income, dif-

TABLE 3.4

Contributions of Individual Components of Drivers of Growth toward Explaining Deviation of SSA's Predicted Growth Relative to the Sample Mean, EAP, and SAR, 1960–2004

| Sub-Saharan Africa | Actual growth deviation | Initial conditions | | | Demography | |
		Income	Life expectancy	Age dependency	Potential labor force growth	Landlocked
Sample mean	−1.12	1.18	−0.79	−0.67	−0.19	−0.12
East Asia and Pacific	−2.78	1.56	−1.06	−1.13	−0.36	−0.21
South Asia	−1.72	0.04	−0.60	−0.68	−0.28	−0.15

Source: Author calculations based on data sources in the appendix.

Note: Calculations based on regression sample only. BMP = Black Market Premium.

ferences in life expectancy with South Asia more than offset the income convergence effect. Against EAP, the net effect from the differences in initial conditions accounts for explaining 0.50 percentage points of the growth gap.

Differences in the level of policy conditions between Africa and the three comparators are smaller than with the previously discussed clusters of growth drivers. Differences in policy disposition contributed to explaining −0.17 and −0.45 percentage points, respectively, of the predicted growth gaps relative to the sample mean and the East Asia and Pacific region only. Africa's policy performance was at par with that of South Asia and therefore does not contribute to explaining the growth gap between the two regions.

Evolution of the Relative Importance of Growth Conditions

The relative importance of different growth drivers has tended to change over time as countries pursue reform programs, undertake investments to compensate for unfavorable endowments, and undergo deep political changes. As we saw earlier in the review of Africa's 45 years of growth experience, the region's growth performance has followed a distinctive U-shaped path, with nearly two decades of growth stagnation sandwiched between an early and later phase of reasonable levels of growth. Figures 3.10, 3.11, and 3.12 depict changes in the relative contributions of the different growth constraints, over these three time phases, to explain the growth gaps with other regions.

| Geography | | Shocks | | | Policy | |
Terms of trade	Trading partner growth	Political instability	Inflation	BMP	Government consumption/ GDP	Residual
0.02	−0.05	0.10	0.00	−0.06	−0.11	−0.38
0.07	−0.34	0.03	−0.05	−0.19	−0.21	−0.81
0.02	−0.08	0.30	−0.05	0.10	−0.05	−0.32

FIGURE 3.10

Regression-Based Decomposition of Periodical Growth Rates, SSA, 1960–74

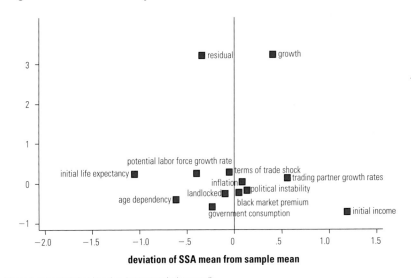

Source: Author calculations based on data sources in the appendix.

Following from the pattern of evolution in the per capita GDP, the nine half-decade observations for each country from 1960 to 2004 are divided into three distinct time periods: the 1960–74 phase, which was character-ized by moderate growth rates; the 1975–94 phase, which represented a deep contraction within the region; and the 1995–2004 phase, which was marked by recovery into moderate growth rates. The actual growth devi-

FIGURE 3.11

Regression-Based Decomposition of Periodical Growth Rates, SSA, 1975–94

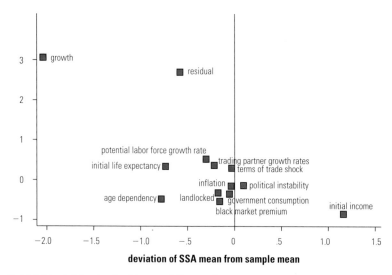

Source: Author calculations based on data sources in the appendix.

FIGURE 3.12

Regression-Based Decomposition of Periodical Growth Rates, SSA, 1995–2004

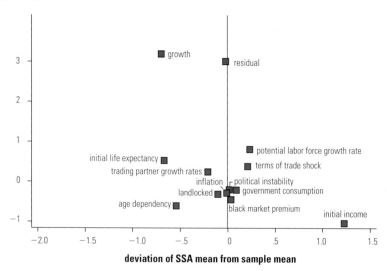

Source: Author calculations based on data sources in the appendix.

ations relative to all the benchmarks reveal the observed U-shaped growth patterns in table 3.5. Not surprisingly, the deviations are much larger relative to EAP than to SAR.

Apart from initial income, initial life expectancy was the most important in explaining predicted growth deviations relative to all three benchmarks. However, the progress that Africa achieved in raising life expectancy has since been eroded by incidence of disease, especially HIV/AIDS in southern Africa. This is apparent in the widening divergence between the second and last phases relative to EAP and SAR.

Age dependency also explains a significant part of the deviation of the predicted growth rate of Africa relative to the global mean. The evolution of the contribution of this driver is consistent with the growth pattern over the three phases, since it rises in the second phase and then declines in the last phase. The initial population explosion that took place in Africa, with the consequence of increasing dependency ratios, was followed by the demographic transition that started in the mid-1980s. However, the persistently large difference with EAP and SAR, even in the most recent phase, clearly continues to account for the largest part of the explanation of the growth gap between Africa and these regions: the population structure continues to be a drag against closing the gap. Policy cluster, exogenous shocks, and the growth of potential labor force seem to track the U-shaped path of the growth performance and become much less important in accounting for the differences in the growth performance in the last phase.

The difference between policy conditions in Africa and other developing regions has narrowed considerably, partly as a result of the reforms of the 1990s. Relative to the global mean, differences in policy conditions accounted for −0.11 percentage points of the growth gap during the early phase and −0.29 percentage points during the period of growth contraction, and they nearly disappear as a factor (0.01 percentage points) in the last phase. The region has also become much more open and better able to make use of opportunities afforded by the global economy, and political instability also appears to be on the wane.

Contribution of Drivers of Growth to Explaining Growth Deviation at the Country Level

Tables 3.6 and 3.7 extend the type of analysis done in the previous two sections at the country level. Table 3.6 presents the contributions for the

TABLE 3.5

Evolution of Individual Contributions of Drivers of Growth toward Explaining Deviation of SSA's Predicted Growth Relative to the Sample Mean, EAP, and SAR, by Periods

Sub-Saharan Africa	Actual growth deviation	Initial conditions		Demography		Geography
		Income	Life expectancy	Age dependency	Potential labor force growth	Landlocked
Sample mean						
1960–74	0.40	1.19	−1.06	−0.61	−0.40	−0.10
1975–94	−2.04	1.16	−0.73	−0.77	−0.30	−0.15
1995–2004	−0.70	1.22	−0.67	−0.55	0.22	−0.09
EAP						
1960–74	−2.46	0.96	−1.01	−0.53	−0.40	−0.19
1975–94	−3.73	1.57	−1.02	−1.27	−0.62	−0.24
1995–2004	−1.03	2.17	−1.27	−1.49	0.19	−0.18
SAR						
1960–74	1.27	−0.19	−0.68	−0.32	−0.31	−0.19
1975–94	−2.97	−0.08	−0.47	−0.73	−0.27	−0.15
1995–2004	−1.74	0.48	−0.78	−0.90	−0.26	−0.12

Source: Author calculations based on data sources in the appendix.

Note: Calculations based on balanced regression sample only.

entire time period, and table 3.7 shows the evolution of the contributions by periods. For each country, the relative importance of each driver of growth is assessed on the basis of the extent to which it contributes to explaining the country's growth gap relative to the global mean. These contributions are also assessed along the three phases of the region's growth path.

We also classify the countries in two groups: high-growth countries and low-growth countries. Gelb (2006) designated 22 African countries, which have taken off well during the period from 1994 to 2003 and have sustained these rates for more than a decade, as high-growth economies. These African countries have posted an average growth rate of 3.86 percent of GDP per capita during this period. The remaining 23 countries for which data are available are categorized as low-growth economies, with an average growth rate of –0.55 percent of GDP per capita. One distinct feature among the high-growth countries is the remarkable improvement of the contribution of the policy variables to explaining growth deviation relative to the sample mean, in the most recent decade of 1995 to 2004.

Terms of trade	Shocks		Policy			Residual
	Trading partner growth	Political instability	Inflation (<500%)	Black-market premium	Government consumption/ GDP	
−0.05	0.54	0.12	0.08	0.04	−0.23	−0.34
−0.03	−0.23	0.09	−0.04	−0.15	−0.10	−0.58
0.20	−0.21	0.08	0.01	0.03	−0.03	−0.03
−0.03	−0.31	0.01	0.08	−0.08	−0.36	−0.60
0.04	−0.38	0.03	−0.10	−0.28	−0.15	−1.30
0.23	−0.23	0.02	−0.08	−0.13	−0.19	0.00
0.01	0.13	0.20	0.04	0.55	−0.15	2.23
−0.02	−0.21	0.35	−0.08	0.01	−0.06	−1.28
0.13	−0.06	0.25	−0.06	−0.10	0.06	−0.32

The situation for low-growth countries remains more or less unchanged, as seen in figure 3.13. This implies that the high-growth countries have to focus their efforts on other aspects of development, such as human development and demographic characteristics, as shown in the regression-based decompositions analysis. Clearly, the countries that have not broken out of the cycle of poverty have a much bigger task of tackling macroeconomic instability first, before embarking on other areas of development. In terms of opportunity groups, policy challenges have been much more acute in resource-rich countries (both landlocked and coastal) following discovery of oil in a number of countries during the 1970s and 1980s. Subsequently, these countries have shown some improvement in terms of reduction in the negative contribution of the policy variables in the past decade.

Finally, in the resource-rich economies, the positive contribution of external factors, such as income effects of terms-of-trade changes, rises sharply in the most recent decade (figure 3.14), providing evidence for favorable movements in terms of trade of these primary commodity economies, maybe owing to changing global conditions that raise their relative prices and demand.

TABLE 3.6
Contributions of Various Factors Influencing Growth at the Country Level
Contribution to deviation from sample mean

Country	Period	Actual growth deviation	Initial income	Initial life expectancy	Age dependency	Potential labor force growth rate	Land-locked	
High-growth countries								
AGO	1960–2004	—	—	—	—	—	—	
BEN	1960–2004	−1.02	1.49	−0.64	−1.02	−0.32	0.09	
BFA	1960–2004	−0.63	1.76	−0.93	−1.34	−0.26	−0.48	
BWA	1960–2004	—	—	—	—	—	—	
CMR	1960–2004	−0.49	0.70	−0.65	−0.63	−0.13	0.09	
CPV	1960–2004	0.58	−0.06	0.43	−0.53	−0.60	0.09	
ETH	1960–2004	−1.22	2.25	−0.99	−0.71	−0.29	0.09	
GHA	1960–2004	−1.52	1.43	−0.48	−0.76	−0.14	0.09	
GIN	1960–2004	−0.36	0.39	−0.86	−0.60	0.34	0.09	
GNQ	1960–2004	—	—	—	—	—	—	
LSO	1960–2004	—	—	—	—	—	—	
MLI	1960–2004	−0.76	1.72	−1.01	−0.98	−0.44	−0.48	
MOZ	1960–2004	3.53	1.74	−1.00	−0.55	0.36	0.09	
MRT	1960–2004	0.68	1.09	−0.86	−0.52	−0.21	0.09	
MUS	1960–2004	1.99	−0.99	0.45	1.01	0.40	0.09	
RWA	1960–2004	−0.14	1.67	−1.04	−1.10	−0.24	−0.48	
SDN	1960–2004	—	—	—	—	—	—	
SEN	1960–2004	−1.96	1.02	−0.95	−0.68	−0.17	0.09	
TCD	1960–2004	−0.97	1.43	−1.12	−0.68	−0.51	−0.48	
TGO	1960–2004	−0.73	1.41	−0.83	−0.75	−0.37	0.09	
TZA	1960–2004	2.43	2.42	−0.96	−0.66	0.30	0.09	
UGA	1960–2004	2.43	2.01	−0.87	−1.22	−0.33	−0.48	
Low-growth countries								
BDI	1960–2004	−2.09	1.96	−0.95	−0.82	−0.16	−0.48	
CAF	1960–2004	−2.34	0.92	−0.98	−0.33	−0.38	−0.48	
CIV	1960–2004	−1.36	0.68	−0.86	−0.70	−0.14	0.09	
COG	1960–2004	−0.45	1.51	−0.85	−0.66	−0.41	0.09	
COM	1960–2004	−3.58	1.00	−0.08	−0.48	0.74	0.09	
ERI	1960–2004	—	—	—	—	—	—	
GAB	1960–2004	−0.04	−0.85	−0.70	0.15	−0.28	0.09	
GMB	1960–2004	−1.19	1.31	−0.85	−0.22	−0.12	0.09	
GNB	1960–2004	−4.25	2.01	−0.93	−0.67	−0.24	0.09	
KEN	1960–2004	−0.51	1.45	−0.50	−1.27	0.07	0.09	
MDG	1960–2004	−2.59	1.51	−0.68	−0.70	−0.06	0.09	
MWI	1960–2004	−0.43	2.16	−1.07	−0.93	−0.32	−0.48	
NAM	1960–2004	—	—	—	—	—	—	
NER	1960–2004	−3.30	1.31	−1.19	−1.26	−0.59	−0.48	
NGA	1960–2004	−0.87	1.55	−0.89	−0.74	−0.28	0.09	

	Trading partner growth rates	Terms of trade shock	Political instability	Inflation	Black market premium	Government consumption/ GDP	Time effects	Residual
	—	—	—	—	—	—	—	—
	0.06	−0.07	0.18	0.07	0.16	0.12	−0.35	−0.79
	−0.51	0.00	0.02	0.09	0.16	−0.15	−0.56	1.58
	—	—	—	—	—	—	—	—
	−0.06	−0.03	0.17	0.06	0.17	0.32	−0.06	−0.45
	−0.51	0.01	0.21	0.12	0.18	−0.24	−1.04	2.54
	−0.30	0.01	0.02	0.08	−0.69	−0.34	−0.61	0.26
	−0.01	0.05	0.12	−0.13	−0.48	−0.09	0.15	−1.26
	−0.04	0.35	0.21	0.08	0.17	0.44	−0.83	−0.10
	—	—	—	—	—	—	—	—
	—	—	—	—	—	—	—	—
	−0.36	0.01	0.14	0.07	0.16	0.11	−0.35	0.66
	−0.33	−0.11	0.12	−0.10	−0.07	−0.25	−0.63	4.26
	0.18	0.02	0.17	0.08	−0.16	−0.70	0.20	1.30
	−0.13	0.26	0.21	0.05	0.15	0.24	−0.57	0.83
	−0.09	−0.11	0.07	0.07	−0.15	−0.14	−0.21	1.62
	—	—	—	—	—	—	—	—
	0.09	−0.01	0.17	0.08	0.15	−0.01	0.25	−1.99
	0.24	0.10	0.05	0.08	0.15	−0.45	0.22	0.00
	0.12	−0.21	0.11	0.08	0.15	−0.19	0.25	−0.61
	−0.34	0.10	0.21	0.09	0.18	−0.23	−1.04	2.26
	−0.30	−0.01	−0.01	−0.30	−0.39	−0.27	−0.57	5.18
	−0.30	−0.05	−0.11	0.03	−0.08	−0.21	−0.40	−0.51
	0.02	0.03	0.13	0.08	0.15	−0.87	0.30	−0.94
	0.06	−0.09	0.16	0.07	0.15	0.17	0.25	−1.20
	0.37	0.42	−0.12	0.08	0.15	−0.72	0.43	−0.77
	−0.33	0.29	0.00	0.08	0.15	−0.37	−0.83	−3.83
	—	—	—	—	—	—	—	—
	−0.06	0.16	0.18	0.07	0.17	0.30	−0.06	0.78
	0.12	0.05	0.18	0.02	0.14	−0.15	−0.40	−1.38
	−0.13	0.65	0.05	0.10	0.18	−0.42	−1.04	−3.91
	−0.14	−0.16	0.16	0.03	0.05	0.15	−0.01	−0.43
	0.17	0.11	0.16	0.04	0.07	0.15	0.24	−3.68
	−0.28	0.02	0.20	−0.02	−0.12	0.09	−0.01	0.33
	—	—	—	—	—	—	—	—
	0.04	0.04	0.14	0.08	0.15	−0.16	0.43	−1.82
	0.05	0.27	−0.06	−0.02	−0.66	0.26	0.15	−0.59

(Table continues on the following page.)

TABLE 3.6 *continued*

Contributions of Various Factors Influencing Growth at the Country Level

Contribution to deviation from sample mean

Country	Period	Actual growth deviation	Initial income	Initial life expectancy	Age dependency	Potential labor force growth rate	Land-locked
SLE	1960–2004	−3.86	1.47	−1.44	−0.50	−0.23	0.09
STP	1960–2004	—	—	—	—	—	—
SWZ	1960–2004	—	—	—	—	—	—
SYC	1960–2004	−3.23	−1.15	0.63	0.94	0.40	0.09
ZAF	1960–2004	−0.75	−0.70	−0.33	0.02	0.06	0.09
ZAR	1960–2004	−3.21	2.02	−0.82	−0.85	−0.41	−0.48
ZMB	1960–2004	−2.48	1.43	−0.83	−0.89	−0.19	−0.48
ZWE	1960–2004	−2.51	0.41	−0.51	−0.93	0.14	−0.48

Source: Author calculations based on data sources in the appendix.

Note: — = not available.

TABLE 3.7

Evolution of Contribution to Deviation from Sample Mean at the Country Level

Country	Period	Actual growth deviation	Initial income	Initial life expectancy	Age dependency	Potential labor force growth rate	Land-locked
High-growth countries							
AGO	1960–74	—	—	—	—	—	—
AGO	1975–94	—	—	—	—	—	—
AGO	1995–2004	—	—	—	—	—	—
BEN	1960–74	—	—	—	—	—	—
BEN	1975–94	−1.52	1.53	−0.69	−1.08	−0.49	0.09
BEN	1995–2004	0.99	1.34	−0.47	−0.80	0.37	0.09
BFA	1960–74	—	—	—	—	—	—
BFA	1975–94	−0.97	1.81	−0.92	−1.45	−0.19	−0.48
BFA	1995–2004	0.39	1.62	−0.96	−1.04	−0.46	−0.48
BWA	1960–74	—	—	—	—	—	—
BWA	1975–94	—	—	—	—	—	—
BWA	1995–2004	—	—	—	—	—	—
CMR	1960–74	0.75	1.02	−0.94	−0.44	−0.64	0.09
CMR	1975–94	−1.09	0.62	−0.58	−0.76	−0.26	0.09
CMR	1995–2004	0.69	0.73	−0.63	−0.29	0.88	0.09
CPV	1960–74	—	—	—	—	—	—
CPV	1975–94	—	—	—	—	—	—
CPV	1995–2004	0.58	−0.06	0.43	−0.53	−0.60	0.09

Trading partner growth rates	Terms of trade shock	Political instability	Inflation	Black market premium	Government consumption/ GDP	Time effects	Residual
−0.24	−0.02	0.01	−0.21	−0.24	0.24	−0.40	−2.39
—	—	—	—	—	—	—	—
—	—	—	—	—	—	—	—
−0.32	−0.69	0.21	0.09	−0.72	−0.49	−1.04	−1.17
0.06	0.01	−0.08	0.05	0.15	−0.11	0.15	−0.14
0.05	−0.21	0.06	−0.39	−0.56	−0.23	0.18	−1.57
−0.10	0.04	0.16	−0.18	−0.41	−0.51	−0.01	−0.51
−0.30	0.08	0.04	−0.18	−0.40	0.01	−0.57	0.18

Trading partner growth rates	Terms of trade shock	Political instability	Inflation	Black market premium	Government consumption/ GDP	Time effects	Residual
—	—	—	—	—	—	—	—
—	—	—	—	—	—	—	—
—	—	—	—	—	—	—	—
—	—	—	—	—	—	—	—
0.03	−0.06	0.17	0.07	0.16	0.12	−0.18	−1.19
0.21	−0.13	0.21	0.10	0.18	0.13	−1.04	0.80
—	—	—	—	—	—	—	—
−0.53	0.02	−0.04	0.08	0.16	−0.20	−0.40	1.16
−0.47	−0.07	0.21	0.11	0.18	−0.02	−1.04	2.83
—	—	—	—	—	—	—	—
—	—	—	—	—	—	—	—
—	—	—	—	—	—	—	—
0.66	−0.03	0.21	0.05	0.18	0.33	1.42	−1.16
−0.21	−0.22	0.16	0.05	0.16	0.33	−0.18	−0.29
−0.16	0.71	0.21	0.12	0.18	0.27	−1.04	−0.36
—	—	—	—	—	—	—	—
—	—	—	—	—	—	—	—
−0.51	0.01	0.21	0.12	0.18	−0.24	−1.04	2.54

(Table continues on the following page.)

TABLE 3.7 *continued*

Evolution of Contribution to Deviation from Sample Mean at the Country Level

Country	Period	Actual growth deviation	Initial income	Initial life expectancy	Age dependency	Potential labor force growth rate	Land-locked
ETH	1960–74	—	—	—	—	—	—
ETH	1975–94	−2.61	2.29	−0.96	−0.62	−0.35	0.09
ETH	1995–2004	0.17	2.20	−1.02	−0.80	−0.22	0.09
GHA	1960–74	−1.18	1.63	−0.79	−0.77	−0.18	0.09
GHA	1975–94	−2.79	1.38	−0.40	−0.81	−0.15	0.09
GHA	1995–2004	0.53	1.25	−0.18	−0.66	−0.05	0.09
GIN	1960–74	—	—	—	—	—	—
GIN	1975–94	—	—	—	—	—	—
GIN	1995–2004	−0.36	0.39	−0.86	−0.60	0.34	0.09
GNQ	1960–74	—	—	—	—	—	—
GNQ	1975–94	—	—	—	—	—	—
GNQ	1995–2004	—	—	—	—	—	—
LSO	1960–74	—	—	—	—	—	—
LSO	1975–94	—	—	—	—	—	—
LSO	1995–2004	—	—	—	—	—	—
MLI	1960–74	—	—	—	—	—	—
MLI	1975–94	−1.49	1.75	−1.00	−0.96	−0.43	−0.48
MLI	1995–2004	2.18	1.60	−1.09	−1.10	−0.46	−0.48
MOZ	1960–74	—	—	—	—	—	—
MOZ	1975–94	2.82	1.86	−0.99	−0.62	−0.43	0.09
MOZ	1995–2004	3.88	1.67	−1.00	−0.52	0.75	0.09
MRT	1960–74	3.01	1.07	−1.17	−0.35	−0.16	0.09
MRT	1975–94	−2.14	0.96	−0.77	−0.71	−0.75	0.09
MRT	1995–2004	0.00	1.26	−0.51	−0.58	0.24	0.09
MUS	1960–74	—	—	—	—	—	—
MUS	1975–94	1.90	−0.73	0.37	0.85	0.33	0.09
MUS	1995–2004	2.13	−1.39	0.57	1.26	0.51	0.09
RWA	1960–74	2.79	1.91	−1.00	−0.85	−0.70	−0.48
RWA	1975–94	−3.22	1.54	−0.94	−1.16	−0.91	−0.48
RWA	1995–2004	4.55	1.81	−1.26	−1.10	1.33	−0.48
SDN	1960–74	—	—	—	—	—	—
SDN	1975–94	—	—	—	—	—	—
SDN	1995–2004	—	—	—	—	—	—
SEN	1960–74	−2.62	0.93	−1.25	−0.61	−0.37	0.09
SEN	1975–94	−2.06	1.09	−0.84	−0.77	−0.27	0.09
SEN	1995–2004	0.44	1.00	−0.51	−0.56	0.80	0.09
TCD	1960–74	−3.06	1.38	−1.40	−0.26	−0.46	−0.48
TCD	1975–94	−0.12	1.40	−0.96	−0.83	−1.15	−0.48
TCD	1995–2004	2.77	1.68	−0.73	−1.49	1.26	−0.48

Trading partner growth rates	Terms of trade shock	Political instability	Inflation	Black market premium	Government consumption/ GDP	Time effects	Residual
—	—	—	—	—	—	—	—
−0.25	−0.04	−0.07	0.05	−1.29	−0.24	−0.39	−0.83
−0.36	0.06	0.11	0.10	−0.09	−0.43	−0.83	1.35
0.38	−0.14	0.06	0.05	−0.29	0.06	1.25	−2.52
−0.27	0.05	0.11	−0.28	−0.96	−0.12	−0.18	−1.26
−0.07	0.34	0.21	−0.12	0.18	−0.25	−0.83	0.63
—	—	—	—	—	—	—	—
−0.04	0.35	0.21	0.08	0.17	0.44	−0.83	−0.10
—	—	—	—	—	—	—	—
—	—	—	—	—	—	—	—
—	—	—	—	—	—	—	—
—	—	—	—	—	—	—	—
—	—	—	—	—	—	—	—
—	—	—	—	—	—	—	—
−0.37	−0.01	0.13	0.06	0.15	0.19	−0.18	−0.34
−0.32	0.10	0.21	0.11	0.18	−0.19	−1.04	4.66
—	—	—	—	—	—	—	—
0.19	0.01	0.02	−0.23	−0.51	−0.55	−0.24	4.21
−0.59	−0.17	0.17	−0.03	0.15	−0.10	−0.83	4.29
0.58	0.01	0.21	0.09	0.12	−0.98	1.25	2.26
−0.07	0.02	0.11	0.06	−0.91	−0.73	−0.33	0.88
−0.16	0.03	0.17	0.09	0.17	−0.24	−0.83	0.28
—	—	—	—	—	—	—	—
−0.16	0.17	0.21	0.04	0.14	0.22	−0.40	0.77
−0.09	0.40	0.21	0.08	0.16	0.26	−0.83	0.92
0.92	0.01	0.21	0.04	−0.33	0.16	0.90	2.01
−0.20	−0.09	0.07	0.10	−0.19	−0.18	−0.18	−0.58
−0.39	−0.21	0.01	0.05	0.02	−0.21	−0.83	5.83
—	—	—	—	—	—	—	—
—	—	—	—	—	—	—	—
0.63	−0.02	0.14	0.09	0.14	0.02	1.25	−3.66
−0.27	0.01	0.21	0.06	0.16	−0.03	−0.18	−1.32
−0.07	−0.07	0.13	0.12	0.18	0.00	−1.04	0.37
0.63	0.03	0.14	0.09	0.14	−0.73	1.25	−3.38
0.01	0.08	−0.10	0.08	0.16	−0.29	−0.40	2.36
−0.25	0.40	0.21	0.09	0.18	−0.12	−1.04	3.07

(Table continues on the following page.)

TABLE 3.7 *continued*

Evolution of Contribution to Deviation from Sample Mean at the Country Level

Country	Period	Actual growth deviation	Initial income	Initial life expectancy	Age dependency	Potential labor force growth rate	Land-locked	
TGO	1960–74	2.79	1.44	−1.09	−0.70	−0.33	0.09	
TGO	1975–94	−2.86	1.30	−0.67	−0.84	−0.69	0.09	
TGO	1995–2004	−2.83	1.73	−0.68	−0.56	0.79	0.09	
TZA	1960–74	—	—	—	—	—	—	
TZA	1975–94	—	—	—	—	—	—	
TZA	1995–2004	2.43	2.42	−0.96	−0.66	0.30	0.09	
UGA	1960–74	—	—	—	—	—	—	
UGA	1975–94	2.68	2.20	−0.76	−1.19	0.08	−0.48	
UGA	1995–2004	2.06	1.73	−1.03	−1.26	−0.94	−0.48	
Low-growth countries								
BDI	1960–74	—	—	—	—	—	—	
BDI	1975–94	−1.06	1.87	−0.89	−0.78	−0.24	−0.48	
BDI	1995–2004	−4.13	2.16	−1.09	−0.89	−0.01	−0.48	
CAF	1960–74	−1.66	0.66	−1.17	−0.10	−0.44	−0.48	
CAF	1975–94	−3.34	0.99	−0.86	−0.46	−0.41	−0.48	
CAF	1995–2004	−0.36	1.47	−0.87	−0.53	−0.05	−0.48	
CIV	1960–74	2.51	0.81	−1.09	−0.69	−0.47	0.09	
CIV	1975–94	−3.20	0.54	−0.68	−0.82	−0.11	0.09	
CIV	1995–2004	−5.66	0.83	−0.87	−0.20	0.70	0.09	
COG	1960–74	0.89	2.00	−0.99	−0.46	−0.31	0.09	
COG	1975–94	−4.63	0.70	−0.67	−0.87	0.03	0.09	
COG	1995–2004	−0.27	0.87	−0.62	−1.04	−1.14	0.09	
COM	1960–74	—	—	—	—	—	—	
COM	1975–94	—	—	—	—	—	—	
COM	1995–2004	−3.58	1.00	−0.08	−0.48	0.74	0.09	
ERI	1960–74	—	—	—	—	—	—	
ERI	1975–94	—	—	—	—	—	—	
ERI	1995–2004	—	—	—	—	—	—	
GAB	1960–74	10.98	−0.69	−0.97	0.55	−0.33	0.09	
GAB	1975–94	−2.27	−0.88	−0.69	0.19	−0.58	0.09	
GAB	1995–2004	−2.14	−0.92	−0.48	−0.42	0.99	0.09	
GMB	1960–74	—	—	—	—	—	—	
GMB	1975–94	−1.24	1.26	−1.03	−0.30	−0.14	0.09	
GMB	1995–2004	−1.08	1.41	−0.48	−0.07	−0.06	0.09	
GNB	1960–74	—	—	—	—	—	—	
GNB	1975–94	—	—	—	—	—	—	
GNB	1995–2004	−4.25	2.01	−0.93	−0.67	−0.24	0.09	
KEN	1960–74	2.81	1.79	−0.71	−1.49	−0.51	0.09	
KEN	1975–94	−1.35	1.34	−0.34	−1.53	−0.02	0.09	
KEN	1995–2004	−2.15	1.31	−0.61	−0.54	0.82	0.09	

	Trading partner growth rates	Terms of trade shock	Political instability	Inflation	Black market premium	Government consumtion/ GDP	Time effects	Residual
	0.55	−0.29	0.12	0.10	0.14	−0.05	1.25	1.56
	−0.16	−0.20	0.08	0.06	0.16	−0.32	−0.18	−1.50
	−0.01	0.00	0.21	0.11	0.18	−0.11	−1.04	−3.54
	—	—	—	—	—	—	—	—
	—	—	—	—	—	—	—	—
	−0.34	0.10	0.21	0.09	0.18	−0.23	−1.04	2.26
	—	—	—	—	—	—	—	—
	−0.26	−0.13	−0.02	−0.57	−0.75	−0.30	−0.40	5.25
	−0.37	0.18	0.01	0.09	0.14	−0.24	−0.83	5.07
	—	—	—	—	—	—	—	—
	−0.34	−0.04	0.05	0.04	−0.05	−0.26	−0.18	0.25
	−0.23	−0.07	−0.43	0.00	−0.13	−0.09	−0.83	−2.03
	0.57	−0.07	0.16	0.09	0.14	−1.31	1.25	−0.96
	−0.37	0.10	0.14	0.06	0.16	−0.75	−0.18	−1.28
	−0.08	0.06	0.02	0.09	0.18	−0.01	−0.63	0.48
	0.55	−0.21	0.21	0.09	0.14	0.23	1.25	1.61
	−0.26	−0.06	0.21	0.05	0.16	0.11	−0.18	−2.25
	−0.17	0.11	−0.18	0.10	0.18	0.20	−1.04	−5.40
	0.65	−0.05	−0.13	0.08	0.14	−1.06	1.25	−0.33
	−0.48	0.22	−0.10	0.05	0.15	−0.41	−0.53	−2.81
	0.39	2.05	−0.10	0.12	0.18	0.00	−1.04	−0.05
	—	—	—	—	—	—	—	—
	−0.33	0.29	0.00	0.08	0.15	−0.37	−0.83	−3.83
	—	—	—	—	—	—	—	—
	—	—	—	—	—	—	—	—
	0.31	0.52	0.21	0.08	0.18	0.37	1.42	9.24
	−0.15	−0.06	0.17	0.05	0.16	0.27	−0.18	−0.67
	−0.06	0.70	0.21	0.14	0.18	0.33	−1.04	−1.85
	—	—	—	—	—	—	—	—
	0.10	−0.02	0.17	0.00	0.13	−0.24	−0.18	−1.09
	0.17	0.19	0.21	0.07	0.15	0.02	−0.83	−1.95
	—	—	—	—	—	—	—	—
	−0.13	0.65	0.05	0.10	0.18	−0.42	−1.04	−3.91
	0.34	−0.02	0.15	0.09	−0.04	0.26	1.16	1.68
	−0.34	−0.09	0.16	−0.02	0.04	0.18	−0.18	−0.65
	−0.20	−0.44	0.17	0.07	0.16	−0.02	−0.83	−2.13

(Table continues on the following page.)

TABLE 3.7 *continued*

Evolution of Contribution to Deviation from Sample Mean at the Country Level

Country	Period	Actual growth deviation	Initial income	Initial life expectancy	Age dependency	Potential labor force growth rate	Land-locked	
MDG	1960–74	−1.94	1.34	−1.03	−0.69	−0.45	0.09	
MDG	1975–94	−3.55	1.48	−0.61	−0.71	0.12	0.09	
MDG	1995–2004	−2.13	1.79	−0.27	−0.70	0.25	0.09	
MWI	1960–74	2.52	2.47	−1.22	−0.88	−0.42	−0.48	
MWI	1975–94	−2.14	2.12	−0.98	−1.02	−0.44	−0.48	
MWI	1995–2004	0.03	1.94	−1.12	−0.82	0.04	−0.48	
NAM	1960–74	—	—	—	—	—	—	
NAM	1975–94	—	—	—	—	—	—	
NAM	1995–2004	—	—	—	—	—	—	
NER	1960–74	−2.97	1.01	−1.38	−1.09	−0.74	−0.48	
NER	1975–94	−3.55	1.54	−1.05	−1.39	−0.47	−0.48	
NER	1995–2004	—	—	—	—	—	—	
NGA	1960–74	1.46	1.49	−1.13	−0.68	−0.60	0.09	
NGA	1975–94	−2.75	1.46	−0.82	−0.85	−0.15	0.09	
NGA	1995–2004	−0.59	1.81	−0.67	−0.61	−0.04	0.09	
SLE	1960–74	—	—	—	—	—	—	
SLE	1975–94	−3.45	1.27	−1.46	−0.47	−0.49	0.09	
SLE	1995–2004	−4.67	1.88	−1.39	−0.57	0.30	0.09	
STP	1960–74	—	—	—	—	—	—	
STP	1975–94	—	—	—	—	—	—	
STP	1995–2004	—	—	—	—	—	—	
SWZ	1960–74	—	—	—	—	—	—	
SWZ	1975–94	—	—	—	—	—	—	
SWZ	1995–2004	—	—	—	—	—	—	
SYC	1960–74	—	—	—	—	—	—	
SYC	1975–94	—	—	—	—	—	—	
SYC	1995–2004	−3.23	−1.15	0.63	0.94	0.40	0.09	
ZAF	1960–74	1.72	−0.49	−0.57	−0.37	−0.17	0.09	
ZAF	1975–94	−2.45	−0.83	−0.16	−0.03	0.12	0.09	
ZAF	1995–2004	−1.07	−0.77	−0.29	0.69	0.32	0.09	
ZAR	1960–74	−0.79	1.57	−0.97	−0.59	−0.27	−0.48	
ZAR	1975–94	−4.52	1.89	−0.70	−0.93	−0.62	−0.48	
ZAR	1995–2004	−4.11	3.29	−0.88	−1.15	−0.05	−0.48	
ZMB	1960–74	−0.74	1.21	−0.90	−0.86	−0.41	−0.48	
ZMB	1975–94	−4.13	1.39	−0.66	−1.00	−0.33	−0.48	
ZMB	1995–2004	−0.92	1.75	−1.11	−0.70	0.28	−0.48	
ZWE	1960–74	—	—	—	—	—	—	
ZWE	1975–94	−0.58	0.38	−0.31	−1.04	0.46	−0.48	
ZWE	1995–2004	−5.41	0.46	−0.82	−0.77	−0.35	−0.48	

Source: Author calculations based on data sources in the appendix.

Note: — = not available.

Trading partner growth rates	Terms of trade shock	Political instability	Inflation	Black market premium	Government consumption/ GDP	Time effects	Residual
0.59	0.01	0.16	0.09	0.14	0.14	1.25	-3.58
-0.07	0.00	0.18	0.00	-0.05	0.12	-0.06	-4.04
-0.09	0.43	0.13	0.01	0.15	0.19	-0.83	-3.27
0.28	0.04	0.21	0.08	0.01	0.14	1.16	1.14
-0.47	-0.05	0.19	-0.01	-0.27	0.02	-0.18	-0.58
-0.48	0.14	0.21	-0.13	0.06	0.19	-0.83	1.32
—	—	—	—	—	—	—	—
—	—	—	—	—	—	—	—
—	—	—	—	—	—	—	—
0.55	0.00	0.18	0.09	0.14	-0.12	1.25	-2.39
-0.34	0.07	0.11	0.07	0.16	-0.20	-0.18	-1.39
—	—	—	—	—	—	—	—
0.41	0.03	0.02	0.08	-0.07	0.45	1.25	0.12
-0.18	0.08	-0.04	-0.09	-0.85	0.22	-0.18	-1.45
-0.02	1.01	-0.20	-0.04	-1.18	0.04	-0.83	0.05
—	—	—	—	—	—	—	—
-0.32	-0.09	0.13	-0.32	-0.43	0.29	-0.18	-1.47
-0.07	0.12	-0.23	0.01	0.14	0.15	-0.83	-4.24
—	—	—	—	—	—	—	—
—	—	—	—	—	—	—	—
—	—	—	—	—	—	—	—
—	—	—	—	—	—	—	—
—	—	—	—	—	—	—	—
—	—	—	—	—	—	—	—
—	—	—	—	—	—	—	—
-0.32	-0.69	0.21	0.09	-0.72	-0.49	-1.04	-1.17
0.42	0.01	0.08	0.09	0.12	0.00	1.25	1.26
-0.06	-0.01	-0.29	0.01	0.16	-0.16	-0.18	-1.11
-0.23	0.07	0.10	0.07	0.17	-0.17	-0.83	-0.29
0.67	-0.50	0.00	-0.03	-0.43	-0.40	1.16	-0.52
-0.18	-0.15	0.12	-0.40	-0.70	-0.31	-0.06	-2.02
-0.52	0.19	-0.03	-1.06	-0.40	0.32	-1.04	-2.31
0.63	0.02	0.21	0.05	-0.24	-0.80	1.16	-0.31
-0.27	-0.16	0.17	-0.32	-0.75	-0.72	-0.18	-0.82
-0.47	0.46	0.08	-0.10	0.12	0.20	-0.83	-0.11
—	—	—	—	—	—	—	—
-0.36	-0.05	0.06	-0.02	-0.33	-0.05	-0.40	1.56
-0.21	0.27	0.01	-0.40	-0.52	0.09	-0.83	-1.87

FIGURE 3.13
Evolution of Contribution of Policy

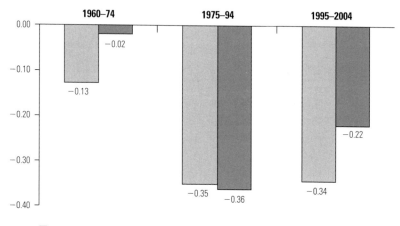

■ high-growth countries ▫ low-growth countries

Source: Author calculations based on data sources in the appendix.

FIGURE 3.14
Evolution of Contribution of Shocks

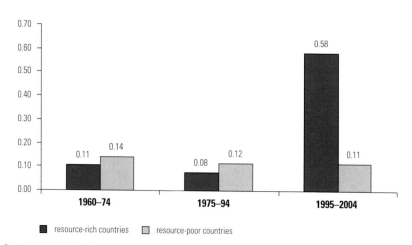

■ resource-rich countries ▫ resource-poor countries

Source: Author calculations based on data sources in the appendix.

Conclusions

Following the unpacking of the clusters of the constraints to growth, it is clear that demographic factors dominate in terms of Africa's contrast to the conditions for growth obtaining in the other regions. Particularly strong among these are age dependency ratios and life expectancy. The former appears to have gotten much worse in the growth contraction phase before starting to improve in the past decade, furnishing evidence for the onset of demographic transition in Africa from the 1980s. However, relative to EAP and SAR, the contributions have deteriorated even in the past decade, indicating that the gap between Africa and the Asian economies is widening with respect to demographic indicators. Life expectancy rates, however, have worsened even in the growth recovery phase, on account of health pandemics like HIV/AIDS. Hence, it is imperative that greater attention be paid to improvement of human development indexes to complement the demographic transition in Africa.

Openness of trade and policy improvement are the other two areas of greatest impact. This is particularly the case for low-growth countries whose growth rates have not even averaged zero percent in the period from 1995 to 2004. Nevertheless, relative to the other developing regions, some significant improvements in policy have taken place, particularly in the high-growth countries in Africa.

Finally, it is clear from the results that Africa needs to pay more attention to factors other than policy in order to compensate for the unfavorable endowments related to geography. The evidence points to significant improvements in policy during the past decade, and probably the payoff in terms of scaling up growth would now tend to be higher from efforts in tackling the other constraints to growth.

Notes

1. Such shortages of foreign exchange during the late 1970s and 1980s, for example, were much less stringent for importing capital goods, since official development assistance, which funded most of the public enterprise investments, precluded financing raw material or recurrent costs.
2. This cost differential is also reflected in the wide divergence between the average share of investment in GDP for Sub-Saharan Africa measured in domestic and international prices. In domestic prices, this ratio for the period 1960 to 1994

(weighted by average GDP at 1985 international prices) was 19 percent compared to only 9.5 percent at 1985 international prices. For East Asia, China, and industrialized countries, there is virtually no gap between the two measures.

3. To show the impact of the costs of doing business, we compare the residuals from two estimations of productivity as follows:

    Gross TFP is estimated as $\ln(\hat{A}_i) = \ln(Y_i - M_i) - \alpha \ln(K_i) - \beta \ln(L_i) - \delta \mathbf{Z}_i$ and

    Net TFP is estimated as $\ln(\hat{A}_i) = \ln(Y_i - M_i - IC_i) - \alpha \ln(K_i) - \beta \ln(L_i) - \delta \mathbf{Z}_i$

    where $_i$ is net TFP, IC is indirect costs, and $(Y - M - IC)$ is net value added.

4. There are other analyses of the role of ethnicity in the private sector in Africa. Most notable is a study by Taye Mengistae, which looks very rigorously at the role of ethnicity in the indigenous private sector in Ethiopia (Mengistae 2001). More recently, Marcel Fafchamps (2004) examined the dynamics of the private sector, including the role of ethnicity, in a comprehensive analysis of markets in Sub-Saharan Africa.

5. The data for the figures are from the 1990s surveys conducted by the World Bank in Africa; this information is not gathered in the current Investment Climate Surveys.

6. We have also tested these hypotheses econometrically, with the use of regression models. We try to determine whether an entrepreneur's access to a university education is significant in determining start-up size, as well as his or her access to a formal loan. Both university education and access to a loan at start-up are also significant for the whole sample. University education is significant for indigenous entrepreneurs in both East and West Africa, and formal loans help only entrepreneurs in East Africa.

7. The deviation of a region/country i's period t average growth rate from the sample mean $(g_{it} - \bar{g})$ can be decomposed into the sum of the observed residual of the region/country i and the regression-weighted sum of the deviations of a region/country i in the growth determinants as:

    $$g_{it} - \bar{g} = -\hat{\gamma}(\ln y_{i,t-k} - \overline{\ln y}) + \sum_j \hat{\phi}^j(x_{it}^j - \bar{x}) + \sum_l \hat{\lambda}^l(z_i^l - \bar{z}) + \hat{\varepsilon}_{it}$$

    The symbol $\wedge$ denotes an ordinary least squares estimate, is the set of factors that vary over time, and l is the set of factors that are time invariant.

CHAPTER 4

Constraints to Growth

Much of the analytical work done to explain the tragedy of the collapse of African growth during the 1970s and 1980s and the slow recovery during the 1990s has focused on correcting policy mistakes, or what Collier and Gunning (1999) referred to as "sins of commission." Indeed, in combination with the sharp paradigmatic shifts away from an emphasis on correcting for market failure to a greater focus on government failure, the thrust of the reforms during this period were on restoring macroeconomic stability, getting the prices right, freeing up markets, and scaling back government involvement in the development agenda. In the process, too little attention was paid to "sins of omission," particularly underprovision of public goods and services essential for reducing firm-level costs and making potential opportunities for investment and trade more profitable.

In this chapter we look more deeply at some of the critical constraints that have been overlooked because of the emphasis on traditional policy approaches. As we saw from the previous chapter, while traditional macro policy shortfalls did reduce Africa's growth rates, many of these policies are now at international norms. We also saw that human development, political, demographic, and geographic variables were much more important in explaining Africa's slow economic growth.

The rest of this chapter tackles three main sets of constraints. The first two are part of Africa's endowments—geographic, i.e., isolation and fragmentation, tropical climates and diseases, the natural resource curse; and the second set is delayed demographic transition. Some constraints cannot be changed; others cannot be changed quickly. But ways to compensate must be developed. The third set of constraints is largely historic, institutional, or policy related and is subject to change and amelioration. This set consists of transaction costs, risks, and capacity limitations.

Africa's Unfavorable Endowments: A Constraint to Growth but Not a Predicament

Africa has atypically large parts of its population living in countries with economic characteristics that globally have been disadvantageous, and a history that has made ethnic and regional polarization a major challenge (table 4.1). A third of its population lives in landlocked, resource-poor countries. Another third lives in countries with large natural resource rents, whose growth performance globally has tended to be significantly poorer than that of non-resource-rich developing countries. Polarization and fractionalization have invariably been major root causes of conflict and have saddled the young African nations (most of them less than a half-century old) with huge costs of nation building and peacekeeping.

Geographical disadvantages account for uncharacteristically high costs of development in Africa (Ndulu 2006b). It has been argued that high transportation costs and an environment favorable for diseases conspire to make capital accumulation and productivity growth much more expensive in Africa than elsewhere in the developing world (Bloom and Sachs 1998; Gallup, Sachs, and Mellinger 1999; Sachs and Warner 1995, 1997, 2001).

Africa's Growth Is Unusually Constrained by Geographical Disadvantages

Distance and being landlocked influence a country's access to international markets, hinder its ability to exploit economies of scale, and lower its production efficiency (Sachs and Warner 1995, 1997, 2001). Being landlocked, remoteness of populations from ports or ocean-navigable rivers, and large overland transportation distances all reduce growth, studies around the globe have found (Bloom and Sachs 1998; Gallup, Sachs, and Mellinger 1999). Economic isolation is more acute in Sub-Saharan Africa, where 31 percent of the countries are landlocked, compared to only

TABLE 4.1
Interregional Comparison of Geographical and Sovereign Fragmentation Indicators

Region	Ratio of number of countries to area ($*10^{-10}$)	Average population density (people per sq. km.)	Average number of borders	Proportion of population in landlocked countries (%)	Average transport costs ($ per container from Baltimore)	Natural resource rents dominance[c]	
						Proportion of natural-resource-rich economies[d]	Share of natural-resource-rich countries in each region[e]
SSA	2.00	77.65	4.00	40.20[a]	7,600	30	34
EAP	1.44	405.50	2.09	0.42	3,900[b]	19	7
ECA	1.17	74.58	4.93	23.06	—	19	12
LAC	1.52	119.92	2.34	2.77	4,600	20	17
MNA	1.60	136.27	3.94	0.00	2,100	63	29
SAR	1.67	382.94	2.75	3.78	3,900[b]	0	0

Sources: Ndulu 2006b and Collier and O'Connell 2006.

Note: — = not available; SSA = Sub-Saharan Africa; EAP = East Asia and Pacific; ECA = Europe and Central Asia; LAC = Latin America and the Caribbean; MNA = Middle East and North Africa; SAR = South Asia.

a. Democratic Republic of Congo, Sudan, and Ethiopia have been treated as landlocked countries.

b. Data on transportation costs are available for East and South Asia regions together (Limao and Venables 1999).

c. An economy is classified as resource-rich if it generates more than 10 percent of its GDP from primary commodity rents (the excess of world prices over production costs). The categories of primary commodities included are energy resources, other minerals and forests. They are also referred to as "natural resources."

d. As a share of the total number of countries in each region.

e. As a share of the total number of "natural resource" economies (41 in the world).

12 percent of all the other developing countries. Nearly 40 percent of the Sub-Saharan Africa (SSA) population lives in these landlocked countries, with high transportation costs and poor trade facilitation (figure 4.1).[1]

Although there are important variations across countries in the region, for most African countries, distance from their primary markets and the high transport intensities of their products (low value–high weight and sparsely produced) are major impediments to production and trade (Esfahani and Ramirez 2003). Frankel and Romer (1999) find that distance strongly undermines growth due to its impact on international trade. Africa is by far the most remote continent by this measure, and trade is an even stronger predictor of growth for African countries than it is for non-African countries (O'Connell and Ndulu 2000). And the situation is much worse for landlocked countries. Relative to other regions, the transport costs of intra-SSA trade are much higher. The median transport costs for intra-African trade, at $7,600 for a 40-foot container, are almost the same as for imports from the rest of the world (involving much longer distance), and it is $2,000 more than for intraregional trade in other developing regions. Nominal freight rates on African exports are normally much higher than those on similar goods shipped from outside the region (AfDB 1999). For example, freight charges on African exports to the United States as a proportion of cost, insurance, and freight value are on average approximately 20 percent higher than for comparable goods from other low-income countries.

The situation is worse for landlocked countries. In 1990, the ratio of freight cost to exports for African landlocked countries, at 30 percent, was twice the average for the region as a whole. Using shipping and CIF-free on board ratio data, Limao and Venables (2001) find that a representative landlocked economy has 50 percent higher transportation costs and 60 percent less trade volume than a typical coastal economy. However, the authors note that landlocked countries are able to offset a significant proportion of this disadvantage through improvements in their own and their transit countries' infrastructure. Sub-Saharan Africa is a highly fragmented region. It has 48 small economies with a median gross domestic product (GDP) of $3 billion (Wormser 2004). For a given geographic area, the region has the highest number of countries, with each country sharing borders with four neighbors on average, often with different trade and macro policy regimes (Ndulu 2006b). This fragmentation has its origin in the region's colonial history, kicked off during "the scramble for Africa." This got worse after independence, with the breakup of federations (for

FIGURE 4.1
Sub-Saharan Africa Geographical Distribution

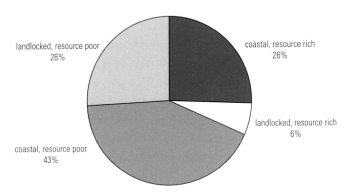

Source: Author calculations based on classification in Collier and O'Connell (2006).

Note: Data are rounded.

example, the Northern Rhodesia Federation), customs unions, currency zones (only the CFA zone [a monetary union] survived), central banks, and immigration systems—as countries established their own trade regimes. This process further fragmented policy frameworks, fractured transportation networks (for example, the disbanding of East African Railways), and led to more transshipments and longer transit times, as well as more limited backhauls. So the problem of isolation is not merely one of market size, but also the absence of cohesion of policy across potentially larger investment areas.

Ndulu (2006b) reviewed the very substantial evidence mustered at macro, meso, and micro levels to show how important infrastructure is for growth—the bulk of it linked to bridging the gaps in geographical dislocation. We highlight here those that have direct bearing on African growth.

At the macro level, the two most recent and comprehensive studies are those by Esfahani and Ramirez (2003) and Calderon and Serven (2004). Esfahani and Ramirez (2003) use a structural model to estimate the relationship between infrastructure and output growth. After accounting for the simultaneity between infrastructure and GDP, they find that the contribution of infrastructure services is substantial and in general exceeds the cost of provision of those services. Drawing on these results, the study finds that if, for example, the growth rate of telephones per capita rises parametrically from about the current 5 percent per year in Africa to

10 percent per year, as in East Asia, the annual growth of GDP would rise by about 0.4 percentage points. In the power sector, an increase of per capita production growth rate from the current 2 percent in Africa to 6 percent, as in East Asia, can raise the annual GDP growth rate by another 0.5 percentage points. Private ownership of infrastructure assets and government credibility—for example, low risk of contract repudiation—matter with respect to infrastructure growth. Because of network properties of infrastructure assets, returns to infrastructure investment rise with population density. Being landlocked or experiencing difficulty of access to international markets has a significant negative effect on steady state investment and productivity in non-infrastructure sectors.

Calderon and Serven (2004) undertake an empirical evaluation of the impact of infrastructure development on economic growth and income distribution using a large-panel data set encompassing more than 100 countries and spanning the years 1960–2000. They consider an aggregate index of infrastructure quantity and quality, rather than concentrating on any single type of infrastructure (for example, roads, power, or transport and communications only). To account for the potential endogeneity of infrastructure (as well as that of other regressors) they use a variety of GMM (generalized method of moments) estimators based on both internal and external instruments, and report results using both disaggregated and synthetic measures of infrastructure quantity and quality. The two robust results of this study are (1) growth is positively affected by the stock of infrastructure assets and (2) income inequality declines with higher infrastructure quantity and quality.

At the meso level, using a gravity model, Limao and Venables (2001) estimated elasticity of trade with respect to transport costs and found it typically to be quite high at –3. Distance to key markets is an important impediment to trade as expected, but in their model, poor infrastructure (measured by an index combining road, rail, and telecom density) accounts for 40 percent of the predicted transport cost for coastal countries and up to 60 percent for landlocked countries.

Applying the results from this analysis to SSA trade performance, they find that whereas a basic gravity model suggests that African trade, both internal and with the rest of the world, is lower than predicted (in contrast to the earlier findings of Foroutan and Pritchett [1993]), augmenting the model to include infrastructure improves the predictive power of the model as the predicted value gets much closer to the actual values. The median landlocked country has only 30 percent of the trade volume of a median coastal country. What is also striking from this study is that holding activity levels and direct distances between trading partners constant, improving landlocked country infrastructure is as important as improving the infrastructure in the transit country.

At the micro level, Elbadawi, Mengistae, and Zeufack (2002) estimate the impact of geography (supplier and market access) on exports of manufactures using an export market participation equation on a sample of 1,400 textile and garment producers from six countries in Africa and two from outside the region. Supplier and market access are essentially measured by the inverse of transport costs (international plus domestic) and trade policy constraints (degree of openness as measured by Sachs and Warner 1995). They find that (1) firm-level exports increase with both supplier access and foreign market access—a doubling of foreign market access would raise exports by 7 percent, whereas exports would increase by 20 percent with doubling of supplier access; (2) the degree of openness has a strong twofold impact on exports; (3) domestic transport costs seem to have significant and much stronger impact on exports than international transport—the elasticities with respect to suppliers' access are much higher and more robust than with respect to market access; and (4) productivity in the firms increases with both supplier access and access to foreign markets. Mengistae and Pattillo (2004) have further evidence of productivity gains through exposure to foreign competition pressure, as well as through technological learning.

Tropical Climate as a Host for Diseases

More than 90 percent of Sub-Saharan Africa lies within the tropics, where the burden of disease is high. This compares with 3 percent for Organisation for Economic Co-operation and Development (OECD) countries and 60 percent for East Asia. Sachs and Warner (2001) and Masters and McMillan (2001) emphasize the high burden of human and animal diseases in tropical climates, and its impact on life expectancy, human capital formation, labor force participation, and economic growth. They also find a significant negative impact of a malaria index on growth. Easterly and Levine (2003) and Acemoglu, Johnson, and Robinson (2001) show an indirect impact of the disease environment on long-term growth. Artadi and Sala-i-Martin (2003) estimate the forgone growth in Africa as a result of malaria prevalence at 1.25 percent per annum, a figure that surely reflects the influence of other highly correlated aspects of the health environment.

Demographic Pressure

African countries' populations grew more rapidly than the non-African developing world had grown *at its peak*. The ratio of (overwhelmingly young) dependents to the working-age population grew steadily, exceeding historical developing-country norms by 1970, and remaining above these through 2000.

The fertility rate began to fall in Africa in the mid-1980s, suggesting entry into the final phase of the demographic transition, but at a slower pace. This observation is further complicated by the huge impact of HIV/AIDS, starting in the late 1980s, on life expectancies. These very distinctive demographic features of Africa compared to other regions weigh unusually heavily on national savings and undermine the building up of the human capital needed for growth. As we saw in the previous chapter, the rapid growth of the population, as manifested by a high dependency ratio, is inimical to rapid economic growth.

The findings in chapter 3 that the delayed demographic transition in Africa has been a substantial drag on economic growth are not surprising. Indeed, there exists substantial literature on the benefits of the demographic transition on economic growth in Asia and elsewhere, which is, after all, the flip side of the coin. For example, Robert Lucas (2003), in an essay on the Industrial Revolution, says the following:

> On this general view of economic growth, then, what began in England in the 18th century and continues to diffuse throughout the world today is something like the following. Technological advances occurred that increased the wages of those with the skills needed to make economic use of these advances. These wage effects stimulated others to accumulate skills and stimulated many families to decide against having a large number of unskilled children and in favor of having fewer children, with more time and resources invested in each. The presence of a higher-skilled workforce increased still further the return to acquiring skills, keeping the process going.

The demographic transition and economic growth. Similarly, Bloom, Canning, and Sevilla (2001) conclude that the demographic transition throughout the world resulted in a changing age structure of the population, with the growth of the working-age population outstripping that of the non-working-age population. They then offer a number of reasons why age dependency has a powerful effect on economic growth. These are labor supply, savings, and human capital.

Labor supply. The transition mechanism here is largely mechanical. The demographic transition, in which mortality rates decline first, followed by fertility rates, leads to a situation in which the population first gets younger (mortality declines are disproportional among infants and children), and then the baby boom becomes a boom in the workforce. It is also likely that declines in childbearing free more women to also participate in the labor force directly.

Savings. The impact of the demographic transition on savings is also largely mechanical. Children and the elderly consume more than they save, while working-age people, for the most part, do the opposite; thus, increasing the proportion of working-age to dependent population automatically increases savings.

Human capital. One of the reasons for declining birthrates is the fact that changes in the economy (rural to urban migration, for example) change, in a fashion explained by Gary Becker, the calculus that parents use in deciding whether it is better to emphasize quality or quantity in their children. Economic development shifts the incentives by providing greater rewards and reduced costs to investing in children, thus leading to higher levels of human capital investment.

As can be seen from table 4.2, in 1960 high-income countries had reduced their age dependency ratios to 0.6, whereas most countries in the rest of the world had high age dependency ratios (Sub-Saharan Africa and Latin America and the Caribbean), and those in Asia were beginning to decline. Over the next decades, East Asian age dependency ratios approached those of the high-income countries, whereas those of South Asia and Latin America and the Caribbean began to decline. The Middle East and North Africa experienced increasing age dependency ratios until 1970, when they began to decline, while Africa's dependency ratios increased until 1990, when declining fertility rates began to have an effect.

TABLE 4.2
Age Dependency Ratios

Region	1960	1970	1980	1990	2000
East Asia and Pacific	0.79	0.81	0.71	0.55	0.50
Europe and Central Asia	0.61	0.60	0.56	0.55	0.50
High-income OECD countries	0.60	0.59	0.53	0.49	0.49
Latin America and the Caribbean	0.87	0.88	0.80	0.70	0.61
Middle East and North Africa	0.90	0.96	0.92	0.89	0.70
South Asia	0.78	0.81	0.77	0.72	0.67
Sub-Saharan Africa	0.87	0.92	0.94	0.95	0.91

Source: World Bank, World Development Indicators 2006.

So what has been the global demographic experience since 1960? The demographic transition information is presented in figure 4.2. In 1962, virtually all regions of the developing world were experiencing the same rate of population growth (between 2.5 percent and 3.0 percent). However, East Asia and the Pacific, and to a lesser extent Latin America and the Caribbean,

FIGURE 4.2
Demographic Transition Information: Rate of Natural Increase

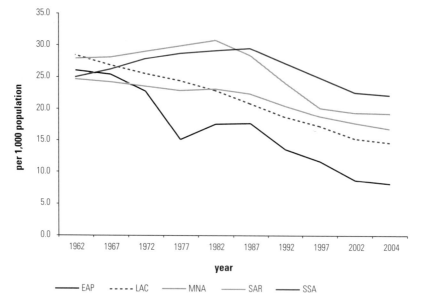

Source: World Bank, World Development Indicators 2006.

Note: EAP = East Asia and Pacific; LAC = Latin America and the Caribbean; MNA = Middle East and North Africa; SAR = South Asia; SSA = Sub-Saharan Africa.

had already begun to experience lower birthrates and death rates. Over the next 40 years, East Asia, Latin America, South Asia, and even the Middle East and North Africa experienced a dramatic decline in population growth because of steady decreases in mortality rates and unprecedented decreases in fertility rates (2.2 percent per year in East Asia, 1.6 percent per year in Latin America, and 1.5 percent per year in South Asia and the Middle East and North Africa). However, it was not until 1980 that African fertility rates began to fall, and then at a lower rate (about 0.8 percent per year). This delay in the demographic transition has probably reduced African growth rates, but it also offers an opportunity for accelerated growth rates if fertility declines can be accelerated.

What causes fertility rate declines? There is a great debate as to the causes of fertility change, but a number of factors have been cited in much of the literature. These include declining infant and child mortality rates, urbanization, increasing incomes, increased levels of education (especially for women), increased female participation in the labor force, and increased access to family planning services. A quick look at some of these variables across regions goes a long way toward explaining Sub-Saharan Africa's delay in reducing fertility levels. These data are presented in table 4.3.

If the variables presented in table 4.3 are indeed associated with or even causative of fertility rates, the reasons for Africa's relatively high fertility rate is readily explicable. Compare Sub-Saharan Africa to the regions that are, on the whole, more developed—East Asia, the Middle East and North Africa, and Latin America. Africa's fertility rate is around twice theirs, its infant mortality rate three to four times as high, its primary enrollment rates for girls about 80 percent of the other three regions, its secondary

TABLE 4.3
Socioeconomic Indicators, 2004

Region	Fertility rate	Infant mortality rate	Girls' primary enrollment rate	Girls' secondary enrollment rate	Percent urban	Per capita income (US$ PPP)
EAP	2.01	36.77	111.75	68.87	40.56	5,335
LAC	2.45	31.37	117.36	84.75	76.81	7,684
MNA	3.04	55.19	96.41	70.84	56.78	5,735
SAR	3.11	91.52	97.99	48.20	28.22	2,876
SSA	**5.31**	**168.19**	**87.56**	**35.00**	**34.73**	**1,871**

Source: World Bank, World Development Indicators 2006.

Note: EAP = East Asia and Pacific; LAC = Latin America and the Caribbean; MNA = Middle East and North Africa; SAR = South Asia; SSA = Sub-Saharan Africa; PPP = purchasing power parity.

enrollment rate for girls about half, its urbanization rate 60 percent of the average of the other three, and its per capita income 30 percent of theirs.

Perhaps the more interesting case is South Asia, which has per capita incomes between those of Africa and the other regions, and intermediate socioeconomic variables as well. Indeed, South Asia is less urbanized than Africa and has female enrollment rates not markedly higher than those of Africa. South Asia still has high infant mortality rates as well, yet its fertility rates are much closer to those of the other regions than to those of Africa. *Nevertheless, over the 44 years between 1960 and 2004, South Asia saw its infant mortality rates decline at 2.2 percent per year, while Sub-Saharan Africa experienced declines of just half of that, 1.1 percent per year.*

One problem, of course, is that all these variables are interrelated. Income growth affects health outcomes directly through better nutrition and better hygiene. Education affects health outcomes as well. Income growth affects fertility, and that, in turn, affects income growth. The bottom line is that while there is no magic bullet, the two areas that are most likely to have spillover effects on fertility behavior are effective health services focused on reducing infant and child mortality, and expand girls' enrollments in secondary schools.[2]

Kahn, Stopnitzky, and El Zayed (2006) examined the relationship between education and fertility in Bangladesh using multivariate analysis and found that education had a strong impact on fertility behavior. On average, women with no education had more than 3.5 live births each, while women with a secondary education had a little more than two.

The literature is ambivalent concerning the impact of family planning programs. Supporters note the large numbers of women who would like to use modern family planning methods but for whom such services are out of reach, either because supplies are limited or the price is too high, and argue that unmet demand indicates that increases in the availability of affordable contraceptives would reduce fertility (Bulatao 1998; Casterline and Sinding 2000). Detractors (particularly Pritchett 1994) argue that fertility behavior and the desire to control fertility behavior are strongly correlated over time, and that it is changing intentions with respect to family size, rather than the supply of contraceptives, that drives fertility outcomes. It is also true that Western countries experienced the demographic transition before the widespread availability of modern family planning methods.

However, there is evidence that family planning programs may be more important in reducing fertility in Sub-Saharan Africa than elsewhere. Westoff and Bankole (2000) note that the percentage of women who want no more children has risen slowly but steadily in Sub-Saharan Africa since the 1970s, having reached a level of 20 to 40 percent in many countries by the late 1990s. Yet overall levels remain far below those seen in Asia and in North Africa, where the level of demand for limiting births clusters in the 40 to 60 percent range. Unmet need for the means to limit births is increasing fairly uniformly for most Sub-Saharan African countries; in contrast, in Asia and North Africa, and Latin America and the Caribbean, it is generally declining with the adoption of contraceptive use. Although the evidence indicates that most women in Sub-Saharan Africa who practice contraception do so to space rather than to limit births, trend data suggest that the proportion of users practicing contraception to limit births has been increasing in recent years; in some countries, this proportion approaches half of all methods used and is higher than expected elsewhere.

Westoff and Bankole (2000, 1) then conclude:

> While demand for contraception is increasing throughout the developing world, most of the demand in Asia and North Africa and in Latin America is already being met whereas much of the demand in Sub-Saharan Africa is not. In both Asia and Latin America, where contraceptive use is already high, providers need to gear their services toward helping clients to continue use and to improve the effectiveness of their contraceptive practice. In Sub-Saharan Africa, where use is low, programs must aim to encourage adoption of modern methods.

Even if supplying contraceptives has a more limited effect on reducing fertility than its supporters maintain, it still may be the most cost-effective approach to the problem. We know fertility is directly linked to income levels, urbanization, and female participation in the workforce, all of which are part of the growth and development process and tend to change slowly. We also know that reductions in infant and child mortality and increased education for girls also reduce fertility, and these should be pursued vigorously in any case. However, although the impact of family planning programs is still debated, there is little doubt that the costs tend to be modest compared to other approaches.

Fraser, Green, and Dunbar (2002), in a megastudy of the costs of family planning in Sub-Saharan Africa, present data that show that, in most countries, family planning costs range from $10 to $20 per couple per year, depending on the method. This would mean in Kenya, for example, with

9 million women between the ages of 15 and 64, and an unmet need for contraceptives of 30 percent, that increasing family planning programs to cover the unmet need would mean spending an additional $30 million to $60 million. How does this compare to improving primary health services or expanding secondary education?

Kenya's education budget in 2003 was $420 million, almost 30 percent of all government expenditures. Per pupil expenditures in secondary school were $95 per student in 2003, with girls' enrollment reaching 1.2 million, or 46 percent of the secondary school age group. To increase the enrollment of girls by 25 percent (an additional 300,000 girls) would cost $29.5 million (assuming one could expand access only for girls). The Kenya health budget was about $6.50 per capita, well below the estimated requirement by the World Health Organization of $12 per capita. Thus a well-funded (though admittedly untargeted) health program would require additional expenditures of around $200 million. Without really knowing the efficacy of these investments in terms of reducing fertility, it would be hard to determine which is more cost-effective, although by any measure, the family planning approach is the cheapest.

Moreover, family planning programs, which, in the past, have been largely funded by donors, have seen substantial reductions in available finance, partly because of shifts to HIV/AIDS programs and partly because traditional supporters have lost interest (box 4.1). At a recent symposium in Mozambique, African health experts lamented the lack of funding for family planning. According to Chisale Mhango, a public health expert at the African Union's Department of Social Affairs, "There hasn't been adequate emphasis on family planning as a strategy, and yet it is a cost-effective thing. . . . When you provide family planning, you are reducing unwanted pregnancies and therefore maternal mortality—including deaths from abortion" (Inter Press Service News Agency 2006).

A United Nations Economic and Social Council (ECOSOC) report issued in January 2005 notes that funding for family planning programs decreased by 36 percent, from $723 million in 1995 to $461 million in 2003. A similar report, released in 2006 by ECOSOC, says that donor funding for family planning continued to decline in 2004.

HIV/AIDS and the Demographic Transition

HIV/AIDS remains a tragedy of overwhelming proportions in Sub-Saharan Africa, even though estimates of prevalence have been

BOX 4.1

The Demographic Transition and Family Planning in Ethiopia

"Capturing the Demographic Bonus in Ethiopia," a draft report produced by the Africa Region of the World Bank (2006a), offers a strong analytical case for expanded support for family planning programs. The researchers examine the proximate and structural determinants of fertility in Ethiopia, the expected development outcomes over the period from 2005 to 2030, the costs of family planning programs, and the links between different demographic scenarios and household and national income. Their conclusions are quite dramatic.

After developing a behavioral model in which the determinants of fertility include, among other things, urbanization, women's education, income levels, employment, and female empowerment, the authors simulate the evolution of fertility behavior between 2000 and 2030. Beginning with estimates of the changes in income, education, and urbanization over the 30 years, they then add the simulations to estimates of the increased use of contraceptives, to present both a low and a high estimate. In the low scenario, the total fertility rate (TFR) declines from 5.9 in 2000 to 3.63 in 2030. In the high scenario, the TFR declines more quickly to 2.87 in 2030.

The authors then examine the differences in population levels, dependency ratios, and income resulting from the two scenarios and compare the gain in long-term income to the costs of family planning programs needed to move from the low to the high scenario in terms of contraceptive use. Under the high-fertility scenario, the Ethiopian population in 2030 would be 135 million and the age dependency ratio would be 0.70; under the lower fertility scenario, the population would be 124.2 million and the age dependency ratio 0.61. The welfare difference between the two scenarios, measured in the present value of per capita consumption, is between $105.00 and $112.50. This is a massive number in a country where the current mean level of per capita consumption is $117. The study estimates the cost of an accelerated family planning program as $52 million annually (less than 50 U.S. cents per capita) compared to the more modest program implicit in the high-fertility scenario.

While any simulation is subject to differing views about reasonable estimates of key variables, as well as questions as to the stability of structural relationships over long periods, the incredible ratio of benefits to costs of family planning are likely to be true under any imaginable scenarios. The report states, "In conclusion, two major messages emerge from the population projections and the simulations: (1) Development is the best contraceptive; and (2) Contraceptives are good for development."

readjusted downward in recent months.[3] The basic facts in Sub-Saharan Africa are as follows:

- Globally, there are 24.5 million people living with HIV; the epicenter of the epidemic is in Southern Africa, where one-third of people infected with HIV reside.

- There are 2.7 million new infections each year.

- The adult prevalence rate of HIV is 6.1 percent.

- Two million people die of AIDS each year. Of those, about 930,000 were living in Southern Africa.

- Three women are HIV-infected for every two men.

- Among young people (age 15 to 24), 75 percent of the HIV-infected population are women.

- About 17 percent of those with AIDS (810,000 people) are receiving antiretroviral therapy.

- Two million children are living with HIV; there were about 12 million orphans living in Sub-Saharan Africa in 2005.[4]

Demographic Impacts

As shown in figure 4.3, there are 4 countries in Sub-Saharan Africa with prevalence rates above 20 percent, another 7 with prevalence rates between 10 and 20 percent, 7 with rates between 5 percent and 10 percent, and 26 with rates below 5 percent. Clearly, the biggest demographic impacts will be on the countries with the highest prevalence rates—the nine countries of Southern Africa and the Central African Republic. The clearest picture of the impact on the age structure of these countries can be seen in figure 4.4.

What is clear is that in countries with high HIV prevalence, the whole pattern of mortality is changed, and changed dramatically. In 10 years, Southern Africa went from having one-third of annual deaths coming from the working-age population to two-thirds. While the AIDS pandemic also affects fertility through a number of channels (increased death rates and morbidity of women of childbearing ages, changes in sexual behaviors, and increased need for women to enter the workforce), it is unclear

FIGURE 4.3
HIV Prevalence in Adults in Africa, 2005
Percent

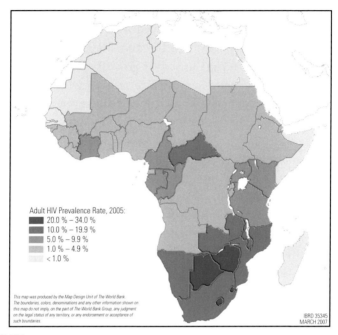

Source: UNAIDS 2006.

Note: For Cape Verde, The Gambia, São Tomé and Principe, and Comoros, the data values are not available.

FIGURE 4.4
Age Distribution of Deaths in Southern Africa

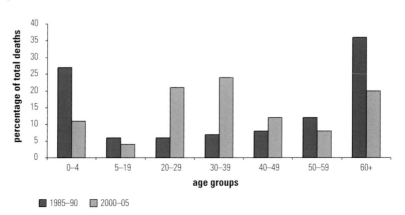

Source: UNAIDS 2006, 23.

whether fertility will increase or decrease. What is certain is that the net effect of the HIV pandemic on fertility and mortality will be to increase age dependency ratios and thus reduce economic growth rates.

The high rates of fertility still common in Africa mean that Africa's demographic transition has been delayed. The current situation results in high levels of age dependency, which reduces saving, reduces investment in human capital, and results in slower growth of the labor force. All of these factors reduce economic growth rates from what they might have been if the age dependency ratio were lower. However, this situation provides a reserve for higher growth rates if fertility rates can be induced to decline.

Declines in fertility rates seem to be linked to income growth, urbanization, girls' education, and reduced infant and child mortality rates, all of which have been delayed in Africa because of stagnant growth rates. Thus, as growth begins to accelerate, as it has in many African countries in the past decade, there is a reserve fuel in the form of declining age-dependency ratios that can accelerate per capita growth rates by 1 percent or more. Given the importance of this issue, and the fact that donors have reduced their funding for family planning programs, it would be well to revisit the relative priority of investments in family planning.

Finally, the HIV/AIDS pandemic increases age dependency, especially in high-prevalence countries. Bearing in mind that investments in preventing and treating AIDS are extremely important from a human point of view, and the reduction of human suffering is clearly the prime motivating force for HIV/AIDS programs, it is good to know that these programs may also, in a minor way, lead to increased economic growth.

Natural Resources—Curse and Potential

Extensive empirical evidence of poor growth performance by the natural-resource-rich economies in Africa, the Middle East, Latin America, and East Asia and Pacific suggests that these resources are another factor that is thought to have negative implications for growth. This is known as the "resource curse" hypothesis because these countries appear to have failed to realize their apparent economic potentials. Added to this is what is known as "Dutch disease," the fact that foreign exchange inflows from natural resource exports may have adverse effects on the domestic economy because they lead to an appreciation of the domestic currency. This hurts other (nonresource) industries because their products become more expensive on the world market, and exports generally fall. A nondiversified primary commodities exporter also becomes extremely vulnerable to exchange rate volatility, as the domestic currency exchange rate fluctuates whenever global demand for the natural resource being exported changes.

As mentioned, about 30 percent of the countries in Sub-Saharan Africa, 19 percent of the countries in EAP, and 0 percent in SAR are resource rich. Resource-rich countries are classified according to a threshold defined as generating more than 10 percent of GDP from primary commodity rents. Because prices of commodities fluctuate, potentially some economies flip back and forth across this threshold year to year, but because most resource-rich countries derive their wealth from minerals, including oil, the majority of them maintained a fairly stable status throughout the period of analysis.

Figure 4.5 plots the performance in terms of average growth rates, dividing countries into four groups: resource-rich coastal, resource-rich

FIGURE 4.5

SSA's Smoothed Average Growth in Real GDP Per Capita, by Opportunity Group

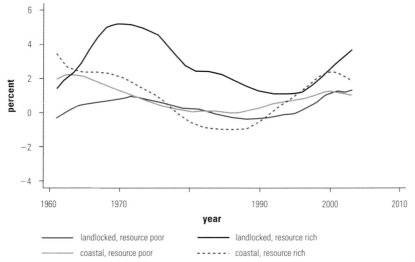

Source: World Development Indicators 2006, PWT 6.1 (Heston, Summers, and Ater 2002), GDN 1998, and Collier and O'Connell 2006.

landlocked, resource-poor coastal, and resource-poor landlocked. In Sub-Saharan Africa, there are only two countries with a full set of annual growth rate observations (Botswana and Zambia) that are categorized as landlocked, resource-rich economies. The evidence is rather ambiguous. If we discard the resource-rich landlocked group because it is dominated by one country with high growth rates—Botswana—the graph suggests that being landlocked and resource poor is a strong constraint. However, coastal resource-rich countries did better than coastal resource-poor countries, except during the 1980s.

Risks and Uncertainty

It is well known that investors make decisions based on a function that includes the rate of return and the risk of any investment choice: the higher the risk, the higher the required rate of return. Each investment carries its own particular risk-return ratios. However, in Africa a number of environmental factors that are external to the individual investment tend to raise the risk, and thus, for any given rate of return, reduce the rate of investment. In this section we will examine two risk-elevating factors: macroeconomic policies and political instability.

Macroeconomic Stability

Africa as a region has made significant progress in the area of macroeconomic stability. From the mid-1990s, inflation—a standard proxy for instability—fell from an average of 24 percent to an average of 13.3 percent for the period from 2001to 2004. However, it is worth noting that despite this recorded improvement, as figure 4.6 shows, average inflation in Africa is higher than in other regions for the later years.

As the yearly averages for the region show, the improvement achieved is even more pronounced. Figure 4.6 depicts a steady decline in inflation to a level below 10 percent in both 2003 and 2004. However, the figure also shows significant variability over the years, which is a definite threat to perceptions of stability. In particular, from around 1990, other regions show much less variability in their inflation rates than Africa (figure 4.7).

It is not only the inflation rate that determines stability, but also its variability over time. Noise in inflation perpetuates the perception of risk in

FIGURE 4.6

Inflation Trends: Regional Comparisons, 1971–2004

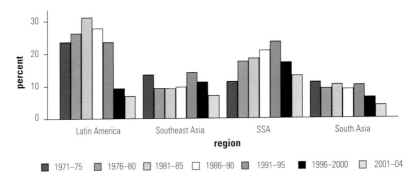

Source: World Bank, World Development Indicators 2006.

FIGURE 4.7

Regional Inflation, 1971–2004

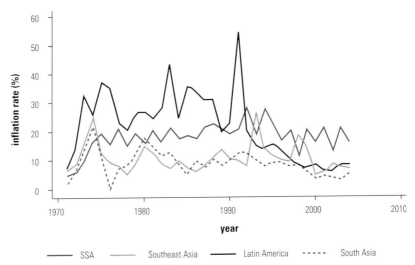

Source: World Bank, World Development Indicators 2006.

the investment environment and also generates skepticism about the authorities' ability to maintain stability. The pervasiveness of this problem is also evident in the high percentage of investors who perceive macroeconomic instability to be a major impediment to investment and growth. For example, in the 2003 Investment Climate Survey for Tanzania (World

Bank 2004a), 43 percent of respondent firms rated macroeconomic instability as a major obstacle to doing business, even though Tanzania has had a steady decline in its rate of inflation, from about 21 percent in 1996 to about 4 percent in 2003. The proportion of entrepreneurs who rate macroeconomic instability as a significant constraint to business is comparable to Uganda and Kenya, at 45 percent and 51 percent, respectively, but for China the percentage is considerably lower, at 30 percent. This gives a clear message that maintaining economic stability should be a priority for African countries.

Table 4.4 shows that the noted recovery extends to other indicators of stability, with the possible exception of external debt. Relative to other developing regions, Africa stacks up very well, again with the exception of debt, where Africa's average does not show any signs of declining and also performs poorly relative to other regions. For example, for the period from 1997 to 2003, the debt–to–gross national income ratio of 133 percent is twice as

TABLE 4.4
Fiscal Policy Indicators for Selected Regions
percent

Region	1971–80	1981–90	1991–96	1997–2003
Sub-Saharan Africa				
Government spending (% of GDP)	16.26	17.48	16.463	15.04
Growth rate of spending	7.48	3.74	1.93	6.20
Fiscal balance	−6.44	−5.74	−5.50	−4.81
Debt/GNI	31.90	91.00	133.33	133.96
Latin America				
Government spending (% ofGDP)	12.99	15.26	12.97	14.55
Growth rate of spending	6.56	2.50	3.68	3.21
Fiscal balance	−2.84	−4.59	−0.73	−2.43
Debt/GNI	33.36	87.17	85.84	61.55
South Asia				
Government spending (% of GDP)	9.25	11.26	11.41	12.36
Growth rate of spending	8.32	6.35	4.87	6.90
Fiscal balance	−6.09	−9.77	−7.24	−5.58
Debt/GNI	22.82	34.48	46.10	44.16
Southeast Asia				
Government spending (% of DP)	14.38	17.54	14.31	12.73
Growth rate of spending	8.14	3.61	6.57	4.50
Fiscal balance	−4.05	−5.58	−2.45	−3.90
Debt/GNI	27.08	56.36	65.12	65.29

Source: World Bank, World Development Indicators 2006.

Note: GNI = gross national income.

high as that for both Latin America and Southeast Asia, and three times that of South Asia.

These observations suggest that while on the whole Africa has made great strides in achieving some measure of stability, the region is not completely out of the woods. Concerted effort now has to be devoted to sustaining the stability, with particular emphasis on prudent management of fiscal policy.

Recent developments, specifically developments in commodity markets and future official development assistance flows, make the issue of fiscal management more urgent. Most African countries rely on primary commodities, whose prices tend to fluctuate significantly. This has in the past resulted in a procyclical fiscal policy that is mainly driven by developments in commodity markets. Further, volatility of commodity prices makes it difficult to stabilize budgetary spending. The current environment of rising oil prices presents a particular challenge to management of windfall gains by oil-producing countries. Dependency on oil tends to be even trickier due to high volatility of oil prices. In addition to high fluctuations, oil price changes are subject to exogenous shocks, which are primarily caused by unforeseen factors and as such are difficult to project. This not only generates volatility in government spending, but also puts pressure on fiscal policy, especially with regard to sterilizing excess revenue for medium- to long-term sustainability.

The donor community has committed to doubling aid flows to Africa over the next few years. This will be, by any standard, a large increase, and while the scaled-up aid will open up fiscal space for African countries, it nevertheless presents a host of challenges to macroeconomic management of recipient countries and could potentially be a source of imbalances. The impact of higher aid flows will depend on policy choices regarding the utilization and absorption of these resources, as well as the interactions between monetary policy, fiscal policy, and exchange rate management. The threats to macroeconomic stability from increased aid include the potential for real exchange appreciations and their effect on exports and competitiveness. Scaling up aid may also generate inflationary pressures from increased domestic demand, unless the liquidity injections are sterilized. Aid flows tend to be unpredictable, which may impede a government's ability to plan effectively. Also related to this unpredictability, governments must make plans for continued spending in the event that donors renege on their commitments. This could lead to increased fiscal deficits.

Political Uncertainty and Conflict

Polarization, Nation Building, and Conflict

The countries of Sub-Saharan Africa came to political independence both later and more rapidly than those of other developing regions. While only Ethiopia, Liberia, and South Africa existed as independent states at the end of 1955, fully three-quarters of colonial Africa, representing the vast bulk of its population and GDP, had achieved political independence by 1966. In 1966, the average independent state in Sub-Saharan Africa had held sovereignty for fewer than 10 years; its counterparts in the rest of the developing world had been independent for the better part of a century.

Colonial structures of political control were both arbitrary—with boundaries cutting across historical patterns of politics and trade—and effective. Their abrupt departure meant that the challenge of economic development was in many cases confounded from the outset with an acute problem of nation building. Nigeria provides a telling example of the impact of ex ante regional polarization on political and economic development. But similar patterns of internal polarization, often created or reinforced in the encounter with conquering European powers, existed throughout the continent in 1960.

While the salience of ethnoregional polarization was clear to political scientists in the early 1960s (for example, Carter 1962, 1963, 1966), economists have only recently begun to come to grips with the implications of nation building for African economic growth. Two approaches have been important. The first is due to Easterly and Levine (1997), who noted that as a legacy of low population densities and arbitrary colonial boundaries, the probability that any two randomly chosen individuals in a given African country would belong to the same ethnolinguistic group is very small. Moreover, on a global basis, ethnolinguistically heterogeneous countries tend to grow more slowly, as a result of weaker public sector performance. Miguel (2004) reports a similar finding for Kenya and Tanzania. Collier (2000) finds, however, that the adverse impact of heterogeneity is strongly contingent on political institutions. In democracies, ethnolinguistic heterogeneity has no impact either on overall growth or on microeconomic efficiency (as measured by the economic return on World Bank projects). In dictatorships, the impact is strong.

Azam (1995, 2005) focuses on polarization, rather than on heterogeneity per se; a polarized society is defined here as one like Nigeria's, in which there are two or three large subnational ethnic groups that dominate population and politics in separate regions. Azam argues that in a situation of ex ante ethnoregional polarization, regionally based redistribution may be required to buy off the threat of armed conflict. The existence of such a risk is consistent with the global evidence of Collier and Hoeffler (2000), who find the risk of civil war maximized under conditions of polarization: homogeneous societies have low exposure to civil war, but so do heterogeneous societies. In cases of ex ante polarization, then, the Azam analysis forces a reinterpretation of distortionary redistribution. If the "good policy" counterfactual involves armed conflict and economic collapse, a redistribution program that distorts efficiency relative to a peaceful counterfactual may be growth promoting (relative to the true counterfactual). This condition shifts the grounds of the governance critique from redistribution itself to the instruments employed to achieve it. Political elites attempting to "buy the peace" should be seen to do so transparently and credibly (perhaps via constitutional means), and with a minimum of distortion, and they should simultaneously employ instruments directly targeted at reducing polarization.

Conflict in Africa

Over the past 40 years, especially in the past two decades or so, Africa has experienced a debilitating descent of states into persistent internal conflict that has become an all-too-familiar phenomenon across the region. In fact, conflicts are now arguably the single most important determinant of poverty in Africa. According to the International Institute for Strategic Studies, in 1999 Africa played host to more than half the world's conflicts as instability not only brewed within countries but spilled over into neighboring states, resulting in catastrophic wars within and among countries. While growing nationalism and ethnicity has typified these conflicts, other factors such as abject poverty, lack of opportunities, and corruption have contributed significantly.

Africa's underlying proneness to rebellion, and hence to civil war, is strongly related to economic conditions. Conflicts affect the economy through reduced investment in both physical and human capital, as well as through the destruction of existing assets, including institutional capacity, and these are reflected in reduced economic growth. Statistics show that countries that experienced a civil war had an average income that was about 50 percent lower than countries that did not experience a conflict, and investment ratios for both physical and human capital were also about 50 percent lower in conflict countries.

Conflicts across the region have profoundly changed the social welfare of affected societies as military spending has diverted increasing proportions of national resources from pressing developmental needs. Local and national economies have suffered huge output losses with devastating consequences to the quality of life as populations became poorer. Conflicts have led to widespread dislocation of populations and loss of household savings. Conflicts have also caused serious reversals in health and other human development aspects. For example, in most war-torn countries old diseases have reappeared and new ones have emerged in situations where health and other social facilities not only were underfinanced but were stretched far beyond their capacities.

A study by Milanovic (2005) finds that war and underlying risk factors are the reasons why low-income countries, and Africa specifically, failed to catch up to the slower-growing developed countries. The poorest countries have lost, on average, some 40 percent of their output through greater frequency of war compared with the rest of the world. Wars alone explain almost the entire relative decline of the less developed countries (LDCs) compared with the middle-income countries. In other words, had prevalence of war among LDCs been at the same level as elsewhere, the LDCs would have at least kept pace with the rest of the world.

Figure 4.8 shows the incidence of civil war in the developing world since 1960. There is a sharp increase in both absolute and relative terms in Sub-Saharan Africa in the early 1990s. Since the mid-1990s, however, there has been a sharp decline in the proportion of countries involved in civil conflict in the region, and the proportion of the African population living in an environment of civil conflict has fallen more sharply, dipping below the average of other developing regions at the turn of the 21st century. Cessation of conflict in Sudan is not reflected in this data and should further reduce the latter proportion. This positive change is corroborated by new global data on the incidence of violent conflicts (Gleditsch and others 2002). Using these data, Collier and Hoeffler (2006, 89–107) show that immediately after the end of the Cold War, the incidence of wars declined. The number of wars peaked in Africa in 1992, and since then the number of civil wars seems to be declining.

The Costs of War

Recent research suggests that the incidence and severity of conflicts in Africa have had a robust, negative effect on the growth rate of income. For

FIGURE 4.8
Countries in Civil War

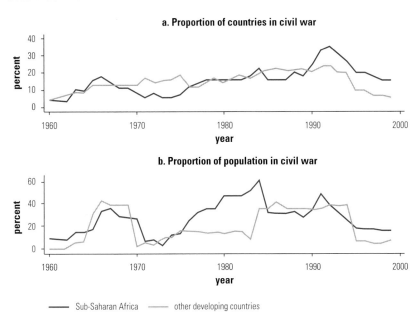

Source: Ndulu and O'Connell 2006a (Sambani's data set).

instance, the data show that countries that experienced civil wars had an average income 50 percent lower than that of countries that experienced no civil war.

The indirect cost of war can be higher than the direct cost. In war-torn countries, many state functions that are essential for a good business environment, such as the judiciary system, are compromised. As a result, the production structure is altered, as agents shift their assets to sectors that are insulated from the disruptions of conflicts. The sectors that produce tradable goods and services and financial intermediation are adversely affected, whereas the agriculture and defense sector grows. After the war ends, there is reversal to the prewar structure, but such reversal occurs gradually, and it can take years before the prewar level of activity is recovered.

A study by Lacina and Gleditsch (2005) estimates the magnitude of the indirect cost of war by comparing the number of battle deaths with estimates of war deaths from other causes, primarily disease and malnutrition. Their findings for a selected number of countries are reported in table 4.5.

The study confirms that the direct costs of war are only a fraction, often less than 10 percent, of the indirect costs. Far more people die from war-related disease and malnutrition than from battle death. These disproportional costs are borne mostly by noncombatants and provide the rationale for intervention.

Collier and Hoeffler (2004) estimate that one year of conflict reduces the country's growth rate by 2.2 percent. Moreover, a civil war typically has an average life of 7 years, implying a 15 percent reduction of the economy. However, these are not the total economic costs of wars. Postconflict, the economy grows at more than 1 percent above the norm, but it takes roughly 21 years to achieve a level of GDP that would have been attained had there been no war. The total economic costs (present value at the beginning of the war) have been estimated at 105 percent of GDP. Military expenditure (as a percentage of GDP) rises by 1.8 percent during the war but declines by only 0.5 percent postconflict. If we assume this lasts for 10 years postconflict, the cost is 18 percent of GDP (present value).

Conflicts affect the growth rate of African economies through reduced investment in physical capital and the destruction of assets, including institutional capacity. Investment ratios and stocks of human capital in civil war countries are at least 50 percent lower than the average for countries that had no civil war.

The results for the effects of conflict on the level of income per capita are mixed. This could reflect the fact that today's level of per capita income is the result of years of policy choices and exogenous shocks. Some authors find no or negligible effects of conflict on the level of income per capita in Africa. Others, using different quantitative estimation techniques, find a robust and negative effect of conflict on the level of income. Artadi and Sala-i-Martin (2003), for instance, find that civil conflict decreased the

TABLE 4.5
Battle Deaths versus Total War Deaths in Selected African Conflicts

Country	Years	Estimates of total deaths	Battle deaths	Battle deaths as a percentage of total war deaths
Angola	1975–2002	1.5 million	160,475	11
Sudan	1983–2002	2 million	55,000	3
Liberia	1989–96	150,000–200,000	23,500	12–16
Democratic Republic of Congo	1998–2001	2.5 million	145,000	6

Source: Lacina and Gleditsch 2005.

average annual growth in Sub-Saharan Africa by 0.5 percent in the second half of the 20th century.

Regional Spillovers

Conflicts are bad public goods. They affect not only the countries involved, but also neighboring countries through the flow of refugees, drug activity, loss of remittances, and loss of export proceeds. Research shows that neighboring countries lose about 43 percent of GDP, and since the average number of conflict-neighboring countries is 2.7, the total cost of a conflict in one country is 115 percent of initial GDP of neighboring countries. The international community intervention is therefore needed not only to help break the cycle of violence, but also to prevent any regionalization of conflicts.

Recent Trends

Even though Africa compares unfavorably with the rest of the world, significant progress has been made recently. The number of actual and attempted military coups has been declining since independence in Africa. In 2004, there were 40 percent fewer coup attempts than in the 1960s, and all failed. There is a decline in the number of international terrorist incidents in Africa, and the number of terror cells in Africa has declined.

The number of conflicts in which a government was one of the warring parties declined from 15 to 10 between 2002 and 2003, while one-sided violence declined by 35 percent. Reported fatalities from all forms of political violence were down by more than 24 percent. Warfare has been less deadly over time. The average numbers of battle deaths per conflict per year have declined, although unevenly.

Despite those positive advances, concerns and challenges remain. The decline in the number and scale of conflicts was gained through preventive diplomacy and an involvement of peacekeeping forces when diplomacy failed. The fact that wars are ended does not necessarily mean that their underlying causes have been addressed. For peace to be sustainable over the long run, the root causes of conflict need to be addressed.

Political Instability, Conflict, and Investor Behavior

As discussed, political instability reduces growth rates. In the case of conflict, it does so by dislocating, injuring, and even killing people; destroying infrastructure; and bringing purposive economic activity to a halt (box 4.2). But political instability, even if it doesn't lead to conflict, creates uncertainty

BOX 4.2

Country Studies

Rwanda. Lopez and Wodon (2005) estimated the cost of armed conflict in Rwanda. They found that without the genocide of 1994, Rwanda's per capita GDP would have been about 25 percent higher in 2001. The study suggests that the economic cost of the conflict was long-lasting, even though Rwanda managed successfully to reverse the decline of some other social indicators, such as the rates of enrollment in primary school and the rate of child mortality.

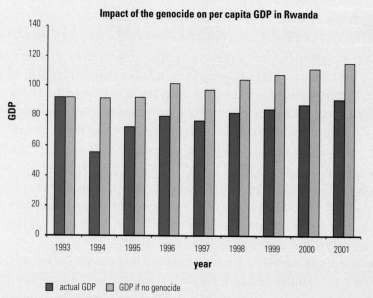

Impact of the genocide on per capita GDP in Rwanda

■ actual GDP   □ GDP if no genocide

Source: Lopez and Wodon 2005.

Mozambique. Mozambique is a former Portuguese colony. The civil conflict, which started with groups funded at Mozambique's independence in 1974, ended in 1992. It is estimated that up to 1986, some 100,000 Mozambicans were killed, mostly civilians. More than 5 million people have been displaced internally, and approximately 1.7 million have been forced to flee to neighboring countries. Long after the war ended, landmines continued to exact a heavy toll on the population.

The economic losses to Mozambique because of the war were $15 billion, four times the 1988 GDP. In addition to the destruction of roads, approximately 45 percent of schools had been destroyed or closed by the end of 1987. By 1993, 48 percent of the total number of health posts had been destroyed. The environment was severely affected too, leading to a fall in the population of elephants from between 50,000–65,000 in 1974 to 13,000 or less in 1990.

The Mozambique case provides a classic example of how conflict in one country can affect the welfare of neighboring countries. Tanzania, Zambia, and Zimbabwe are the countries that suffered the brunt of the Mozambique war. Their economies have been affected because of increased defense spending, and the additional costs of transportation throughout South Africa, as the facilities in Mozambique became unavailable. The use of these ports is estimated to have cost Southern African Development Community (SADC) countries $300 million a year. By 1988, Malawi had lost approximately 40 percent of its GDP, Zimbabwe 25 percent, Zambia 20 percent, and Tanzania 10 percent. The conflict created an environmental problem as a result of the massive displacement of population. Malawi in 1989–90, for instance, had lost approximately 12 million trees to building and cooking supplies.

Democratic Republic of Congo. Since independence in 1960, the DRC has been almost continuously racked by conflict. The first five years after independence were extremely bloody, with assassinations and secessions by Katanga and Kasai provinces the order of the day. In 1965, Lieutenant-General Joseph Mobutu overthrew President Kasavubu and began 32 years of despotic, but in Congolese terms, peaceful rule. Mobutu, in turn, was overthrown by a foreign-backed rebellion led by Laurent-Desire Kabila in 1997. This was followed by what has been called the Second Congo War, in which troops from Uganda, Rwanda, Zimbabwe, Namibia, Angola, Chad, and Burundi were aligned with various internal forces. An estimated 4 million people have died, most from starvation and disease, and the Eastern Congo continues to be the site of periodic conflict.

In 1974, GDP equaled about $8.0 billion; it fell by 14 percent to $6.8 billion in 1982 and rose again to a peak of $8.4 billion in 1989. Since that time, as a result of misgovernment and increasing conflict, GDP fell to $4.2 billion in 2002, 50 percent of what it was in 1989. With a rapidly growing population, the average person in the DRC saw his or her income decline from $241 to $82, a decline in welfare that is largely unprecedented in the modern era.

as to the direction and stability of economic policy, and thus raises the risk-
iness of investment. In unstable times, only those investors who expect
very high rates of return will invest in physical capital, while others will put
their savings in land or other safe investments, including capital flight.

Weak Institutional Capacity

A detailed discussion of the weaknesses of Africa's institutional capacity,
along with a discussion of strategies to invigorate capacity in both the state
and nonstate sectors, can be found in "Capacity Building in Africa" (World
Bank 2005b). Suffice it to say that only four countries in Africa are above
global averages for state effectiveness and societal engagement. With few
exceptions, the first three decades of state capacity building—1960 to
1990—produced poor results. Efforts at indigenizing the inherited, colonial, extractive, and elitist state were often swamped by patronage and
clientelism and unsustainable expansions in the scope of government
(Levy and Kpundeh 2004). For many Sub-Saharan countries, independence was followed by a period of political and economic instability that
was not conducive to capacity development. The postindependence instability was related variously to wars (both civil and cross-border), repres-
sion, autocratic rule, clientelism, and revolutionary socialism.

Even under these often turbulent conditions, Africa benefited from
islands of excellence in the public sector's organizational capacity and performance. The well-managed public entities included central banks,
finance ministries, revenue-generating agencies, and offices of political
leaders (presidents, prime ministers, and cabinets). They depended on
explicit decisions by political and administrative leaders to establish the
key elements of public sector management needed to run the state and
maintain power, showing that strong, committed leadership matters for
capacity development. Nevertheless, key institutions, both public and private, necessary for private sector growth are largely weak and ineffectual.
Of particular importance are the institutions serving the financial sector.

The Financial Sector as a Constraint to Growth

This section discusses the structure of African financial sectors as it influences
private sector activity, economic growth, and poverty alleviation. Particular

emphasis is placed on obstacles and challenges they present to host economies, specifically financial depth, access, and efficiency. A vibrant, competitive, and efficient financial sector that reaches the majority of an economy's population is a cornerstone of sustained high levels of economic growth and development. Financial markets enhance economic growth through various channels that include mobilization and pooling of resources, increased allocative efficiency of savings, expansion and diversification of opportunities, risk sharing, and easier exchange of goods through effective payment systems. Better functioning financial systems are particularly instrumental in reducing external financing barriers and thus enabling entrepreneurial activity and firm expansion through increased lending activity.

Financial sectors in Sub-Saharan African countries, however, have not contributed significantly to economic growth. African financial sectors, especially in low-income countries, are among the least developed in the world. The systems are shallow relative to the size of the economies. The range of institutions is narrow and dominated by commercial banks. Limited access to basic financial services, including credit availability, continues to pose a major obstacle to entrepreneurial activity and welfare improvement. It is worth noting that some progress is being made as financial systems continue to institute reforms, broaden their product base, deepen their lending, and increase their reach. However, given that deeper and more efficient systems are critical for growth prospects, clearly much more needs to be done if financial sectors are to be in the vanguard of engineering economic growth. Decisive initiatives are required to turn the tide and make financial sectors major players in economic growth.

Financial Sector Development

Formal financial systems have been very shallow in African countries, and they are even more so in low-income countries. Table 4.6 shows that in terms of both M2/GDP (ratio of money and quasi money to GDP) and private sector credit, Africa has the lowest averages. The M2/GDP ratio of about 27 percent for the period from 2001 to 2004 is considerably lower than the 43 percent for South Asia and 50 percent and 56.9 percent for Latin America and Southeast Asia, respectively. These comparisons are also reflected in the private sector credit averages for the same period, whereby Africa scores 16 percent against 26 percent for South Asia, 44 percent for Latin America, and 45 percent for Southeast Asia. Moreover, while other regions have had the latter measure increasing, the average for Africa has tended to stagnate.

TABLE 4.6
Indicators of Financial Development: A Regional Comparison
Percent

	Sub-Saharan Africa		Southeast Asia		Latin America		South Asia	
Indicator	1996–2000	2001–04	1996–2000	2001–04	1996–2000	2001–04	1996–2000	2001–04
M2/GDP	24.4	26.7	49.6	56.9	43.1	50.0	38.5	43.6
Private sector credit	17.1	16.5	44.9	45.4	43.2	43.9	22.7	26.4
Liquidity liabilities	31.9	32.3	54.3	61.1	48.0	54.8	42.7	47.8

Source: World Bank, World Development Indicators 2006.

Within the region itself, there are significant differences in the financial development of individual countries. Not surprisingly, higher-income countries appear to have more depth than their low-income counterparts (figure 4.9). Low-income countries in Africa attained an average of 25 percent and 12.6 percent, respectively, for M2/GDP and private sector credit in the period from 2001 to 2004, compared to 32.8 percent and 35.5 percent, respectively, for middle-income countries.[5]

Inefficiency in the Banking Sector

Interest rate spreads throughout the region have remained high, with little indication of converging with global levels. Banks in Africa have been more inefficient than in most other developing regions, as indicated by the interest rate spread that is highest among African countries and widest among all developing regions, at a median of 13 percent (figure 4.10). The main factors causing high spreads can be grouped into high operating costs, perceived risk from policy frameworks and lending environments, lack of competition, and high concentration.

In most of Africa, lack of competition is pervasive, so banks do not have to alter their way of doing business or their pricing structures to get a fair share of the business. In addition, the small size of markets across Africa results in diseconomies of scale and consequently leads to high fixed and operating costs. These, compounded by the inadequacy of infrastructure, result in high transportation and telecommunications costs. All these factors translate into high costs of intermediation, which are, in turn, reflected in wide interest rate spreads.

FIGURE 4.9
Financial Development in SSA

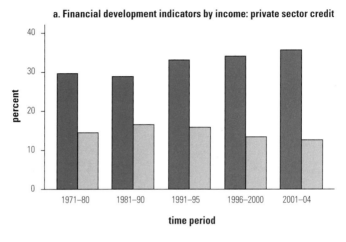

a. Financial development indicators by income: private sector credit

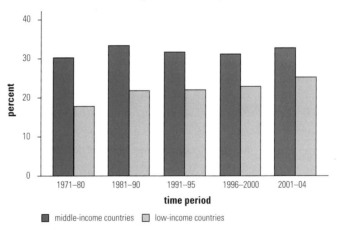

b. Financial development indicators by income: M2/GDP

■ middle-income countries ☐ low-income countries

Source: World Bank, World Development Indicators 2006.

The lending environment across Africa is characterized by a poor credit culture, poor contract enforcement, and lack of protection of creditor rights. Coupled with a lack of collateral and inability to prove creditworthiness on the part of potential borrowers, these elements have resulted in a higher perception of risk and higher external finance premiums. The prevalence of nonperforming loans in banks' portfolios add to these costs as banks compensate for the cost of forgone interest income by charging higher lending rates to performing loans.

FIGURE 4.10
Median Spread: A Regional Comparison

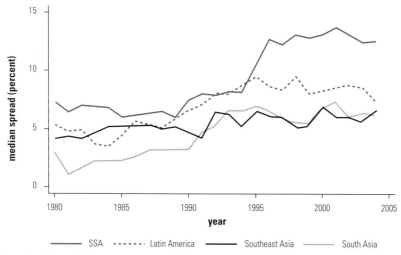

Source: World Bank, World Development Indicators 2006.

Access to Finance

A key characteristic of African financial sectors is low access to financial services.[6] A disproportionately small fraction of the populations across the region is served by formal financial institutions. Data on access to financial services are scarce, and most conclusions reached are from anecdotal but compelling evidence.[7] Figure 4.11 nevertheless gives a good idea of the extent of this problem.

Lending to the private sector remains an impediment. Access to credit in Africa has been a problem, particularly for small and medium enterprises, the informal sector, low-income people, and agricultural sectors. Figure 4.12 shows that for the selected sample of African countries, not only is credit extended at a much lower rate, but lending conditions, captured by the interest rates and collateral requirements, are more stringent.

The limited contribution of African financial sectors to their private sectors is evident in the level of resource intermediation relative to their most productive uses. Evidence suggests that Africa has a very low propensity to on-lend mobilized deposits. This is reflected in low ratios of loans to deposits. The average ratio for the region is around 32 percent, with a tendency for higher-income countries to have better performance ratios.

FIGURE 4.11
Access to Finance: Africa Relative to Other Regions

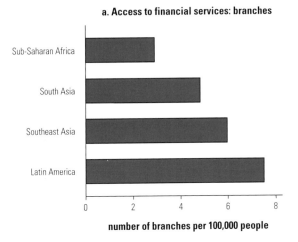

a. Access to financial services: branches

number of branches per 100,000 people

b. Access to financial services: deposits

deposits per 100,000 people

Source: World Bank 2006c.

What factors impede lending in Africa? Structural problems in financial systems explain a large part of why access to credit remains a key obstacle to African enterprise. These deficiencies include information problems, limited bankable projects, perception of high risk, and in some lingering cases, regulation of interest rates. Problematic contract enforcement, characterized by lengthy and cumbersome processes of recovering claims or realizing collateral, also features prominently in banks' lending decisions.

FIGURE 4.12
Access to Financial Capital

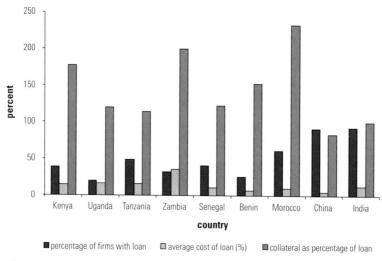

Source: Ramachandran, Tata, and Shah 2006.

Government borrowing has crowded out private credit and has effectively hampered economic activity. Over the past few decades throughout
the region, banks have relied extensively on government paper. Historically, instruments such as treasury bills offered higher interest rates
despite their being relatively risk free. As shown in figure 4.13, Africa has
one of the highest growth rates of government claims, but the main difference is in the growth rate of claims against the government relative to
claims against the private sector. Moreover, in all other regions, claims
against the private sector have been growing faster than claims against
the government. In Africa, the opposite has been true. This increased borrowing by African governments has resulted in banks having little incentive to seek lending opportunities in the private sector and possible
compromised development of new products and innovative ways of doing
business.

Low Savings

Mobilization of domestic savings in Africa remains at the center of the
debate over ways to harness resources for development in Africa. It is pre-

FIGURE 4.13
Portfolio Allocation Trends

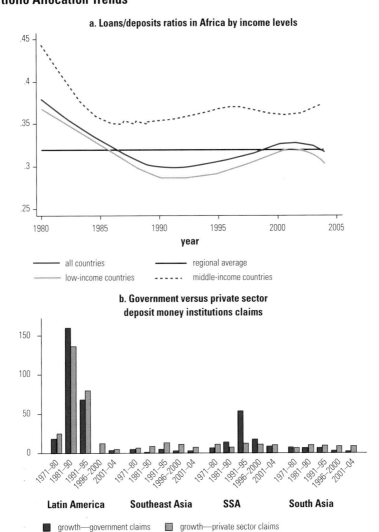

a. Loans/deposits ratios in Africa by income levels

b. Government versus private sector
deposit money institutions claims

Sources: World Bank 2006c; IMF EDSS 2005.

sumed that higher investment rates will lead to higher growth. Thus, domestic savings is considered an important determinant of growth in developing countries. Foreign savings is also important, but investment financed with domestic savings is considered not only less costly but also more permanent and durable. However, Africa has had the poorest savings performance in the world.

Saving rates in Africa have remained far below those of other developing regions. As figure 4.14 shows, as a region, Sub-Saharan Africa has not
only had low savings, but starting in the early 1970s, the savings rate has
declined significantly, especially in the 1980s. This trend has begun to
reverse itself with a notable increase, but the rate remains significantly
below the regional average achieved in the 1970s. The poor performance
of Africa becomes even starker when compared to other regions, especially
with respect to South Asia. In the early 1970s, the average savings rate in
Sub-Saharan Africa was higher than in South Asia. However, while the
savings rate in Africa has trended downward, South Asia has experienced
a sustained upward trend, so that by 2003 the average savings rate had
exceeded 20 percent, compared to a mere 9 percent for Africa.

The situation is even worse if one excludes resource-rich countries,
which have relatively high savings rates. Without these outliers, the average savings rate for the region would be even lower. In fact, when we
exclude these countries from the sample, the average savings rate falls from
5 percent to about 3 percent in 2003. Over the period under consideration,
the savings rates in the majority of African countries have averaged below
10 percent of GDP, with some countries actually recording negative rates.

Over time as well, individual country performance has varied significantly. Some of these differences are depicted in figure 4.15. With the

FIGURE 4.14
Saving Trends: Regional Comparison by Decade

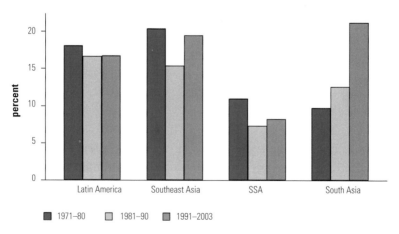

Source: World Bank 2006c.

exception of Botswana, Cameroon, and Mauritius, all countries suffered declines in saving rates in the 1980s. The declines in the average savings rates for the decade varied significantly, from as low as 1 percent to as much as 20 percent.[8] However, even though the saving rates for most countries bounced back in the following decade, for some countries the falls were sustained. Some of the countries whose declines lasted into the 1990s have started experiencing upswings in their saving rates. The declines have been more stubborn in a few countries. A case in point is Kenya, whose savings rate of 19 percent in the 1970s has dropped each decade to an average of 8.6 percent, achieved since the turn of the millennium. A similar situation exists in Malawi, where the savings rate also dropped dramatically, from 14 percent in the 1970s to a current average of negative 5 percent.

Overall, the decade starting in the 1990s is marked by improvements in savings. However, as the figure below shows, more than 25 percent of the countries experienced declining savings rates.

Another fundamental feature of domestic savings in Africa is the prominence of public savings as a determinant of savings rates—a feature that is absent in other developing regions where savings rates are driven by private savings. Indeed, for Africa it has been found that where savings have declined, public savings deteriorated at a faster rate than private savings

FIGURE 4.15

Saving Trends in SSA, 1980–2004

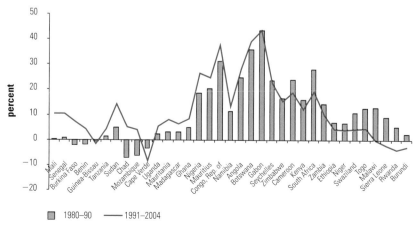

Sources: World Bank 2006c.

(Aryeetey and Udry 2000). This observation necessitates looking separately at the individual components of savings, because the behavior in the two sectors, that is, public and private, is likely to be determined by different sets of factors. This kind of decomposition may also provide better insights into which of the sectors is a major contributor to a nation's savings, as well as give a better indication of where efforts should be directed.

We benchmark the performance of Sub-Saharan Africa with respect to these components against the performance of other developing regions. Figure 4.16 shows that Africa's performance in both public and private

FIGURE 4.16
Savings Decomposition

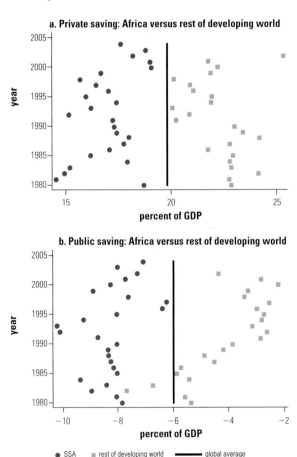

savings falls below that of other developing regions. Africa's averages in all time periods are below the averages for the developing world. Conversely, the averages for the rest of the developing world are in almost all cases above the global average. However, it is also clear from the figures that Africa's performance is even worse in terms of public savings.

In the end, there are many reasons for low measured savings rates. These include low per capita incomes, low deposit rates that reduce incentives to save at financial institutions, and institutional impediments such as the distance to formal financial institutions. Moreover, in rural areas, substantial amounts of savings may be in the form of physical capital—livestock, trees, and land improvement. A case in point is provided by Aryeetey and Udry (1998) in their study of savings in Ghana. According to the national accounts, gross domestic savings were 8 percent of GDP, but a household survey of Ghanaian farmers done a year later found that the median household saved over 30 percent of its income. The nonmonetization of savings can be attributed to the complexity, or lack thereof, of economic activity. Specifically, where markets are shallow and fragmented and small-scale production activities are dominant, then household portfolios will tend to comprise a higher proportion of physical assets. Finally, the poor have developed their own informal savings and credit institutions that overcome, in part, the obstacles presented by failures of the formal system. What are needed are mechanisms to link these informal institutions to the formal financial sector, thus deepening the resources available for intermediation.

Conclusions

We have presented in this chapter a number of constraints that need to be addressed in order to reinvigorate economic growth in Sub-Saharan Africa. We have characterized them as constraints that are difficult to address but that can be ameliorated, and constraints that are more amenable to being addressed. The former group includes geographic disadvantages, high population growth, and low levels of human development. The second group includes institutional, political, and policy failures, which decrease the return to private investment—high transaction costs, high levels of risk, and weak institutions. The final chapter presents a growth strategy for Africa that is largely centered on dealing with both sets of constraints.

Notes

1. We include Sudan and Democratic Republic of Congo in this group, given the high concentration of their population in remote areas.
2. Most studies indicate that the impacts of expanded secondary education on fertility are much greater than the impact of expanded primary school enrollment.
3. Prior to this year, estimates of HIV prevalence were largely drawn from testing pregnant women at antenatal clinics and extrapolating to the population at large. However by the end of 2005, national population-based surveys were available for 20 countries, 19 of which were in Sub-Saharan Africa. These new surveys indicated that, except for Uganda, levels of prevalence were generally lower than the antenatal clinic surveys. For example, antenatal prevalence in 2003-04 in Botswana was 38.5 percent, whereas the national survey showed a prevalence rate of 24.0 percent; similarly, in Ethiopia the prevalence rates have been adjusted downward from 8.5 percent to less than 3.5 percent.
4. The data in this section come from UNAIDS (2006).
5. We have included South Africa in the middle-income group, which is certain to skew the average as South Africa is definitely an outlier with a much more developed financial system.
6. We define access as "ensuring provision of financial services that entail appropriate products, reasonable cost and physical proximity."
7. There are some commendable efforts devoted to filling this gap and some indicators are becoming available. See, for example, Beck, Demirguc-Kunt, and Peria (2005), and FinScope (2005).
8. These rates exclude declines for countries that were in conflict, such as São Tomé and Principe and Rwanda, which suffered declines in excess of 25 percent.

CHAPTER 5

Tackling the Challenges of African Growth

Africa is on the move and appears to be perched on the cusp of breaking out of the long economic stagnation of the 1970s and 1980s. The past 10 years have seen renewed growth and improved governance across a number of African states, setting the stage for taking advantage of opportunities that are emerging from a rapidly changing world economy. The average growth rate in African countries for 2005 is about 4.3 percent, with 17 countries growing at 5 percent, and 9 growing at approximately 7 percent or more. As reported in *Doing Business in 2006* (World Bank 2005c), Africa has moved from last to third among regions on the pace of reforms, ahead of the Middle East and Latin America. Africans at the grassroots level are hopeful and are striving to do better for themselves. A recent Gallup poll shows that Africans are more optimistic about their future than people in many other developing regions. Following a wave of democratization in the region since the early 1990s, there are now 31 young democracies in the region, representing more than two-thirds of the countries. Apart from serving as a platform for good governance, this change presents a real opportunity for switching to peaceful regimes via elections instead of the coups that dominated the transfer of power in the 1970s and 1980s, often punctuating the development process. The number of countries in conflict likewise has come down sharply, from 15 in early 2000 to 5 currently.

The global economy continues to grow quickly, driven by a phenomenal expansion in trade and investment. The rapid expansion of China's and

India's economies has more recently anchored this growth and has helped raise the prices of primary commodities, particularly basic metals, reversing the downward trend for some of the key commodity prices that a significant number of countries depend on, such as copper for Zambia. Perhaps more significant is the advent and dominance of the new information-based technologies as the main driver of productivity growth. This technology is much cheaper to imitate than older mechanical technologies, and it is based on two nondepletable resources—silicon and brain power.

This chapter draws from the analysis of the first four chapters to lay out the strategic elements for scaling up and sustaining African growth in the medium term. It goes beyond the focus on correcting policy failures—an approach dominant in the 1990s—to identifying growth opportunities and binding constraints to exploit these opportunities—and it offers ideas for prioritizing areas for action by African countries and regional authorities. Given the diverse opportunities and constraints each country faces, as well as the specificity of each country's history, growth strategies have first and foremost to be country specific. Therefore the aim here is to offer a menu of strategic options and ideas that draw, from the global and country-specific experiences, lessons for country strategies and cross-cutting regional initiatives.

The rest of this chapter is organized as follows. The next section draws key lessons from the preceding analysis of a half-century of the African growth experience, as well as that of other developing regions, to inform growth strategies in Sub-Saharan Africa. The following section then documents the revival of growth that got under way in the mid-1990s and identifies opportunities from the changing global economy. The underlying influential factors behind the recent revival of African growth provide a foundation on which to build the next stages of the region's growth strategy. We emphasize that Africa now faces a window of opportunity, with a growing number of politically stable countries facing the prospect of mutually reinforcing declines in fertility rates and increases in capital formation and growth.

The strategic agenda builds upon this platform and rests on five pillars, which primarily target resolution of the constraints discussed in chapter 4, and integrates the lessons just discussed. The focus is on a medium-term strategy that hinges on taking action in four areas (characterized as the four *I*'s): steps to improve the *investment climate*, a big push toward closing the *infrastructure* gap with other regions of the world, a greater focus on *innovation* as the primary motor for productivity growth and enhanced competitiveness, and *institutional* and human capacity. These areas were identified using the analysis of what matters most for growth and based on country-specific, cross-country, and microanalysis done in chapter 3. Finally, we offer a few suggestions on how to finance such a strategic approach, mainly emphasizing domestic resource mobilization.

Lessons from a Half-Century of Africa's Growth Experience

We draw six key lessons from the previous analysis to inform the growth strategies in Sub-Saharan Africa. First, African countries' growth experience is extremely varied and episodic. However, from a regional strategic perspective, addressing two challenges peculiar to the region is the key to success: the slow growth of large countries and the extreme instability of growth across a large number of African countries. Countries with large populations, such as the Sudan, the Democratic Republic of Congo, Nigeria, and Ethiopia, will have to grow more rapidly and on a more sustained basis in order to improve the livelihoods of a "typical" African and to generate regional traction through positive spillover effects, similar to the experiences in Southern Africa and East Asia. Nigeria and Ethiopia appear to be on track and need to sustain recent gains in reviving growth. The region's stake is particularly high in reviving growth in the postconflict economies of Sudan, Côte d'Ivoire, and the Democratic Republic of Congo. Another cross-cutting challenge for the region is how to best manage responses to shocks, particularly in the resource-rich countries, where their fortunes are closely tied to the fortunes of key minerals in the world market.

Second, while lower levels of investment are important for explaining Africa's slower growth, it is the slower productivity growth that more sharply distinguishes African growth performance from the rest of the world. Investment in Africa yields less than half the return, measured in growth terms, found in other developing regions. This situation clearly calls for looking beyond the creation of conditions for attracting new investors to more explicitly pursuing measures that help to raise productivity of existing and new investments. These include reducing transaction costs for private enterprise, particularly indirect costs; supporting innovation to take advantage of new technological opportunities; and improving skills and institutional capacity to support productivity growth and competitiveness. African countries and populations are still highly dependent on agriculture for food, exports, and income earning more broadly. Productivity in this sector lags far behind the phenomenal progress made in Asia and Latin America and should be a key target for raising overall productivity of African economies.

Third, consistent with much of the cross-country growth analysis, evidence from the research reviewed earlier suggests that policy and governance matter a great deal for growth. Taking a half-century of African growth experience as a whole and controlling for differences in the composition of opportunities, the impacts of poor policy have been shown to typically account for between one-quarter and one-half of the difference in predicted growth between African and non-African developing countries (Collier and O'Connell 2006). However, the evidence also suggests that the importance of policy in explaining the growth differential between African countries and others may have waned since the 1990s as a result of major reforms implemented in the region, which have moved policy performance in African countries much closer to the global average. Thus, while it is imperative for countries to identify and address other binding constraints, sustaining these gains in the improvement of the policy environment will have to be a permanent feature of any growth strategy a country adopts. More specifically, it means maintaining durable macroeconomic stability and continued propping up of efficient market functioning.

Fourth, the evidence also suggests that overcoming disadvantages arising from geographic isolation and fragmentation, as well as from natural resource dependence, will be necessary if Africa is to close the growth gap with other regions. Estimates referred to earlier show that taking actions to compensate for these disadvantages may facilitate closing up to one-third of the growth gap with other developing countries (Collier and O'Connell 2006). With much higher proportions of countries and populations in Africa being landlocked and resource rich, it is necessary to compensate for these disadvantages, primarily by closing the infrastructure gap and better managing and using resource rents.

Fifth, the results from the foregoing empirical analysis, and indeed from a large body of other studies, suggest a very powerful influence from the growth of trading partners' economies. The key transmission mechanisms are trade and capital flows, requiring greater openness, strengthening of capabilities for taking advantage of the rapid growth in the global markets, and improvement of the investment climate to make African countries better destinations for global capital than in the past. On the side of trade, evidence shows that integration with global markets is associated with higher growth,[1] underpinning the need for growth strategies to emphasize scaling up and diversifying exports. Enhanced competitiveness and reduced barriers to trade are the two critical areas of action. It is important to note that, while concerns with border trade policies and facilities are still crucial (for example, port capacity and efficiency), increasingly, constraints such as infrastructure, standards, and access to information have become much more binding. There is growing evidence that high trade-transaction costs can be an important factor in harming export competitiveness and ability of countries to attract foreign direct investment (FDI) (for example, results of Integrated Framework studies in Madagascar and Cambodia). A core part of any growth strategy, therefore, will need to target reducing the costs of transacting trade—particularly reducing supply chain costs—as well as the cost of trade processes (Braga 2006).

Finally, our analysis points to a very large role played by the delayed demographic transition in Africa in explaining its relatively slower growth performance. In all the empirical estimates discussed in chapter 3, differences in the demographic variables consistently predict two-thirds of the observed difference between average growth in Sub-Saharan Africa and other developing regions. Two types of consequences from this delayed transition are particularly important. The first and probably the biggest challenge is the uncharacteristically high level of age dependency, with its implications on fiscal and household/parental pressure for taking care of the overwhelming number of the young (and, indeed, achievement of the Millennium Development Goals [MDGs]). The second relates to the rapid growth of the labor force, potentially a positive driver of growth but also possibly a negative force if employment opportunities do not keep pace. The latter concern relates to the growing potential instability from rapidly rising youth unemployment. It is possible to turn this potential risk into an opportunity, since the youth are likely to be the drivers of innovation in the region with appropriate human capital and technological investment. In any case, they now constitute a large portion of the Africans in the diaspora as they migrate in search of opportunities. Thus, while the strategy needs to address the fundamentals of the slow transition, such as how to speed up reduction in fertility, appropriate actions are also needed to increase employability of youth and expand opportunities to engage in a growing private sector at home.

Changing Contexts and Emerging Opportunities

Over the 10-year period since 1995, Sub-Saharan Africa has seen both a revival and far greater stability of growth in several countries. Twelve countries have had annual gross domestic product (GDP) growth in excess of 5 percent,[2] up from only five countries during the previous decade (1985–94). Excluding the oil-producing countries (which account for 29 percent of the region's population), income per capita in the fastest-growing one-third of African non-oil-producing countries grew at a median rate of 3.5 percent, twice the pace of the bottom one-third. These countries, together, account for 35 percent of Sub-Saharan Africa's population. By 2005, nine countries were near or above the 7 percent growth rate threshold needed for sustained poverty reduction.[3]

What is also striking in this recent experience is the sharp decline in the number of countries that on average posted negative growth rates during the period, down to four from about a dozen African countries during the first half of the 1990s. Many of the fast-growing countries have accomplished this for sustained periods. Any fluctuations appear to have much smaller amplitudes, and bad years still register respectable growth rates. Diversification of the economy and exports has been the main source of this greater stability. Some of the fastest-growing countries have also done relatively well in terms of poverty reduction, as demonstrated by a group of seven low-income African countries,[4] which succeeded in reducing poverty at an annual rate of 1.5 percentage points over the past decade (World Bank 2005e).

Sub-Saharan Africa's recent improved economic performance reflects some important underlying changes that are taking place across the continent. Policies and institutions are improving, peace and security is returning to the region, and African governments are increasingly taking control of their own economic destinies. Higher levels of political participation and competition also give Africans a greater stake in their own future. Perhaps the most significant change is that since 1983, African demography appears to have taken a turn toward a transition that will reduce pressures on fiscal resources, encourage savings, and support productivity growth. We elaborate on each of these areas of progress in turn.

A significant and durable improvement in the policy and institutional environment has been observed across a growing number of countries in the past 10 years. During that time, a large number of reforming African countries have succeeded in reestablishing sustained macroeconomic stability, more open and liberal markets, and better conditions for private sector involvement in the economy. The following are the prime indicators of this progress. Unweighted consumer price inflation persistently and sharply fell within a decade, from 27 percent in 1995, to about 6 percent by 2004. In a median African country, government spending as a proportion of GDP also fell sharply in the past decade, as it has in other developing countries in the world, and the average fiscal deficit was halved to 2 percent of GDP by 2000. Except in a few countries, black market exchange rate premiums now average just 4 percent. Through unilateral trade reforms, African countries have also compressed tariff rates; the average rate is currently 15 percent. And as mentioned previously in the *Doing Business in 2006* report (World Bank 2005c), Africa has moved from last to third among regions on the pace of reforms in improving business environments, ahead of the Middle East and Latin America. Two countries are in the world's top 10 reformers (Tanzania and Ghana) and two-thirds of African countries made at least one pro-business reform, up by 25 percent from 2005. In these respects, the continent now more resembles other developing regions, where reforms have been pursued in earnest for prolonged periods.

Peace and security are spreading in the region after decades of conflicts. As we saw earlier, since the mid-1990s there has been a sharp decline in the proportion of countries involved with civil conflict in the region, with the number of countries in conflict falling particularly sharply since 2000, from 15 to 5 currently. The proportion of the African population living with civil conflict has fallen even more sharply, dipping below the average of other developing regions at the turn of the 21st century, reflecting the end of conflict in countries with large populations, such as Ethiopia, Sudan, and the Democratic Republic of Congo. Southern Africa is now a region of stability after the end of conflicts in Mozambique, Namibia, Zimbabwe, and Angola, as well as the resolution of tension between South Africa and its neighbors. West Africa likewise has seen the end of conflicts in Guinea Bissau, Senegal, Chad, Sierra Leone, and, most recently, Liberia, although the emergence of conflict in Côte d'Ivoire in that part of the region is a major setback, considering in particular the economic spillover impacts for neighboring countries whose economies were and are still closely linked to Côte d'Ivoire's economy. In Central Africa, recent resolutions of conflicts in Burundi and the Democratic Republic of Congo have taken place, and if peace holds, together with Rwanda the opportunities for progress in the Great Lakes will substantially improve. The end of conflict in southern Sudan considerably expands the possibility of benefiting from the peace dividend in Eastern Africa and the Horn of Africa.

Increased political participation gives Africans a greater stake in their own future, laying a stronger foundation for domestic accountability and restraint against policy syndromes.

A central theme of the recent African political reforms is the restoration of institutional constraints on the power of African political elites. A wave of democratization swept through the continent between 1989 and 1994, which fostered a much faster improvement in the political and participatory processes (Bates 2006). There are currently 31 mostly young democracies in Africa. Figure 5.1 shows, for Sub-Saharan Africa and for four other developing regions combined, the percentage of countries in each year that had chief executives selected by competitive, multiparty elections. In 1982, only one-tenth of African countries and two-tenths of other developing countries had competitively elected executives (Ndulu and O'Connell 2006b). As late as 1991, Africa showed virtually no improvement, while other developing countries had doubled their figure to 40 percent. By 1995, however, the gap was nearly closed, despite continuing increases in other regions. In 2002, Africa was ahead of the other regions by about 8 percentage points. Notwithstanding the early challenges from democratization, the political democratization drive in Africa has created space for peaceful regime changes, deeper debates about societal development visions, and greater respect for human rights. Although there has been some speculation that the initial wave of democratization was associated with a sharp rise in civil conflict in the region, this situation appears to have reversed itself, as democratic practices are taking hold in most countries.

There is now a significant revival of interest in regional integration initiatives in Africa, with a change in focus from preoccupation with preferential trade arrangements to an approach that emphasizes market integration and promotion of the region as an attractive investment destination for foreign and African capital. The African Union and New Partnership for Africa's Development (NEPAD) have embraced the latter two

FIGURE 5.1
Share of Countries with Competitively Elected Chief Executives

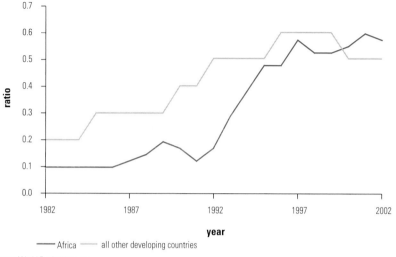

Source: World Bank 2005a, 18.

objectives and are developing plans for pursuing these by promoting a critical mass of countries with a policy environment friendly to capital accumulation and private business (under the African Peer Review
mechanism); improving cross-country infrastructure links; reducing the
level of risks, particularly associated with conflicts, which scare away capital (own and foreign); more vigorously employing risk-mitigating instruments, particularly for transnational projects; coordinating management
of pandemics such as HIV/AIDS and malaria and protecting regional commons such as the Nile River Basin and the Great Lakes; and strengthening
as well as helping to retain the pool of human skills in the region.

The Changing International Economic Environment—
New Opportunities and New Challenges

The past 20 years have seen enormous changes in the international economy. Of particular note has been the rapid rate of growth of international
trade, which has risen by an average rate of 5.8 percent a year. This means
that between 1950 and 2000, world trade increased 17-fold. This growth
in trade has been associated with high rates of growth in countries that

have been called "globalizers" (Collier and Dollar 2002). These have led a major shift in developing countries' export structures, toward more manufactured goods and fewer resource exports (figure 5.2). The change is significantly larger in low-income countries than in middle-income countries, underlining the real possibility of this taking place in African countries. It is also significant that developing countries are moving up the technological ladder as the high-tech content of their exports has risen sharply (see figure 5.3).

The rapid globalization of the past 25 years has been associated with high growth not only by international standards, but also by important shifts in the pattern of that growth. Since 1981, China's share of world GDP increased from 3.3 percent to 14.0 percent, while India's share increased from 3.5 percent to 6.2 percent. Export volumes of emerging Asian countries increased by a factor of 14 (10.7 percent per year) between 1981 and 2006, while imports increased by a factor of 11.6 (9.5 percent per year). This new strength of the emerging Asia in the world economy presents both opportunities and dangers.

Already, the rising demand in East Asia has reversed the decline in prices for many primary commodities and led to record prices for oil and

FIGURE 5.2
World Trade Trends: Composition of Exports, 1981–2001

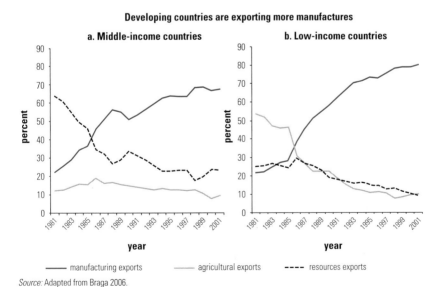

Developing countries are exporting more manufactures

Source: Adapted from Braga 2006.

FIGURE 5.3
Developing Countries' Share of Exports, 1981–2001

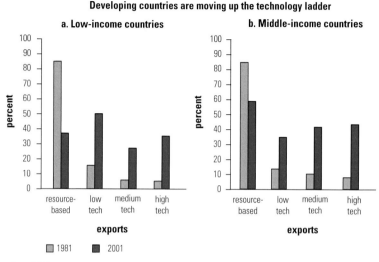

Developing countries are moving up the technology ladder

a. Low-income countries   b. Middle-income countries

□ 1981   ■ 2001

Source: Braga 2006.

copper, as just two examples. Asian investment in Africa is growing rapidly and represents an important diversification FDI sources to Africa. The
rising wages in East Asia could, in the future, make certain labor-inten-
sive manufactured goods more costly to produce, and thereby expand the
potential market for manufactured goods from Africa. However, China
and India have taken advantage of the end of the Multifiber Agreement,
with exports of textiles and clothing increasing by 46.3 percent and 22.2
percent, respectively, in 2005, while exports from Sub-Saharan Africa
declined. African countries must find ways to take advantage of their low
wages to compete effectively with China and India in the global market,
including in South-South trade.

One of the hallmarks of global economic activity in the 21st century is
the importance of information. This is exemplified by the increased importance of trade in services and of outsourcing of simple services such as
accounting, bookkeeping, and telephone ordering, as well as more complex
services, such as radiology and software production. But information is not
only embedded in services, it is also embedded in products and processes.

Floriculture is a good example. The development of flower exports from
Africa has depended on creating new supply chains, identifying new end

users, and being able to get flowers to Europe overnight. But moving beyond the production of red roses will require a much more attenuated knowledge of tastes and market opportunities, nimbleness in the ability to adjust production to take advantage of new opportunities, and a research capability that will enable flower growers to produce those specific blooms that will pay the highest prices.

Information is the one factor of production that is not used up in production and the one factor of production that is cheap to acquire. Being effective at using information requires access to cheap communications technology, as well as a high level of human capital to manipulate the information productively. But if, as we have seen, being a latecomer confers advantages on a country, then that advantage is multiplied in an era in which information is a key factor of production. One needs only to look at the huge success of mobile phones in Africa to see what is possible. Cheap, and relatively free from excessive state control, mobile phones have provided fishermen, farmers, and other small entrepreneurs with cost-effective information on markets and investment opportunities, increasing the productivity of capital.

Opportunities and Options for Growth Strategies

The rapid growth of Asian countries and Chile over the past quarter-century makes it clear that growth constraints are not insurmountable. The experiences from these countries also present options that various African countries could pursue, depending on their endowments and starting points.

Manufactured Export-Led Growth

Some African economies can realistically hope to follow the main Asian model, in which a central component of growth is manufactured exports. This strategy has the advantages of generating broad-based benefits because it creates many jobs and enables very rapid growth. One small African country, Mauritius, has already transformed itself from an impoverished sugar island to a middle-income, diversified modern economy through this strategy. Others, such as Ghana, Kenya, and Madagascar, could follow. The basic conditions for success include a good coastal location, a supportive investment climate, and reduction in the trade transaction costs in order to enhance competitiveness.

Natural Resource–Based Equitable Growth

Some African countries have abundant, valuable natural resources, so their most likely route to prosperity is through the equitable exploitation of their resource base. Another small African country, Botswana, has already transformed itself from an impoverished desert country to middle-income status via this route. Resource-rich coastal countries, such as Nigeria, the Democratic Republic of Congo, the Republic of Congo, and Cameroon, could also use these rents judiciously to support diversification of their export bases, thereby reducing their dependence on volatile resource rents.

Natural Resource–Based Export Diversification

Some countries may be able to follow the emerging Latin American model of modern agriculture. One possibility for these countries is to diversify within the primary sector itself (such as agribusiness in Chile, Costa Rica, or Colombia) or move toward natural resource–based, export-oriented industrialization (as in the case of Indonesia or Malaysia). The latter case would entail adding value to the exports through processing, or using rents and revenues from natural resources to finance export-oriented industrialization. Landlocked countries pursuing this route could focus on high-value, low-weight products, since they can more effectively absorb the high trade-transaction costs associated with their location disadvantages.

Labor Export and High-Value Service Sector

Some countries may well be so disadvantaged that prosperity for their populations will depend upon employment opportunities in more fortunate neighboring economies or, like India, their pursuit of the high-value service sector—the office economy. Landlocked countries in the Sahel, and Southern African countries, have a long tradition of intercountry migration (for example, Swaziland and Lesotho vis-à-vis South Africa, or Burkina Faso vis-à-vis Côte d'Ivoire), and it is likely to be a feature of a prosperous future. Investment in human capital would also be supportive of building such high-value service sectors.

Key Strategic Challenges

The diversity of country endowments and history demands that country strategies be specific to their circumstances. However, there are four areas of action that are common to the majority of African countries. These underpin the ability of countries to integrate into the global economy, mobilize resources that can be invested, and raise the productivity of physical and human capital engaged in the growth process. They are a package of what we refer to as the four I's—investment climate, infrastructure, innovation, and institutional capacity.

Investment Climate: Reducing the Cost of Doing Business

In chapter 3, we identified the main challenges for improving investment climate to be the following: reducing indirect costs to firms, mainly related to the costs of infrastructure services, with energy and transport topping the list; and reducing and mitigating risk, particularly affecting security of property related to contractual effectiveness, crime, political instability, and corruption. These measures should be complemented at the regional level by developing subregional cohesive investment areas through measures that promote collective good reputation (peer pressure), policy coordination, and coordinated infrastructure investment to enhance connectivity. A separate paper, prepared for this study (Ramachandran and Shah 2006), lays out a more detailed strategy. Apart from dealing with the challenges of the investment climate more generally, it also considers those challenges more specific to the development of an indigenous African private sector, partly as a way to strengthen the domestic constituency for private sector development.

As we saw previously, African countries are generally at the high end in terms of the costs of doing business (World Bank 2006b). Some of these costs arise from a legacy of distrust of the private sector, some from excessive and inefficient bureaucracy, and some from corruption. These causes are linked. Distrust leads to more regulation, inefficiency increases the cost of this regulation, and corruption arises from the power given officials to regulate. But deregulation, given some of the political-economy realities discussed below, is difficult and requires clear and dedicated political leadership.

One promising example of reform within Africa is Senegal, which has significantly lowered its costs of doing business relative to other countries in the region. The investment climate data clearly reveal a lower set of costs in this country as opposed to the others surveyed in Africa. The Senegalese case needs to be explored in much further detail, with a focus on understanding the political incentives for reform and the process of implementation. The *Doing Business in 2007* (2006b) report from the World Bank highlights 10 countries in Africa that have reformed select business indicators, such as the time to register a business (World Bank 2006b); again, it would be useful to understand the political dynamic behind these efforts.

But beyond deregulation is the need to actively develop institutions, both public and private, that will encourage private sector activity. The list is quite long: grades and standards agencies, particularly for exports; regulatory agencies for monopolies and quasi-monopolies; public research institutions to promote new technology development and application; export processing zones; business schools; and a plethora of new or more effective financial institutions such as capital leasing companies and export credit lines, a more competitive banking system, mortgage companies, stock markets, and venture capital firms. Some of these issues are taken up later under sections that deal with infrastructure, institutional capacity, and innovation.

Leadership is the key ingredient. President Park Chung Hee of the Republic of Korea became so certain that Korea's national security lay in economic growth and that growth depended on export promotion and diversification, that he set weekly export targets for large exporters and met with them each week to determine whether they were meeting their targets. When they failed, he stimulated their ardor, using a number of carrots and sticks that he controlled. This is not a model that translates easily to Africa, nor should it. What is important, however, is Park's single-mindedness and his focus on growth.

Leadership can come from many different quarters, necessitating a broad engagement of interested parties and actors. Examples from the Ugandan experience are instructive. Justice James Ogoola has championed a highly effective commercial court structure in Uganda, which relies on pushing routine disputes into mediation and getting settlements in a matter of days, rather than months or years. Similarly, Dr. William Kalema returned from a prestigious career in the United States to dedicate himself to building the private sector in Uganda. Individual entrepreneurs have often played a role in shaping their country's policies and in changing attitudes toward entrepreneurial activity.

The government's role in improving the investment climate is pivotal and we want to highlight here this particular dimension of the challenge. The Washington Consensus focused on reforming government by, among other things, privatizing state enterprises, liberalizing foreign exchange markets, bringing government accounts into balance, liberalizing trade, and reducing government controls over other markets. What is clear in hindsight, particularly in contrast to the experiences in Asia, is the lack of emphasis on the important enabling role the government can and must play in encouraging private investment. Given the African experience of weak public institutions, developing a strong positive role of government that will reduce market failures and avoid government failures will be a difficult, but necessary, task in most countries.

Infrastructure: A Big Push Necessary to Make a Difference

Analyses of investment climate surveys clearly show that investments in infrastructure are bound to benefit all firms, large and small, minority and indigenous. It is also very clear from available evidence that good-quality roads and a steady, reliable supply of electricity are in very short supply in many African countries (see chapter 3). A separate flagship study on infrastructure is under way, which will drill down through the detailed elements of the strategy. We will restrict ourselves here to the broader elements of the required strategic interventions, particularly with respect to supporting growth.

Overcoming neglect. The sheer magnitude of the problem and long-term neglect of infrastructure in many African countries demand a big-push solution. During the 1990s, African governments and development partners sharply reduced the share of resources allocated to infrastructure in favor of scaling up spending in social sectors. Several reasons were behind this shift. One was the specter of the "white elephants" of public infrastructure projects that suffered particularly from inadequate provision for recurrent costs, unrealistic pricing, and a wide range of regulatory forbearance. Second, the 1990s and the early 2000s saw an expansion of divestiture programs and increased participation of the private sector in infrastructure, particularly in telecommunications, water, and power. Finally, the deliberations of the Copenhagen Social Summit in 1995 provided a powerful platform for a shift in the structure of spending toward social sectors. In connection with that, several African governments made commitments to achieve the International Development Targets (IDT), primarily limited to social well-being, and the structure of official development finance was commensurately aligned to meet those targets (Ndulu 2006b, 10).

Two decades of neglect currently manifests itself in the form of huge infrastructure gaps relative to needs in the region and compared with other developing regions. It is estimated that Sub-Saharan African countries need $18 billion a year in infrastructure financing in order to achieve the much higher 7 percent economic growth target needed to halve extreme poverty in the region by 2015; and to achieve the MDGs, Sub-Saharan Africa would need another $18 billion a year (Wormser 2004).

It has also become clear that for the foreseeable future, the drive to fill the investment gap will have to be led by the public sector—either directly funding the buildup of infrastructure assets or underwriting risk to crowd in private investment. The past decade has seen a sharp drop in private investment in this area as investors have become more risk averse. It has also become clear that public-private partnerships in infrastructure are more effective than when either of the two parties goes it alone. This is particularly the case for the transportation, energy, and water subsectors.

The response to these gaps should be pursued in three areas: scaling up financing of infrastructure, reorganizing the way the sector is managed for greater effectiveness, and exploiting the scale and coordination of regional approaches to infrastructure investment and management of services.

Financing. African countries can absorb more financing for infrastructure and gainfully make use of it. The rates of return to infrastructure projects appear to have improved quite substantially with increased private sector participation and improvement in the financing of recurrent costs. Recent analysis of World Bank infrastructure projects' economic rates of return (ERR), for example, not only show high rates of ERR, averaging 35 percent between FY 1999 and FY 2003, but also show that these rates are a considerable improvement over the 20 percent average ERR for the preceding 40 years (Briceno, Estache, and Shafik 2004). Furthermore, with the participation of the private sector in infrastructure investment and service delivery, capacity constraints have been significantly relieved. The main challenges relate to availability of financing and efforts by African governments to reduce investor risks.

Financing needs for improving access to quality infrastructure services in Africa are huge. Fay and Yepes (2003) estimated the financing requirements for meeting projected worldwide demand for infrastructure services between 2000 and 2010. Using country-specific growth projections (from Global Prospects Data, World Bank), they derive the needs for infrastructure services for production and consumption. The infrastructure investment and maintenance requirements are then estimated given the stock of assets in 2000. Given these estimates, to meet the needs for ensuring quality infrastructure services, Sub-Saharan African countries would on average need to spend 5.6 percent of their GDP in the next five years to meet their demands for quality infrastructure services (excluding electricity transmission and distribution).

The public sector has to play a much larger role in financing infrastructure than envisaged in the past two decades. Despite the changes that have taken place since the 1990s, the domestic public sector remains the most dominant source of financing for infrastructure in the developing world, accounting for 70 percent of current infrastructure spending. The private sector and official development assistance (ODA) account for 20 to 25 percent and 5 to 10 percent, respectively, for the developing world as a whole (Briceno, Estache, and Shaflik 2004). The private sector is, in fact, a much smaller contributor for Africa. Between 1990 and 2002, private commitments for infrastructure in Sub-Saharan Africa totaled $27.8 billion, compared to $804.9 billion for the developing world as a whole. Nearly two-thirds of this amount ($18.5 billion) was for telecommunications. And as African countries were gearing up to attract private participation, many sponsors were pulling out of developing countries, driven by pressure from shareholders to exit uncertain markets and reduce risk (Estache 2004). Inclusive of a risk premium, the cost of capital (and indeed the hurdle rate of return) in this sector is quite high and may shoot past the point where most new infrastructure projects could generate adequate private returns. The risk premium is exacerbated by the significant currency mismatch that exists in many infrastructure transactions, where revenue streams denominated in local currency do not match foreign currency debt service obligations (Ndulu 2006b, 14).

More recent data now show some reversal of the decline in the infrastructure investment flows. Private investment has doubled from $3 billion in 2002 to $6 billion (World Bank, PPI data).[5] ODA flows likewise appear to be on the rise, for example, increasing from $3 billion in 2003 to $4 billion in 2004. Nontraditional donors, particularly China, are increasingly and rapidly expanding their involvement in the region, with tentative estimates of around $2 billion in flows to African countries in 2004 and 2005 (Honohan and Beck 2006).

Innovative financing arrangements and instruments are emerging and should be encouraged. One such arrangement involves ODA being used to leverage private sector finance by underwriting risk in public-private partnerships in infrastructure investment and service provision. An example here is the South Africa Regional Gas Project, which has mobilized about $1 billion in private sector investment—equivalent to one-third of Africa's total private sector investment in infrastructure in 2002—by combining a World Bank partial risk guarantee and Multilateral Investment Guarantee Agency political risk guarantees with International Finance Corporation (IFC) equity (World Bank 2003a).

Regionwide infrastructure funds are another new instrument that can be expanded considerably to scale up funding of infrastructure projects. Three of these are already in existence. The oldest among these is the Southern Africa Infrastructure Fund, sponsored by the African Development Bank, Standard Investment Corporation, and South African institutional investors, with a commitment of $130 million in infrastructure projects in Southern Africa. The second is the AIG African Infrastructure Fund, sponsored by the U.S.-based AIG insurance company and IFC, with a goal of funding infrastructure projects in reforming African countries in the form of equity, quasi-equity, or convertible debt, with rates of return ranging from 25 percent to 35 percent, net of local taxes. This fund has targeted $500 million and had already committed $400 million by 1999. The third is the $350 million New Africa Infrastructure Fund, sponsored by the Overseas Private Investment Corporation, with private management, targeting infrastructure projects in Sub-Saharan Africa countries.

Increase in the productivity of existing infrastructure and new investments. Obviously, the most cost-effective way of increasing infrastructure services and productivity is to improve the productivity of investments already in place. Moreover, most of the steps necessary to do so are also important for increasing or maintaining the productivity of new investments. The key strategic areas are improving maintenance capacity; improving data, monitoring systems, and accountability; providing financing mechanisms for maintenance and rehabilitation; improving management in the various infrastructure subsectors; and strengthening regulatory systems. This agenda is absolutely essential if infrastructure investments are to have consistently high rates of return.

This is not the place to go into detail as to how to ensure that the requisite software is in place, but it would be useful to make several observations. First, data gaps are so large that they impede effective monitoring of performance. We know less about access, efficiency, and equity in infrastructure investment worldwide—much less in Africa—than we do about virtually any other key sector (Estache 2006). As a consequence, accountability in infrastructure is weaker locally, nationally, and globally than other development sectors. Thus, it is incumbent upon all actors to upgrade their performance in this area.

Second, improved regulation is critical, not only of private sector monopolies such as power systems, but also of public sector infrastructure such as roads. Regulatory systems in Africa are weak and subject to corruption. Strengthening of these institutions requires some emphasis on accountability and transparency.

Key reforms are under way in strengthening maintenance capacity and regulatory institutions. By 2000, at least 20 Sub-Saharan Africa countries had established road funds and boards. A primary focus of these agencies is maintenance of infrastructure and judicious selection of new investments. Thirty percent of countries in Sub-Saharan Africa now have autonomous regulatory agencies for the electricity sector, while 75 percent have regulatory agencies for telecommunications (Estache 2005). The primary purpose of these is to ensure fair competition and efficiency in service provision. Strengthened regulation is a necessary condition for efficient private participation, to which we will now turn.

Public-private partnerships. One of the major reasons that donors turned away from investing in infrastructure in the 1990s was a belief that the private sector would step in and fill the gap. Since many infrastructure investments could be expected to be profitable in more liberalized environments, donors could turn to providing truly public goods. Unfortunately, these expectations were not realized. For Africa, only 41 percent of sample countries have private participation in electricity generation, 28 percent in electricity distribution, and 20 percent in water and sanitation (Estache and Goicoechea 2005). Private participation has taken many different forms, including asset sales/privatization, concessions, build-own-operate and build-operate-transfer schemes, management contracts, and leasing (Estache 2004).

The main brake on private investment in infrastructure is limited profitability. Estache and Pinglo (2004) suggest that returns to capital in low-income countries have to be at least 2 percent to 3 percent higher than in richer developing countries, and twice the returns expected in developed countries. This means that, *ceteris paribus*, the average tariff required to generate the minimum required rate of return will have to be higher than elsewhere. This is a difficult position for governments to take, and the mechanisms and fiscal resources to subsidize services to make them more affordable may not be present.

The very factors that raise the costs for private investment in general are also relevant with respect to private sector investment in infrastructure. High risks, whether from unstable government policy or other commercial risks, and high transaction costs raise the cost of doing business. Thus, while public-private partnerships offer some obvious advantages in expanding infrastructure services, it is no panacea.

Lorrain (1999) offers the following lessons from the experiences of the 1990s to guide the development of public-private partnerships:

- Pragmatism and ad hoc project organizations adapted to each legal and economic context have been shown to be superior to the application of strict a priori models.

- The development of an appropriate institutional framework is vital; such a framework must evolve from a lengthy institutional learning (capacity-building) process.

- The public-private partnership constitutes a long-term association. This association must be able to adapt to unforeseen events.

- The regulatory system must often rely on the involvement of an independent body.

- Public-private partnerships are meant to be long lasting and entail a certain degree of risk between partners; all parties must be tolerant of these risks as the project evolves.

Although market-oriented reforms of infrastructure in developing countries have tended to focus primarily on commercially viable services in urban areas, an increasing number of countries are beginning to experiment with extending the market paradigm to infrastructure services in rural areas that are often less attractive in commercial terms. One approach

combines financing for targeted subsidies to lower the cost of private participation, and gradual tariff reform (using a liquidity backstopping instrument). For example, for small power projects in Uganda, explicit subsidies
are provided through grants to make investment more attractive for the
private sector (for example, by subsidizing the electricity connections to
poor households). More generally, Wellenius, Foster, and Malmberg-Calvo
(2004) argue that in these cases, subsidies are used to close the gap
between market requirements and development needs and are increasingly determined and allocated on a competitive basis.

Regional approaches. Given the geographic disadvantages referred to in
chapters 3 and 4, particularly the number of landlocked countries and the
small size of markets, infrastructure investments should be part of a
regional or subregional strategy. The emergence of regional investments in
energy—the West African gas pipeline and the Southern Africa and West
Africa power pools, in particular, are examples of how important it is to
think regionally. Africa's historic borders have little to do with coherent
economic units. River basins, for example, can involve more than a dozen
countries. Getting all these different interests on the same page is not easy,
but the success thus far of the Nile River Basin shows it is possible.

For landlocked countries, investment in transport links to ports is critical. This involves not only roads and railroads, but dedicated port facilities and improvement in facilitation at cross-border checkpoints. But
beyond the problems that landlocked countries face is the need to escape
from the traps imposed by small markets. Most African countries have
GDPs of less than $5 billion. While exports offer access to a dynamic
world economy, the importance of being able to trade with one's neighbors cannot be overstated. Investment in a shoe factory becomes much
more economical when the potential market is not 5 million consumers,
but 30 million.

Infrastructure is one of the key areas of collective regional interest that
NEPAD and a number of subregional integration initiatives have recently
become interested in. The objectives here are partly to foster integration of
African markets through improved connectivity, and partly to facilitate
cross-country investment within Africa. Where improvements in infrastructure services entail the use of shared natural resources, such as the
Nile Basin and the Great Lakes, African governments have also collectively
sought to protect them as regional commons and to avert potential conflict

in relation to their use (for example, hydroelectric power sharing under the Nile Basin Initiative).

The high proportion of landlocked countries necessitates cross-border trade facilitation and coordination in transboundary infrastructure investment. In other cases, transboundary cooperation in the provision of infrastructure services could lead to a substantial reduction in costs among members and could enhance the reliability of services. A good example of potential here is the West Africa Power Market Development Project (WAPP), where there is great potential for significant reduction in power generation costs. Nigeria and Côte d'Ivoire could reduce their oil thermal generation costs of $.08 to $.10 per kilowatt hour to $.035 to $0.45 per kilowatt hour.

Two approaches are being pursued for regional infrastructure initiatives: regional or multicountry projects, and coordination among individual country projects to maximize the cross-country synergetic effects of infrastructure projects. Examples of the former include the gas pipeline project between Mozambique and South Africa, the Nile Basin energy and conservation projects, and the planned West African gas pipeline project. An example of investment coordination is the Southern Africa Power grid sharing and the roads program under the East African Community.

Investment guarantees for long-term ventures, and funds to cover transfer risks, are widely used in other regions to leverage private investment in non-export-generating activities (for example, power). Credit guarantees by multilateral development banks, such as the Andean and the ASEAN Development Banks, are used as catalysts for cofinancing arrangements for long-term investment. Since the gaps are more severe for cross-national undertakings, loan guarantees by creditworthy regional and multilateral development banks can be particularly helpful in financing public-private infrastructure projects for improving regional connectivity. Furthermore, a Currency Convertibility Fund for cross-national guarantees would help reduce transfer risks associated with the nonexport orientation of such ventures.

Innovation to Underpin Productivity Growth and Competitiveness

African countries can exploit their status as late starters to intermediate technologies by adapting and applying available technological inventions.

Like a big book in the sky, technological knowledge and inventions are a global public good. But one can only use them if one can reach the book, turn the pages, and read from it. Juma (2006, 3–4) identifies the conditions that helped emerging economies do this effectively:

> First, these countries invested heavily in basic infrastructure, including roads, schools, water, sanitation, irrigation, clinics, telecommunications, and energy. The investments served as a foundation for technological learning. Second, they nurtured the development of small- and medium-sized enterprises. Building these enterprises requires developing local operational, repair, and maintenance expertise, and a pool of local technicians. Third, government supported, funded and nurtured higher education institutions, as well as academies of engineering and technological sciences, professional engineering and technological associations, and industrial and trade associations.

Recent economic history demonstrates that successful innovation requires careful action by growth-oriented governments. Chandra and Kolavalli (2006) point out that their study of 10 successful examples of intervention required a common set of industry-specific measures to promote technological innovation (see box 5.1 for details):

- Governments set goals to support a nascent or nontraditional industry because it was a valuable source of export-led growth.

- Political commitment sometimes took the form of a guiding national vision; in other cases, it involved taking actions to help the industry, even in an otherwise closed economy.

- Governments rewarded winners and abandoned losers, using success in the world market as an indicator.

- With a few important exceptions, governments did not pick winners, they rewarded winners.

- Governments supported competition among both domestic and foreign firms.

- Governments supported the rule of law and enforcement of contracts.

We have earlier noted the unique position of knowledge as a factor of production, and its importance in the global economy. Some knowledge is embedded in particular pieces of capital, while other knowledge exists

BOX 5.1

Technology, Adaptation, and Exports: How Some Developing Countries Got It Right

As global markets have become more deeply integrated and competitive, the challenge of diversifying away from dependence on primary commodities has become more daunting. Not only are small local markets and poor business environments constraining competitiveness, but there is also a gap in sophistication of standards and productivity. Technology can help bridge this gap, but individual firms often lack the incentive, expertise, and resources to pursue the required innovation.

In a volume that draws lessons from 10 cases of developing countries that successfully adapted new technologies to catch up with developed countries—both in specific industries and across a wide range of income levels—Chandra and Kolavalli (2006) draw the following key lessons.

1. Latecomers can leapfrog across several stages of development. India's global share of outsourced information technology has grown from less than 1 percent in 1996/97 to 3.3 percent in 2003/04 with sales increasing from $1.86 billion to $15.6 billion within this period. Taiwan (China) increased its per capita income 10-fold within four decades, largely on the back of rapid expansion of electronic exports (accounting for nearly 13 percent of global total). Malaysia has moved from exporting crude palm oil processed in Europe and only 10 percent of global processed palm oil in 1995 to 50 percent of processed oil by 2001. Chile raised its share of world production of salmon from 1.5 percent in 1987 to a whopping 35 percent in 2002 and increased its share of wine products from 0.5 percent in 1988 to 5 percent in 2002. Kenya's floriculture exports grew 300 percent between 1995 and 2003, and Kenya is currently the world's third-largest exporter of cut flowers. In all cases, economic activity in the industry was either nonexistent or at best nascent until public support kicked in and other conditions changed in favor of harnessing technologies.

2. Technological learning was the key channel of innovation behind their successes. Along with Lall (2000), the study attributes significant differences in economic performance among countries with similar levels of technology investment to technological learning—*technological mastery* at

(Box continues on the following page.)

BOX 5.1 *continued*

first and *technological deepening* later. The channels of technology transfer are multifaceted, and the countries and industries studied followed a variety of them. These include the following:

- Within-firm transfers through FDI (from parent to subsidiaries—for example, electronics in Malaysia and Taiwan, floriculture in Kenya, Nile perch fisheries in Uganda, and wine and salmon in Chile).

- Licensing, contracting, and subcontracting (buyers must develop own marketing capabilities). This is a more limited channel.

- Capital goods imports in the presence of capabilities to use and adapt the technology embodied in the imports.

- Local adaptation or development through interactions between firms and technical institutional training abroad (for example, India and Chile).

- Contracts and consultants to meet product or service specifications (for example, Nile perch processing in Uganda).

- Formal research and development.

- Harnessing of the diaspora to disseminate technological knowledge to local firms (for example, Indian software and Taiwanese electronics).

3. Underproduction of technology requires public action to support acquisition of knowledge necessary for using technology assets. For example, leading industrial clusters in Organisation for Economic

independently of any material investment. That knowledge, although sometimes protected by copyrights or patents, is often free; however, using it in a developmental way may have some costs. Information or knowledge can be used effectively under two conditions—the presence of a skilled labor force that is able to manipulate complex ideas and, in fact, to build new knowledge on the base of the old, and the existence of a dense network of modes of communicating that knowledge, in other words, information technology.

As Sebastian Edwards (2001) notes in the case of Latin America, for example, growth acceleration in the region will require a significant boost

Co-operation and Development economies, including in Singapore and Taiwan (China), owe their existence to government actions (Yusuf 2003). There are several reasons for the apparent market failures. Collective benefits exceed those accruing to innovating firms with traditional spillover effects (Ruttan 2001): market prices do not reveal the profitability of investments in new technology, deferring discovery (*informational spillover*), and large-scale complementary investments are required prior to new investment in technologies becoming profitable (*coordination spillover*; Rodrik 2004). The key preconditions are capable institutions, mainly for enforcing property rights and contracts (Porter 1990); infrastructure; and skills.

4. The following are key areas of public support. (a) Negotiating with multinational corporations for technological transfers (Taiwan [China] and Malaysia), including the use of fiscal incentives and other forms of lures; (b) providing financial support to domestic firms and research organizations to help spin off firms (for example, Fundación Chile and Corporación de Fomento starting off first commercial-scale salmon fishing); (c) providing technological extension services across a wide range of these cases; (d) promoting exports to help reach new markets and develop new products (for example, export processing zones offering generous incentives and infrastructure services); (e) providing nonforbearing regulatory services and enforcement of standards, particularly for exports of fresh produce and phytosanitary standards; and (f) investing to meet technical manpower needs (for example, by investing in science and technology education and promoting in-house training within firms).

in productivity. Productivity growth associated with the wave of market reforms has waned, and a second wind of faster productivity growth will depend on expanding the role of technology, the Internet, and the *new* economy. In order to take full advantage of this new technology, Edwards argues, Latin American countries will have to make major investments in the complementary areas—research and development, education, and infrastructure, as well as institutional and economic reforms (including more flexible labor markets).

Information and communications technology (ICT) is now the main technological driver for productivity growth. Its importance has recently received empirical support in OECD country studies. For example, Nordhaus (2001) uses a new data set to conclude that for the U.S. business sector, information technology accounts for a little over one-third of recent productivity acceleration. Jorgenson and Stiroh (1999) and Jorgenson (2001) found that information technology has contributed 1 percentage point per year on average (1996–99) to U.S. output growth. Investment in ICT facilitates innovation, primarily through organizational changes (Brynjolfsson and Hitt 2000, 5). The following are two main channels through which investment in information technology influences aggregate growth: (1) a higher stock of ICT will make investment in human capital and in organizational capital more productive, and (2) investment in information technology will have a direct effect on growth. The effect of investment in information technology on GDP growth will depend on the levels of both human capital and organizational capital (box 5.2).

BOX 5.2

ICT Helping to Improve Financial Services in Africa

Financial services in most of Sub-Saharan Africa are limited for a number of reasons, including high information and transaction costs, governance issues, and lack of competition. If financial services are to be provided to a broader group of savers and borrowers, then innovations, both organizational and technological, are necessary, particularly to reduce costs. Some of these innovations are now being introduced or have already begun to spread in certain areas.

Smart Cards—the Remote Transactions System (RTS) in Uganda. Three microfinance institutions are piloting the RTS, which allows the processing of loan payments, savings deposits, withdrawals, and transfers. Each client or client group purchases a smart card with a given value. At the front end of the technology is a point-of-sale device that reads the cards and is networked to a server, which is then linked to the institution's management information and accounting systems. The technology has challenged the limits of local infrastructure (unreliable electricity supply and erratic telephone connectivity) and the literacy of the customers. Moreover, the pilot program demonstrated that it would only be economical at a scale that required the different financial institutions to share the infrastructure.

According to a study by the Centre for Economic Policy Research, a country that has reached a level of mobile phone penetration of 10 percent of the population adds 0.59 percent to its GDP per capita growth rate. Furthermore, strong empirical evidence exists (see figure 5.4) that investment in ICT improves competitiveness (WEF 2006). Historically, African countries have not treated ICT as an important sector for economic growth and prosperity. For example, in 2003, Internet access in a sample of African countries cost an average of $78 per month, while the cost in a set of other developing countries was $19.40. In 2002, there were only 1.5 million Internet users in all of Sub-Saharan Africa, half of whom were in South Africa. Typically, African governments have tried to monopolize Internet usage, charged high tariffs, treated imported computers as consumer rather than investment goods (in terms of external tariff rates), and done little to encourage growth of the ICT sector.

Cell phone banking. Celpay is a payments company that works in the Democratic Republic of Congo and Zambia. To make a payment, a customer sends a text message with the details to Celpay, which then returns a text message requesting the customer's personal identification number. Once that is done, Celpay transfers money between the participants' accounts. Currently, there are 2,000 users in Zambia who make one to two transactions per month at a cost of 1 to 2 percent of the transaction.

International remittances. The volume of identified international remittances into Africa in 2005 reached $8 billion, almost double the 2004 level. For some countries with large numbers of workers overseas, such as Lesotho and Cape Verde, remittances can reach from 15 to 30 percent of GDP. Transaction costs here are high, and there are substantial legal and regulatory barriers to formal remittance avenues. The potential for using cell phone technology is very high. The *Washington Post* (October 3, 2006) described the current use of cell phones in remittances by providing an example from the Philippines, where an uncle living in London transferred small amounts of money to his niece living in Manila. The article goes on to say, "With cellphone use booming across the developing world, handsets that cost as little as $30 are enabling struggling nations to leapfrog past the need for landline phones and ATMs."

Source: Honohan and Beck 2006.

FIGURE 5.4

The Global Competitiveness Index: Impact of Investment in ICT

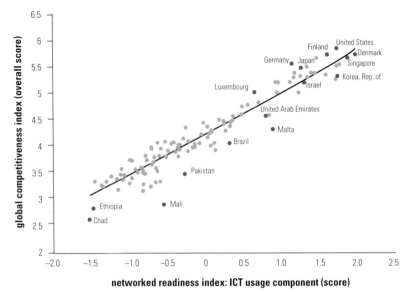

Source: WEF 2006.

The one exception has been mobile phones, which have been lightly regulated, and whose development has been the responsibility of private firms, some indigenous and some foreign.

The result has been perhaps the most breathtaking success in recent African economic experience. From Somalia to Nigeria, mobile phone growth has been spectacular. Since 1998, the number of mobile phone subscribers in Africa has increased from 2 million to more than 100 million. Access to mobile phones is much greater since many businesses have sprung up renting mobile phones for periods of 10 minutes up to 10 days or more. In fact, a burgeoning market for air minutes has been created, generating new employment on its own. In Tanzania, it is estimated that 97 percent of the population has access to mobile phones.

This simple technology has increased the productivity of indigenous business in myriad ways, as in the following examples: A Kenyan farmer can easily find the best prices for the watermelons she sells. A black nursery owner near George, South Africa, always had difficulty selling to white consumers because of their security fears; now they call him and he delivers, and his business has taken off. A fisherwoman on the Congo River, with no electricity, keeps her catch alive in the water tethered to a line. Her customers call her with an order and she prepares the fish for sale.

Moreover, as phones become more sophisticated, they will probably be the key step to expanding Internet connectivity, freeing consumers from the constraints of inefficient landline technology and intermittent power availability. In five years, 200 million Africans will have access to the Internet, and thus to the global economy.

Investment in higher education is shown to strongly boost competitiveness, partly by allowing better use of ICT. Hence, investments in human capital and ICT are key components of the growth agenda.

The challenge of human capacity gaps. African countries cannot build competitive economies and raise productivity without having the human capacity to harness knowledge and technology to complement the other efforts being made to improve the business environment. In this global economy, a competitive edge is largely associated with higher productivity. Diffusion of innovation is crucial for the achievement of productivity gains and successful competitive performance more generally. However, as Chandra and Kolavalli (2006), Utz (2006), Edwards (2001), Ho and Hoon (2006) emphasize, effective diffusion of innovation requires skills and incentives for spreading innovation into the economic environment. For example, information technology enables producers to do more and better individually and as organizations when there is the capacity to use it. This is demonstrated in figure 5.5, where the correlation between economic competitiveness and investment in tertiary education is clearly demonstrated.

Countries in East Asia that saw this potential early positioned themselves to exploit this technology very successfully. A good example is what happened under the initiative of (the Republic of) Korea 21. The Korean government invested heavily to prepare the country for the 21st century. This program targeted what the Korean government considered to be the seven most important fields in science and technology required to enhance Korea's competitiveness in the global economy. As is now clear, the results were phenomenal, and Korea, which started out as a developing country barely four decades ago, has now joined the ranks of OECD status.

Progress in overcoming shortages of skilled and trained manpower in Africa seems to be disappointingly slow, despite substantial resources devoted by both governments and donors to this effort during the past four decades. According to the Institute of Statistics of the United Nations Edu-

FIGURE 5.5

Education Investment Impact on Competitiveness

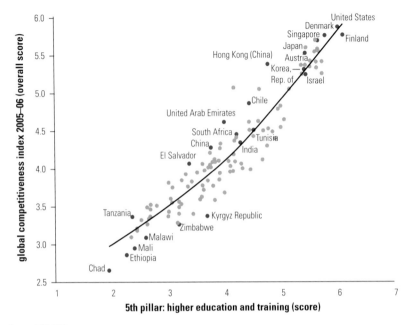

Source: WEF 2006.

cational, Scientific, and Cultural Organization, African countries not only stand at the bottom of the pile in terms of tertiary education enrollment and achievement, but also have the lowest proportion of students graduating with educations focused on science and technology. A major challenge for African countries, therefore, is closing the digital divide.

The problem of deficiency in human capacity has now received a new sense of urgency in the region. Accelerated progress toward meeting the MDGs faces major capacity gaps to implement needed programs. The sheer scale of what needs to be done to meet these targets dwarfs the weak capacity on the ground, particularly skills required for supporting growth and implementing health, education, and other programs. What is worse is that what little human capacity African countries produce is hard to keep. Africa is losing a very significant proportion of its skilled and professional workforce to other markets and is increasingly dependent on expatriates for many vital functions. Emigrants from the region to developed countries are disproportionately higher skilled. For example, the International Organization for Migration in 2000 estimated that there are more

African scientists and engineers working in the United States than there are in Africa. This not only exacerbates the relative scarcity of these skills, but more important, it demobilizes middle- and lower-level skills because of the absence of supervisory capacity. South Africa's Bureau of Statistics estimates that between 1 million and 1.6 million people in skilled, professional, and managerial occupations have emigrated since 1994, and that for every emigrant, 10 unskilled people lose their jobs. This is aside from the fact that the region is losing its potentially most enterprising and ambitious young people, stifling the development of a more dynamic private sector at home.

The losses of human capacity are not only to other regions but also to pandemics. HIV and malaria have grown to be major challenges to African livelihood and development. At the same time, Africa is rapidly losing much-needed health care workers (doctors and nurses) to the developed world, where they are relatively less needed. It is estimated that there are more than 21,000 Nigerian doctors practicing in the United States alone. About 60 percent of all locally trained Ghanaian doctors left the country in the 1980s, and very few have returned. In spite of the huge HIV/AIDS pandemics in Southern Africa, countries in that part of the continent continue to lose medical personnel in droves. Out of all the medical graduates produced by the University of the Witwatersrand in South Africa in the past 35 years, more than 45 percent (or 2,000 physicians) have left the country. In the 1980s, Zambia had 1,600 doctors in the country. The number has since plummeted to 400. Health care in some of these countries is on the brink of collapse. It is a very serious crisis that needs an urgent and major response.

In the longer term, Africa needs to reverse the growing dependency on outside experts for essential decision-making and managerial functions. It has been estimated that annually 100,000 foreign experts are deployed in African countries at a cost of nearly $4 billion per year. The OECD Development Assistance Committee's estimates of technical cooperation assistance to Africa in 2004 reached nearly $6 billion, a significant increase from its level in the mid-1990s. Technical assistance often targets short-term alleviation of capacity shortfalls. In this form, it often discouraged efforts to build and retain local capacity in government, and has tended to engender psychological dependence on expatriate capabilities.

How should Africa and its partners respond to this challenge? African countries should expand tertiary education enrollment and achievement as part of a growth and competition strategy. After decades of decline, many African universities are reforming themselves, pursuing self-sufficiency in finance, improving management, and partnering with the private sector (Bollag 2004). In fact, there has been a mushrooming of private universities, and this development should be pursued by both the for-profit sector and the faith-based communities. Composition of disciplines should lean away from their earlier bias toward social sciences and move toward science and technology and business education. A major challenge will be to reform traditional public-funded universities to be more responsive to the changing needs of their clientele and be more cost-effective. A related challenge will be to build quality-assurance mechanisms (for example, independent postgraduation certification that will help users determine the type of products they are getting from the skyrocketing number of tertiary educational institutions).

African countries also must stem the tide of skills emigration. They cannot contain the problem of brain drain by erecting hurdles to contain emigration. The region could not arrest the flight of its financial wealth by erecting barriers. Success in reversing capital flight has begun in those countries that have created attractive investment climates and expanded opportunities for investors. A similar strategy is needed to contain human capital flight. Talent will flee from where it finds no gainful use. Expanding opportunities for gainful and well-remunerated engagement is part of a lasting solution to the brain-drain problem. In a virtuous circle, better skills lead to higher growth, and in turn, higher growth leads to increased demand for skills. The two main sources for expanding opportunities for gainful application of skills are private sector growth and professionalization of the public sector. In the current era of globalizing production systems, people move and jobs move. Globalization therefore has raised the potential for relocating skilled jobs to Africa through foreign direct investment and outsourcing, which has been a significant factor behind East Asia's phenomenal growth experience. In combination with ongoing public service reforms, which partly aim to reintroduce meritocracy in public service and restructure incentives in favor of a professional cadre, the potential for raising the demand for skills and productivity at home is real.

The countries should make better use of the skills of Africans in the diaspora. Some of these skilled personnel could temporarily return to perform specialist functions when needed. A qualified doctor, for example, would be helped to return home to teach, perform operations, and share skills for a limited time period. Information technology can also enable a virtual return through skill sharing, teaching, mentoring, and even marking exam papers via the Internet and video conferencing. This approach is considered particularly attractive because of its cost-effectiveness. Others may make an economic return by encouraging African professionals with adequate capital or access to it to invest in their home countries or the region. African governments could provide information on investment opportunities and facilities for channeling capital to the region.

Another way the African diaspora skills can be utilized is as technical assistance in place of foreign experts. The policies for deployment of technical cooperation have largely precluded the use of nationals even if they are qualified. A study by Haque and Khan (1997) has shown that deploying national emigrants for technical assistance is not only likely to be more cost-effective, but also likely to get those in the hard-to-get higher end of the skill profile. The argument advanced by the authors is that for each skill category, the emigrant would be willing to accept a much smaller premium to return and perform the required task than would a foreign national. This is not surprising, as one of the important features of African migrants is that most maintain social and cultural links with their home countries.

Strengthening Critical Institutions for Growth

African countries tend to cluster in the lower ranks of institutional performance measures that are correlated with growth. While economists still know relatively little about how durable improvements in public sector performance are achieved, three observations seem relevant to the African situation. First, when institutions are initially weak, the resultant institutional vacuum leaves too much discretion and too little accountability in the hands of political elites. Much then depends on the quality and disposition of the leadership in power (Reinikka and Collier 2001; Glaeser et al. 2004). Wherever political leaders were unable to reconcile the benefits of a market-friendly institutional environment with their own priorities, institutional performance deteriorated and growth suffered. Second, as Collier (1991) argued, donor conditionality was ill-suited to fill the institutional vacuum or act on behalf of the disenfranchised African population. Donors had their own constituencies and could not credibly threaten to terminate aid on the basis of poor policy performance. Third, in the 1990s there was too much focus on correcting "sins of commission"—that is, what governments had done wrong—and too little attention on "sins of omission"—underprovision of public goods and services to reduce costs to firms and make potential opportunities more profitable. A key strategic challenge faced by many African countries is, therefore, that of strengthening the role of the government in supporting the growth process without encumbering private initiative and efficiency.

Consistent with experiences in East Asia and Botswana, for example, successful states followed the market where it led (Wade 1993), and predominantly initiated projects that were viable ex ante at shadow prices (Ndulu 2006b). Success also depended partly on the institutional capacity of a state to pursue this prudent path[6] and partly on government's committing itself to credibility and tying its own hands through effective political restraint mechanisms.

Strengthening state capacity entails three dimensions—capacity of individuals (manning the institutions), organizational effectiveness, and rules of the game. It is clear that there are a whole range of African institutions, both public and private, that need to be strengthened for both growth and poverty-alleviation purposes. While there has been a strong emphasis in recent years on institutions of financial accountability, particularly because of the increasing emphasis on providing programmatic assistance, we will focus on a few key areas here that will have the biggest payoff in terms of private sector–led growth: the enforcement of contracts; exercise of voice as an agency of restraint; revenue transparency, particularly in natural resource–rich countries; and reduction of corruption, particularly in critical areas that undermine confidence.

Enforceability of contracts. Economic activity requires trust. Each nonsimultaneous purchase requires an implicit or explicit contract, and thus depends on a belief that the contract will be adhered to, and, if it is not, that there is a mechanism to enforce its terms. In fact, Nobel Prize winner Douglas North has written that nonenforcement of contracts is perhaps the single most important determinant of underdevelopment. Other scholars believe that weaknesses in formal systems of enforcement, such as courts, can be balanced by a network of trust. In Africa, much of this trust comes from various forms of affiliation—family, village, ethnicity, and history. This works well in small communities or along ethnic and linguistic lines. But by their very nature, these networks limit the potential size of the market, and thus limit the degree of specialization. Formal enforcement institutions become necessary as markets expand and as corporate businesses become part of the picture.

Richard Messick (2004) lays out several lessons that the World Bank has learned around the world in supporting judicial reform. These include the following:

- Judicial reform is harder than project designers believe.

- Projects cannot be developed on the cheap. It is especially important to invest in developing quantitative indicators of performance before moving forward with the project.

- Altering incentives is crucial. This is true not only for judges, but also for clerks and other actors in the system.

- Speedier case disposition in and of itself does not constitute reform.

- Too little attention is paid to alternative dispute mechanisms.

Exercise of voice. As Pritchett and Woolcock (2002) emphasize, while markets create managerial discipline and induce efficacy through the exercise of private choice, governments are principally disciplined through the exercise of voice to enforce representative public choice. Inclusiveness is, therefore, a crucial feature of a developmental state and can be broadly characterized by representational political processes, accountability and openness, a participatory process in national policy choice, and feedback on outcomes and impact in the delivery of public services. Space for the exercise of voice in the development process is necessary for sustaining reforms and achieving results from public programs on the ground. This is a theme that the *World Development Report* (World Bank 2004) pursues in remarkable detail, following on the equally remarkable work on voice in the earlier *World Development Report* (World Bank 2000b). Conceptual underpinnings and systematic empirical evidence linking participation and inclusiveness to efficiency are at an early stage of development (Cleaver 2000; Mansur and Rao 2003); however, substantial work in this direction increasingly supports these assertions.

Governments should commit with credibility, administrative systems should be accountable, political and economic environments should minimize risk to enable longer time horizons for actors, domestic politics should encompass most interest groups, and the political system should be open to contestation. In the same vein, devolution of decision making and development management to subnational levels (local governments and communities) is important, not only for ensuring better use of funds but also as part of a strategy for better governance.

Domestic politics will ultimately dictate the speed with which African countries can move toward more transparency and increased accountability and good governance, which cannot be sustained in an environment that is characterized by exclusive politics (Hamdok 2002: 19, 27). Political contestation is a means of tying the hands of governments through a credible but peaceful threat of regime turnover. It encourages greater transparency and increased accountability. As the rapid process of liberalizing political systems continues, there is mounting pressure for greater inclusiveness of stakeholders in designing development programs. This development poses perhaps the greatest challenge to reformulating the aid relationship. The current dual-accountability system of recipient governments to donors and the local constituency may need to be reconfigured into a single integrated system. The growing emphasis on a partnership approach and local ownership is a very useful response. But to make partnership and local ownership a reality, the immense challenges of surmounting attitudes and changing procedures for aid management first must be faced.

One weakness of the main model of inclusiveness presented in this paper and much of the related literature is that it glosses over the question of whether participatory political institutions necessarily produce policy choices that serve the public interest. Quite often, inclusive or participatory political systems have an encompassing point of view, but it does not follow that (for example) a majoritarian political system, which may be viewed as highly participatory, would succeed in aggregating many individual interests into a truly encompassing welfare function. It is possible to envisage such regimes leading to populist results, for example, with a high tax rate on capital that seeks to finance progressive redistribution but fails by undermining growth. In nascent democracies, such as Ghana, there could be fitful policy performance due to emergence of populist pressures during and after the transition to democracy. Developing a system with a high degree of resistance to populist pressures is a constitutional problem (such as that studied in the Federalist Papers), and it confronts us with the fairly deep question of whether participation and ownership as a domestic political process can potentially be prone to populism and other *mistakes*.

What would be sufficient conditions for emerging encompassing regimes to generate sustained pro-growth policies?

Moreover, there is a political economy conundrum that needs to be addressed by asking a difficult question: what are the incentives for African governments to develop a broad-based private sector? Many African governments have created business environments in which minority-owned firms have been able to perform better than indigenous firms. This may partly be a side effect of poorly formulated and misguided policies, but it may also be a result of the underlying structure of incentives. Is it truly in the interest of governments to facilitate a broad-based private sector? Or is it safer to have a private sector that is dominated by ethnic minorities who do not pose a significant threat to political power but can provide a steady stream of rents? Tangri (1999) argues that the minority Asian community in East Africa, which has thrived even in difficult times, often coexists with a small, wealthy, indigenous private sector. This group relies on its political connections and its rent-sharing arrangements with the government for its survival. The government, in turn, relies upon it for extrabudgetary revenues. This suggests that one has to consider the difficult problem of dismantling some of the key control points that certain governments continue to maintain, which are used to penalize firms that represent a political threat (Ramachandran and Shah 2006). While the situation on the ground is changing, what some governments still seem to fear the most is a private sector that generates wealth independent of government controls and that makes its own unfettered decisions.

It is worth pointing out that in some cases, the unease on the part of government officials exists on purely economic grounds, arising from real concerns about protectionism in developed country markets or lack of domestic demand. In other cases, it is the uncertainty that arises from a lack of control over the generation of wealth, particularly where the private sector is dominated by a few players.

The key question that arises from these concerns is how African governments can be encouraged to take steps to develop a broad-based, relatively unfettered private sector, even when this may be against their short-term interests. There is a chicken-and-egg problem here. Even in a democratic system, the crystallization of politics based on economic interests takes time. In Africa, most politics are regionally, ethnically, or personality based. It takes the rise of a middle class to move toward economics-oriented politics. But without such politics, it is less likely that political decisions will be oriented toward rapid economic growth and the development of the middle class. It is critical to strengthen those institutions that promote voice and accountability and those institutions that speak for an indigenous, export-oriented private sector.

But real accountability is more than the possibility of regime change. The *World Development Report* (World Bank 2004) develops an analytic framework that defines accountability as a relationship among actors that has five features: delegation, finance, performance, information about performance, and enforceability. Thus, an employee is given a set of tasks (*delegation*), and paid a wage (*finance*). The employee works (*performance*), the contribution of the employee is assessed (*information*), and the employer rewards or punishes the employee (*enforceability*). This is quite similar to a government's provision of services, such as infrastructure. A well is to be built (delegation to provider), finances are made available, the well is built (or not), the potential users have the information to know if the well is working, but they may not be able to enforce needed changes if it is not.

The last two links—information and enforceability—are critical for making government accountable. For many, if not most, aspects of service provision, information is usually available, at least to clients. A road is built or is not, drugs are available at a clinic or not, teachers come to the classroom or they do not. What is less easy to determine is their quality, and what contracts the government has made with frontline providers.

One example of the importance of information is the famous Uganda primary school case. In 1991–95, only 13 percent of per-student capitation grants actually made it to the schools. The Ugandan government then began publishing data on monthly transfers in newspapers and on radio. This information could be used by parents and local leaders to make schools and school officials accountable. In 1995, the median school received zero capitation funds; by 2001, they were receiving 80 percent of the funds. In this case, information was enough. Parents were able to enforce performance because the embezzling officials were known locally and were subject to enormous pressure.

In the mid-1980s, Mali, Benin, and Guinea were in economic and fiscal crisis. One result was a decline in public resources for health clinics and the effective elimination of public clinics as a source for health care and medicines. Health status indicators plummeted. The three governments became participants in the Bamako Initiative, an effort by West African governments and donors to revitalize rural health provision (Knippenberg et al. 2003). The basic strategy was to do the following:

- Decentralize decision making and management from the national to the local level.

- Institute community cost-sharing and comanagement of health services.

- Ensure the availability of affordable medicines by allowing communities to control their own resources.

Health care providers and health care financers were now accountable to local communities. There were a number of important technical reforms that made care cheaper and more effective, but the core of the program was accountability through decentralization and a public-private partnership. Health outcomes for all three countries improved as a result of this initiative.

In the case of voice, improvements may need to be made at a number of levels:

- *Delegation.* For example, performance-based contracts between the government and the providers can be introduced. So, if the job of the customs official was twofold—collecting revenues and ensuring rapid movement of goods through the port—and if his performance was measured and incentives created to encourage performance, then importers might receive more effective services.

- *Information.* By being clear and specific about expected results and by collecting relevant data and publishing the data, key clients can glean the information they need to determine whether providers are performing as expected and intended.

- *Enforceability.* The key process here is to decentralize both politically and administratively to give clients the ability to enforce performance.

Of course, effective voice means the opening of space for nonstate actors—media, civil society, and parliament—to have a larger share in the public discourse. The better trained and the more accountable these actors are, the more effective their voices will be as an instrument of accountability.

Revenue transparency. We have noted before that mineral resources, particularly oil, can lead to weak governance and high levels of corruption, which can reduce economic growth rates in the nonmineral sectors. One way to mitigate this result is to strengthen public finance institutions that manage mineral rents and taxes and that spend these resources for public investment and consumption. A first step is to make the relationship between the government and the mineral producer transparent, in the hope that transparency will lead to better behavior. This turns out to be a complicated problem. In 2003, the United Kingdom launched the Extractive Industries Transparency Initiative (EITI), which built on the non-governmental organization campaign Publish What You Pay (PWYP). Both aim to enhance the transparency of natural resource revenue. PWYP strives for mandatory disclosure of payments by extractive industry companies; the EITI aims for voluntary disclosure by governments as well as companies. In the EITI, companies and governments use similar templates for reporting all revenue flows, whether accruing directly to government or through a national oil company. Any discrepancies become evident by comparing the templates. More than 20 oil-producing countries have endorsed the EITI, and most have started to implement it. The United Kingdom currently provides a secretariat, and an international advisory group is preparing proposals for a future management structure and a monitoring and validation system.

Of the 22 countries that have signed on to the EITI, so far only Azerbaijan, Gabon, the Kyrgyz Republic, and Nigeria have published EITI reports, and they all reveal serious deficiencies in coverage or government accounting procedures, or both. These deficiencies will have to be addressed through broader public finance reform for the achievement of genuine political accountability for the spending of mineral revenues. Nevertheless, real progress is being made. Nigeria, the largest oil and gas producer in Africa, is probably a poster child for EITI. President Olusegun Obasanjo committed to EITI in November 2003 and launched Nigeria EITI (NEITI) in February 2004. The National Stakeholders Working Group (NSWG) steers implementation and is composed of 28 individuals from civil society, media, and government, as well as national and multinational companies.

On March 16, 2005, a consortium led by the London-based Hart Group signed a contract to audit Nigeria's oil revenues. The NEITI process consists of three stages. The first audit is aimed at reconciling information on payments and receipts. A second audit is focused on amounts of oil and gas produced, lifted, lost, refined, and exported. A third audit reviews the transparency and appropriateness of the industry processes and makes recommendations for improvement. In addition, all the information and data on the extractive industries is made public through a communications strategy and the engagement of regional civil society groups.

On April 26, 2006, the NSWG announced the results of the Hart Group audits for the period from 1999 to 2004. Based on EITI criteria, these audits examined financial and physical data from private and state-owned companies, national and international companies, and regulatory authorities. The report included a set of recommendations that the government wants to translate into a time-bound plan of action to correct the identified weaknesses and improve the relevant systems to avoid future failures. The NEITI bill, which was approved by the House of Representatives of the National Assembly on January 19, 2006, is now awaiting passage by the Senate. This legislation will guarantee mandatory annual audits of the extractive industries sector, oil companies will be legally required to disclose all payments made in its operations, and the recently established Oil Revenue Monitoring Unit will be made independent from the Finance Ministry and merge with the EITI Secretariat.

Obviously, reforming the revenue side is not sufficient, although it is an important first step. Whenever the audits are complete, Nigerians will know exactly how much money is flowing into the government's coffers from oil rents, and the public audits should reduce or eliminate leakages. The next step is to improve management of the spending side, and that will be even more difficult. For it is in spending, as well as in revenue collection, that the opportunities for fraud, waste, and abuse are manifold.

Reduction of corruption. Corruption is now recognized as one of the major obstacles to development. It manifests itself through rent-seeking behavior that raises the transaction costs on many public and private activities, including bribes to pass goods through customs and highway checkpoints and bribes to police officers to be permitted to do something that might be illegal. Corruption not only raises the costs of doing business and leads to squandering of public resources, it also is corrosive to the national psyche. It erodes the culture of trust that is necessary for the deepening and broadening of markets.

The World Bank's strategy for reducing corruption has five elements:

- Increasing political accountability

- Strengthening civil society participation

- Creating a competitive private sector

- Strengthening institutional restraints on power

- Improving public sector management

We have already dealt with many of these topics—voice and accountability, deregulation of private sector activity coupled with effective regulation of monopolies, and transparency of mineral revenues. Others are somewhat beyond our scope—such as political institutions, which have been shown to be very important. In this section, we want to focus on a few small points that have not already been made.

Andersen and Rand (2005) empirically tested the proposition that investment in ICT will reduce corruption. They point out that as governments use the Internet more broadly, more of their economic workings will be made public. For example, the Nigerian EITI Web site publishes every audit of the oil revenue system. Second, the Internet allows an informal press to flourish. In China, a number of investigative reporters have been very effective by traveling the country reporting on corruption and publishing the results on the Internet. Andersen and Rand's regressions demonstrate that an increase of one standard deviation in Internet users per thousand leads to roughly a 0.58 standard deviation increase in the Corruption Perception Index. In 2002, moving Vietnam up one standard deviation in Internet usage would have resulted in moving it from 100 to 86 in the Transparency International Corruption Perception Index ranking.

Just as ICT development can reduce corruption, so can increased economic openness. A number of studies (for example, Bonaglia and Bussolo 2001; Gatti 1999) have demonstrated that trade reform is associated with reduced levels of corruption. Fisman and Gatti (2000) have found that decentralization is associated with reduced levels of corruption, presumably because clients at local levels have increased information and increased ability to enforce good behavior.

Preventing and resolving of conflict. Some of the methods for solving conflicts have been tested, while others are still under consideration. One major preventive tool at the disposal of policy makers is economic policy. Equity and governance in the context of a growing economy can help reduce the base upon which rebellions thrive. However, economic policy making by major development agencies does not take into account the unique challenges faced by countries on the brink of war. Policy makers often complain that they lack the fiscal space they need to effectively implement the required redistributive policies due to commitment they made to international financial institutions.

In societies on the brink of war or the ones surrounding them, a case can be made for a proactive investment in infrastructure in order to prevent war—that is, offer a bribe to avoid conflict. Thus, roads can be built, and airports and transportation infrastructure investment can be front-loaded in the areas most likely to be affected (Azam 2006). This exercise may raise awareness of the involved parties about the cost of war beforehand, and this awareness may elicit additional efforts to prevent or contain conflicts. It is interesting to note that the World Bank can play a unique role as an independent evaluator of the required investments and can alert donors accordingly.

Well-designed institutions can be effective channels for the peaceful resolution of conflicts between individuals, groups, or nations. Every time violence is observed, it is important to thoroughly investigate whether improvements in the design of institutions could have prevented it. The institution that has received the most attention is democracy. Improved governance and transparency in the conduct of public officials can help reduce support for groups motivated by grievance to start a conflict. Improved governance and transparency are also necessary for the design of sound and sustainable economic policies.

While it is clear that a well-functioning democracy is more adept at peacefully managing conflicting interests, other types of institutional designs have received some attention. Elbadawi and Sambanis (2000), for instance, suggested that democracy alone may be insufficient to prevent conflict. They view innovative arrangements as more effective conduits to peacefully resolve grievances and make optimal decisions. Decentralization is an example of such an institutional innovation. By giving regions enhanced autonomy and ownership of their decisions, it is expected that the motivation to rebel is reduced.

A special mention and encouragement needs to be given to initiatives by third-party countries and regional and international institutions in conflict prevention and resolution. A case in point is that of African countries that have been involved in peacekeeping and conflict resolution in the region. Nigeria's leadership was decisive in the resolution of the conflicts in Liberia, Sierra Leone, Gambia, Côte d'Ivoire, and the Sudan. South Africa, too, has been heavily involved in preventive diplomacy to contain the conflicts in the Democratic Republic of Congo, Côte d'Ivoire, and Burundi.

At the regional level, the African Union's Peace and Security Council, inaugurated in 2004, was set up to prevent and help in the resolution of conflicts within the Union. Other institutions exist, such as the West African Monetary Union in West Africa. As illustrated by the recent conflict in Sudan, the main limitations of African institutions for conflict prevention and resolution is the lack of resources. The emphasis on consensus before any action is taken has also been criticized as conducive to delays and a slow response to conflicts. A rapid reaction force is being contemplated in response to these concerns.

During hostilities, a priority of the international community is to provide emergency relief and secure cessation of hostilities. In a comprehensive study of postconflict countries, Collier and Hoeffler (2002) find evidence that aid ideally should be phased in during the decade after hostilities end. However, aid historically has not been higher in postconflict countries. Instead, it tended to diminish over the course of the decade. The authors also find that policy improvements tend to have higher impact on growth in postconflict countries.

Mobilizing Resources for Growth

There is no doubt that accelerating African growth will require substantial increases in resources for investment, coming from both external and domestic sources. Shanta Devarajan of the World Bank has estimated the increase in external resources needed to meet the MDGs as $40 billion to $60 billion worldwide (Africa would require half that). However, despite the need for additional external financing, it is also important that domestic resources be mobilized, especially as growth proceeds, to avoid increased aid dependence.

Prospects for Aid Financing

Donor commitments of increased aid made at Monterrey, Gleneagles, and other venues promise at least a doubling in aid to Africa in the next six years, rising from $30 billion to $60 billion in 2004 dollars. Aid levels to Africa had dropped substantially in the 1990s, but by 2004 were slightly higher in real terms than 1993–94 levels. However, a large share of the recovery has come in the form of emergency aid and debt relief, which do little to expand fiscal space for African governments. In fact, aid going directly to governments, aid that could open fiscal space, declined from $24 billion to $20 billion in real terms between 1993 and 2004. Over the same period, aid going to emergency and debt relief grew from 15 percent to 32 percent of total ODA.

Moreover, there has been an important shift in the sectors ODA supports. Between 1994–95 and 2003–04, the share of aid going to the social sectors went from 27 percent to 43 percent; aid to productive sectors went from 16 percent to 12 percent; and program aid went from 20 percent to 11 percent. This suggests, then, that it is perhaps unfair to evaluate the effectiveness of aid in terms of growth when aid was not intended to promote growth. Any growth strategy will require a rebalancing of this allocation toward the productive sectors. Finally, the expected increases in assistance are heavily back-loaded, with aid increasing by 10 percent per year between 2005 and 2006, and by 20 percent per year from 2007 to 2010.

Aid brings with it a number of problems. Too much of current aid is duplicative and ill-targeted. Donors bring their own agendas with the aid, and often those agendas clash with those of the recipients. Aid in Africa is extremely intrusive, providing up to 50 percent of government resources in some cases, and the large numbers of donors and projects undermine ownership and lead to inefficiencies in investments. Implementing the Paris Agenda for improved harmonization and alignment is crucial to improve the effectiveness of aid. In addition to the institutional and strategic dependencies implicit in high levels of aid, financial dependency is also a problem. Expanded investments in economic and social services bring with them a commitment for long-term recurrent finance. The history of the volatility of aid flows leads to great uncertainty as to whether new investments can be supported over the medium and long terms.

There is need to enhance aid targeting so as to reduce or eliminate aid dependence, at least in the long term. This requires a careful balancing act between social development and growth-enhancing goals, with the recognition that high growth rates are critical for pulling countries from under the burden of dependence. The concern that in the past aid did not generate economic growth is valid. Exploring reasons why aid underperformed in the past is a first step toward ensuring effectiveness of present and future assistance, and it is one of the purposes of the present study. One main rea- son for the failure of aid in accelerating growth and development is because these were not always among the stated objectives. The past 15 years have seen a clear shift in the allocation of ODA away from infra- structure and agricultural development and toward social expenditures. The question here is whether, in the absence of growth-oriented invest- ment, it will be possible to sustain these expenditures. This shift does not respond to the priorities African countries themselves have set. It is now broadly accepted that countries must lead in defining strategies for scaling up development, national plans, and aid priorities, and donors should align their programs and projects to these national strategies and priorities.

Increased levels of ODA, therefore, require African countries to boost capacity for mobilizing domestic resources. There will be a need to sustain spending once aid is withdrawn or phased out to keep the growth momen- tum going. Given the current situation with domestic savings, what meas- ures need to be taken to reverse the trend? From the earlier discussion on determinants of savings in Africa, there are some factors that will take a long time to reverse. In particular, widespread poverty will remain a chal- lenge for some time. However, several factors present a window of opportunity.

A major problem that has been identified by numerous scholars (for example, Aryeetey and Udry 2000) is that the bulk of savings by African households is in nonfinancial assets. Several factors are responsible for this, but some stand out, namely, the structural and institutional impedi- ments that make it difficult for formal financial institutions to offer services to certain types of clientele, particularly low-income populations, clients in remote areas, and the informal sector. In some cases, however, there are clear indications that formal financial providers are disinclined to serve these particular clients and have designed measures intended to dissuade this clientele from seeking the services of the intermediaries. This is evi- dent in the operational procedures of these institutions that entail meas- ures such as prohibitively high minimum balances and astronomical transaction costs. In yet other cases, the conditions in the financial sector itself, such as weak balance sheets and bank distress, discourage monetiza- tion of assets by those the institutions target.

These represent a source of resources that can be tapped into immedi- ately. The question is whether we can realistically expect African banks to reform quickly enough to be able to overcome these constraints. Unfortunately, the reform agenda remains formidable, especially when the returns from marginal clientele are perceived as being too low to warrant the effort of designing suitable instruments and delivery mechanisms (box 5.3).

If we accept the possibility that the formal financial bodies are not the answer to the problem of access for everyone, at least in the foreseeable future, what are the alternatives? Can microfinance and other semiformal institutions be the remedy and effectively provide services to the underserved? In most societies, microfinance is increasingly being pursued as a potentially effective tool for delivering financial services to those not served by the formal sector. However, microfinance frameworks need to be strengthened in order to be successful. Structural inadequacies hamper their effectiveness. Generally, microfinance institutions manage to mobilize only a small pool of savings, have limited coverage, and have narrow areas of operation. Furthermore, cost management has been a persistent problem, with excessive overheads being the norm, leading to negative net worth positions and higher probabilities of failure. Regulatory frameworks also tend to be deficient, with consequent loss of confidence.

There is no doubt that microfinance is well placed to fill the existing gap; hence, it is considered a complement to the formal sector, rather than a substitute. Yet more needs to be done to render it more effective in fulfilling the required mandate. Proper legal, policy, and regulatory frameworks have to be developed. Policy makers have to build or strengthen institutional capacities in order for microfinance institutions to be self-sustaining and competitive. A few countries have gone some way in this direction. In Benin, positive profits and self-sustenance came through expansion of deposits and loan portfolios combined with recovery of nonperforming loans, whereas in Ghana and Guinea, performance has improved as a result of enhanced commercial orientation, better loan management, and better financial reporting (Basu, Blavy, and Yulek 2004).[7] There is a need for operational skills in the different areas, particularly supervisory personnel who have the competence to effectively monitor the sector.

While in the short term the formal financial institutions may not be in a position to serve marginal clientele, this should be a medium- to long-term objective. In fact, the formal financial sector should be a catalyst in mobilizing domestic resources. Thus, continued efforts to reform and strengthen formal financial sectors are crucial for enhanced savings mobilization from both the excluded clientele and the clientele already served.

BOX 5.3

Banking Sector and Savings Mobilization in Zambia

Zambia has had a very pronounced shift in its saving pattern. Starting with very high savings rates in excess of 35 percent in 1971, Zambia currently has savings rates of 18 percent, but the period in between has been marked by significant variability in the savings rate.

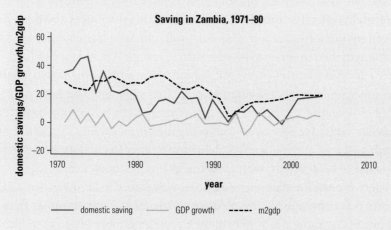

From the picture, we see a significant drop from the middle of the 1970s that is sustained well into the 1980s before a short period of recovery. This decline in the savings rate was precipitated by adverse developments in the terms of trade that turned out to be permanent because, following the 1973 collapse, copper prices never recovered. Government savings collapsed

We made a case for microfinance institutions being a complement rather than a substitute to formal finance in that they serve those members of society that are excluded by the other sector. But there is a two-pronged caveat to this argument. Microfinance institutions are not in a position to fill the entire gap left by the formal sector. But more important, formal financial institutions should have the lead in providing financial services. In fact, Honohan and Beck (2006) argue that the formal financial sector has a natural advantage over their informal counterparts, which emanates from the severe decline in copper-related revenues. In addition, wide-scale impoverishment of the general population emerged. Zambia went from having one of the highest per capita incomes in Sub-Saharan Africa, to being one of the poorest countries in the region, with a per capita income of $366. This general impoverishment contributed significantly to the decline of the savings rate as more people were reduced to levels of subsistence consumption. This situation was further compounded by the emergence of macroeconomic instability characterized by high levels of inflation.

The generally poor state of the economy also manifested in declining profit margins, particularly for banks. To compensate, some banks took greater risks, which consequently led to distress in the banking system and subsequent closure of three banks in 1995, including of the largest banks. The closure of banks resulted in a general loss of confidence in the banking sector, which fell disproportionately on local banks. Unprecedented deposit withdrawals resulted from this and generated severe liquidity problems, which precipitated more bank failures in 1997 and 1998. The effects of these bank failures on the savings rate are evident from the figure, as again the rate declined following these episodes. These failures dissipated public confidence in the banking sector, especially the local banks, and resulted in a general flight to quality, not only from local banks to foreign banks but also from financial to nonfinancial assets. Some of these shifts were imposed by the banking system. Anecdotal evidence suggests that Zambia is one of the countries that suffer great bias against small depositors. Foreign banks in Zambia require higher minimum balances and are reluctant to open accounts for individuals not in formal employment. These practices have excluded a large proportion of private savings.

Source: World Bank, World Development Indicators 2005.

from its ability to provide a broader range of services and its head start on product design and delivery. The authors argue further that considerable progress in access of formal financial services is imminent, especially through new technology aimed specifically at overcoming barriers to finance in Africa.

Elsewhere in the developing world, financial institutions are being reorganized to efficiently extend services to marginal clients. Through innovative product design and technology, intermediaries are finding new ways of expanding access by providing low-cost and convenient products. This active pursuit of small depositors recognizes that the aggregate volume of resources is not negligible. But more important, as the innovators scale up, large institutions are beginning to reassess their decision to stay out of these markets Honohan and Beck (2006). There are now concerted efforts in most of Africa to come up with innovative ways of reaching the untapped markets (see box 5.4). The spillover of these efforts is that combining technology and financial innovation to lower costs benefits the served clientele and increases their use of formal financial services.

Public revenues in African countries are too low. In the short to medium term, it is unlikely that the public sector will be able to mobilize significant levels of resources. The expenditure burden that most African states shoulder makes it very difficult for the governments to achieve any significant savings, particularly in the absence of sustained growth.

The low levels of public revenues in Africa are due in part to domestic revenue bases that are too small. This is not a case that is unique to Africa but applies to most developing countries. In particular, Tanzi and Zee (2001) find that tax revenue as a ratio of GDP in developing countries was 18 percent, compared to 38 percent for industrial countries. This ratio is much lower for low-income countries, but more so for low-income Africa, with countries like Chad and Madagascar having ratios well below 10 percent, while ratios for countries like Tanzania and Uganda hovered around 11 percent.

For a self-sustaining process of development, African states benefit by enhancing public revenues. In particular, the countries that have been enjoying reasonable growth rates will likely show some impact on public revenues. From the figures, it is clear that for many countries, the task of boosting government revenues is quite formidable. However, it is by no means insurmountable.

Currently, the biggest obstacle to the mobilization effort is the inefficiency of tax systems. The systems are characterized by loose laws with numerous loopholes that encourage and enable tax evasion. Poor enforcement of tax laws is rife, hampering tax collection efforts. The complexity of tax legislation makes identification and assessment of tax liabilities difficult. Finally, there are numerous exemptions, some of which do not serve any beneficial purpose, that encourage corruption and are poorly targeted.

Thus, efforts at improving revenue collection should aim at simplifying the tax systems and broadening tax bases. These reforms have been under-

BOX 5.4

Some Initiatives to Expand Access and Encourage Enhanced Savings

Innovations made possible by financial engineering and information and communication technology offer definite opportunities to overcome some of the obstacles to doing business. In addition to having barriers removed, the innovations need to have low unit costs. Several countries are currently spearheading these efforts through new measures and some re-vamped methods.

In South Africa, banks have taken decisive measures to expand provision of basic first-level financial services to low-income populations and other un-banked people. One such initiative is a low-cost account intended to provide access to affordable banking services. The account known as *Mzansi* was launched in October 2004 and is offered by the four main banks in South Africa. To ensure simplicity of use and also low cost, the account is a basic standardized debit-card-based transactional and savings account, with transactions limited to deposits, withdrawals, and debit card transactions Kirsten (2006). To ensure access, the banks have shared ATMs within a 10 kilometer radius of the clients in the townships and rural areas. Although the scheme is relatively new, the prognosis is good. Over the first seven months of its existence, 1.6 million accounts were opened, with total balances of some 325 million South African rand. But most important, of the accounts opened, more than 90 percent are held by the previously un-banked population, and about 54 percent of all accounts are held by women. In October 2005, a new money transfer service was added to the account.

The not-so-new but revamped initiative is the use of mobile banking units, which travel to areas where there are no bank branches. Equity Bank of Kenya has reintroduced mobile banking units that combine the use of vans and laptop computers linked to a branch, enabling the bank not only to reach a wider client base but also to provide a wide menu of products. In addition, the bank is providing saving services more adapted to the needs of low-income clientele with small, high-volume transactions. There are also signs of possible success with considerable net savings (Honohan and Beck 2006).

taken in most countries, but results have yet to be realized. Consumption taxes have been the most common means of simplifying tax regimes. In the past, most countries had adopted sales tax, but increasingly countries are switching to value added tax (VAT) as an alternative that can broaden the tax base without compromising simplicity. Generally, the VAT is a flat rate that is levied on a broad base and exempts a few selected services and some goods that are typically used by low-income households.

Other measures of simplifying tax systems include removing tax exemptions and treating fringe benefits as part of taxable income. These measures have been adopted in South Africa, where before some foreign companies were exempted from some taxes as an incentive to invest in the country, while a substantial proportion of the remuneration package was in the form of nontaxable fringe benefits. These actions achieve both simplification and base broadening of objectives. In addition, the reforms by South Africa included the strengthening of the tax authority, and this has so far been successful.

In addition, any effort to enhance public revenues will benefit from improvement of the tax administration. Done properly and not in isolation from other reform measures, improvement of tax administration can increase tax collection for both direct and indirect taxes.

Many African countries have created revenue authorities with the objective of enhancing the capacity and efficiency of tax administration. Success of these developments has been, at best, questionable. While Kenya has had relatively high tax revenues, with an average of just over 20 percent of GDP, most of this was realized from corporate taxes, and it was clear that with additional reforms and other measures, there was potential to increase income from taxes. The Kenya Revenue Authority was established as one such measure. However, it did not result in increased ratios of tax revenue to GDP. This failure has been attributed to the structural weaknesses of the economy. In essence, the small size of the formal sector workforce has meant that income taxes have a limited coverage, constraining capacity for revenue expansion. In Tanzania and Uganda, reforms of the tax administration resulted in revenue increases, but these could not be sustained over a longer term. Failure in both cases emanated chiefly from fiscal corruption.

A missing component of the reforms has been providing autonomy to tax authorities. In addition, there has been a lack of political will and transparency. And despite extensive reforms, tax systems remain complex in most of Africa.

The recommended agenda for enhancing public revenue includes reforms to improve tax structures and simplify tax systems. Excessive and arbitrary taxation have been major disincentives to meeting tax obligations, while nontransparency and complex tax structures have aided corruption and encouraged tax evasion. These reforms also aim to ensure cost-effectiveness of revenue collection, as well as to reduce excessive tax burdens to the economies. Some of these reforms will have long-term effects, such as the elimination of ineffective tax preferences.

Simplified tax systems and improved tax structures require proper administration. However, tax administration reforms are more effective when applied to transparent and less complex systems. Thus, reforming tax structures would necessarily precede tax administration reforms. African countries have instituted a vast menu of reforms to tax collection mechanisms. However, there is a need to take stock, to look at what reforms were instituted and, particularly, how these reforms were sequenced.

Remittances

Remittances constitute a significant proportion of funds flowing to developing countries and more so in low-income countries. African countries have received their own share of remittances, and though they are the lowest as a proportion of remittances to the entire developing world, these flows are still substantial. More important, remittances to Sub-Saharan African countries now exceed the flows of ODA, but they also have been found to be more stable. As of 2004, remittances to Sub-Saharan Africa totaled $160 billion, from $58 billion in 1995, while ODA flows in 2004 were $79 billion, relative to $59 billion in 1995 (Africa Partnership Forum 2006). Not only are African countries receiving substantial remittances, but these have grown very rapidly over the past decade, growing more than twofold. Within the region, the remittances vary widely, with Nigeria receiving the highest amount in absolute terms; however, as a percentage of GDP, Lesotho has the highest share, at about 26 percent. These figures represent recorded transactions, but anecdotal evidence suggests that the use of informal means is rife, primarily because of high transaction costs and weaknesses in the banking sector. Given the current situation with outward migration from Africa, it can be reasonably expected that the remittances will remain a significant part of the flows to Africa, at least in the medium term.

The question that has been raised is whether remittances contribute to economic growth and can therefore be considered part of the developmental resources. Remittances indeed contribute to economic objectives of recipient countries in numerous ways. There is conclusive evidence that remittances reduce poverty as they expand the budget, allow more consumption, and fund other developmental activities such as schooling. Adams and Page (2005) show empirically that a 10 percent increase in international remittances reduces poverty by 3.5 percent in developing countries. But whether remittances contribute to growth depends on their use. If they are used for consumption only, then their impact on growth is transitory. However, if some or all of the remittances are invested, either directly or indirectly through deposits, they have the potential to affect growth. Again, empirical evidence and country studies show that remittances are used for investment and savings and have contributed to productive activity. Quartey (2006) shows that in Ghana about 17 percent of remittances were used for investment purposes; most migrants invest in activities such as small and medium enterprises and improved agricultural supplies. Further, remittances used for activities related to education made up 27 percent of the total. These proportions are significant and suggest that migrant remittances have substantial long-term effects on the economic goals of recipient countries.

Clearly, remittances are going to be an integral part of the African developmental agenda for some time to come and as such will receive a commensurate part of the resource mobilization effort. In particular, the developmental potential of remittances can be increased through measures that would not only increase the flow but also encourage a larger proportion of remittances to flow through formal channels. This implies addressing the bottlenecks that presently exist. Paramount to all this is efforts to reduce transaction costs of remitting money. The current high costs discourage remittances and can be regarded as a regressive tax on migrants, who usually can afford to send only small amounts of money (Adams and Page 2005). Evidence suggests that banks in most developing countries have not shown any particular interest in entering the remittance arena, mainly because of complicated procedures for what are, at most, low-value transactions. Honohan and Beck (2006) conclude that Africa is not using the formal remittance infrastructure to its full potential. The ability to tap into remittances is hampered by the low level of access to formal banking services. Efforts may also be aimed at enhancing the safety of funds as well as improving the infrastructure, including the payment system. Also, remittances are subject to complex paperwork and documentation that causes delays in processing transactions, and the process could be simplified. These recommendations will improve the efficiency of remittance services and possibly encourage an increase in remittances.

Evidence from other developing regions shows that strategic alliances between local banks and their international correspondents or between banks and transfer companies lower transaction costs substantially, while financial instruments tied to remittances act as an incentive to have a larger share flowing through the banking system. These are areas worth exploring.

Conclusions

We have laid out a set of actions that, if taken, will accelerate economic growth in Africa. The experience of a number of African countries over the past 10 years shows that accelerated growth is possible in a variety of settings. We have pointed out how important it is for the continent as a whole to have its largest countries—Nigeria, Ethiopia, Sudan, and the Democratic Republic of Congo—make the decisions necessary to grow faster. It is important to emphasize that each country situation is unique, with individual constraints and opportunities. The broad strategic approaches presented here can be tailored to the specific situation of each country, following specific analysis of each country setting. The approaches can then be converted into specific action plans that reflect the political, social, and economic environments.

There are lessons to be learned from the experiences of East and South Asia, as well as from the successful countries on the continent. What does Botswana have to teach African countries about managing mineral wealth? What does Mauritius have to teach about export diversification? What can be learned from Mozambique's transformation from a postconflict country to one of the fastest growing countries in the world?

Can Africa learn from the rest of the developing world, such as India? While there is no doubt that India's reform processes have a long way to go, there are likely some lessons, particularly on the political economy front. How did India reduce the regulatory burden on the private sector? What are the underlying forces that have transformed, and are continuing to transform, political will and attitudes toward the private sector? The emerging literature on India's reforms point to three things: the demonstration effect of India's success in the high-tech sector, the emergence of *MBA politicians* who are focused on improving the productivity of the private sector, and the realization that public revenues generated from higher rates of economic growth may well be more beneficial than fluctuating rents. It is well within the capabilities of several countries in Africa to replicate some features of the Indian success story. Call centers and back-office processing firms in Ghana and South Africa, and high-tech firms in Madagascar and Mauritius, are all emerging as strong competitors in the international arena. These and other firms will need the support of their governments and a business environment that will provide a reliable supply of power and water and a transparent system of taxation and regulation.

We have not emphasized the importance of ensuring that growth effects are broadly shared, not only because growth that does not reduce poverty does not meet Africa's and the world's goals, but also because inequality itself undermines growth and stability. Therefore, it is vital that growth be shared. We have also not gone into detail about a number of specific areas that will be the subject of other Flagship studies—infrastructure, financial markets, and agriculture. Finally, we support the expansion of aid but emphasize the requirement of dealing with capacity constraints to make aid effective, the importance of improved efficiency through harmonization and alignment, and the absolute necessity to ensure that aid does no harm, either through undermining capacity, undermining leadership, or undermining incentives for domestic resource mobilization.

In the end, decisions must be made about priorities, specific actions, and modes of financing. The central question is leadership. Political leadership that makes growth the number one priority and focuses the efforts of both government and nongovernment on achieving accelerated growth cannot fail. None of the steps necessary to achieve levels of growth sufficient to reduce poverty is easy. There will be political, technological, and capacity constraints. But these can be overcome, and African countries can succeed if the will to succeed is present.

Notes

1. The World Bank publication *Global Economic Prospects, 2001* (World Bank 2001) shows that countries with increasing export share also tend to grow faster.

Although not a causality statement, raising export orientation of the economy conditionally also raises the probability of experiencing higher growth.

2. They include Angola, Botswana, Cape Verde, Chad, Equatorial Guinea, Liberia, Mali, Mozambique, Rwanda, Sudan, Tanzania, and Uganda.

3. These are Angola, Cape Verde, Democratic Republic of Congo, Ethiopia, Mozambique, Republic of Congo, Sierra Leone, Sudan, and Tanzania.

4. These countries include Burkina Faso, Cape Verde, Ghana, Mozambique, Senegal, Tanzania, and Uganda.

5. PPI data is from the Private Participation in Infrastructure database at: http://ppi.worldbank.org/explore/ppi_exploreRegion.aspx?regionID=1.

6. Robert Wade's (1993) distinction between two types of government interventions—"leading the market" and "following the market"—is relevant here. Leading the market means that government initiates projects that private business people would not undertake at current prices (ex ante unviable at current prices but viable at shadow prices or unviable at both current and shadow prices). Following the market means that the government assists in projects that the private businesses want to undertake at current prices (market-oriented dirigisme).

7. While commercial orientation is a healthy practice with visible benefits, it nevertheless can defeat the purpose for which microfinance is being promoted. Commercialization of institutions sometimes comes at the expense of the very poor. There is evidence to the effect that successful microfinance tends to target the higher ends of the excluded populations, as well as the population already served by the formal sector, leaving those in poverty outside the loop.

Empirical Analysis of Influential Factors of Growth in Africa

Estimating the Growth Model

In this appendix, we assess the importance of major factors influencing growth, which were identified in the growth literature and discussed in detail in chapter 4. We update the analysis conducted under the African Economic Research Consortium (AERC) growth research to identify channels through which these drivers operated (see O'Connell and Ndulu 2000; Ndulu and O'Connell 2006a; and Hoeffler 1999/2000). The main objective here is not to establish causality but to infer the relative significance of the drivers for growth and to use the results for conditional prediction by isolating variation in the determinants of growth. By identifying systematic features of the growth process and documenting their relative importance on a global basis, growth regressions can direct country-level work into its most productive areas (Collier and Gunning 1999).

We estimate a pooled conditional model using a least squares approach in a global regression setting. These ordinary least squares (OLS) regression models have very strong descriptive content and provide a reliable basis for conditional predictions within any sample drawn from the joint distribution that produce the data at hand.[1] Although the primary objective is to determine which factors explain Africa's growth performance, the global regression is necessary here, partly to compensate for data limitations for individual African countries, and partly to infer the relative importance of different factors from the global experience.

We are aware of the many pitfalls in the use of growth regressions, particularly the problem of endogeneity—reverse causalities from growth to the right-hand-side variables, that is, the factors affecting growth. For example, policy variables that have been used as right-hand-side variables—inflation, black market premium, and ratio of government consumption to GDP—have also been found to be subject to reverse causations. These are included in the model to investigate their effects on growth rates. However, one can expect that macroeconomic stability and growth tend to mutually reinforce each other. Greater stability, in this sense, reduces investment uncertainty and hence is supportive of higher long-term growth. Conversely, strong and sustainable growth makes it easier to achieve greater macroeconomic stability, by enhancing the sustainability of domestic and foreign public debt. For this reason, OLS regressions do not give a causal relationship; instead, they give us conditional expectations. That is, the coefficients can be interpreted as conditional on a given level of the included determinant prevailing/observed in a typical country, and average growth rates are expected to be increased or reduced to the extent of the estimated coefficient (Ndulu and O'Connell 2006a).

There are primarily two sources of endogeneity: one from true simultaneity—investment determines growth, but growth also determines investment—and the other from the omission of key determinants that are correlated with the included variables. Instrumental variables have often been used to circumvent this problem. For example, instead of using investment rate as an explanatory variable for growth, demographic variables are used. These factors affect investment in the form of national saving, and yet they are plausibly more predetermined (or slow moving) over the five-year span of country observations. However, it is a daunting task to find good instruments for all the potentially endogenous variables in the growth framework.

If endogeneity arises from the omission of unobserved but time-invariant attributes of countries, a second approach is to eliminate all cross-country variation from the data. This can be done by estimating the regression model using deviations from country averages (the "fixed effects" estimator). The cost here is that many of the most important growth determinants (for example, geography) vary more strongly across countries than within countries; a substantial amount of information is therefore lost. Column 2 of table A.1 reports the OLS regression with country-specific clusters, since we expect errors to be correlated for different half-decadal observations of the same country. As suspected, the landlocked factor drops out of significance.

Influential Factors of Growth and Data

Unless specifically mentioned, the majority of the data are derived from the Global Development Network (GDN) database, for the period 1960 through 1997, and subsequent updates from the World Development Indicators (GDF and WDI, April 2006) database. Apart from the initial conditions mentioned later, the original annual data for the set of remaining drivers are averaged over a five-year period. The dependent variable is growth in real gross domestic product (GDP) per capita, which is the average growth rate of real GDP in constant local currency for the half-decade. Data were supplemented using the Penn World Table (PWT) 6.1.

Human Development

Under this category we include three variables, all related to demography and human development. One of these enters the regression in the form of initial conditions–life expectancy, and the other two enter as half-decadal averages of the annual data recorded for age dependency and potential labor force growth rate.

Initial life expectancy at birth in years for the total (male and female) population is either the data observed or recorded for each country in the first year of each half-decade or the values linearly interpolated or extrapolated to the initial year where necessary. Figure A.1 depicts the trend in the evolution of life expectancy rates prevailing in Sub-Saharan Africa as opposed to those in the other developing regions over the period from 1960 to 2004. The downward trend is unmistakable after the new millennium started. Countries like the Seychelles and Mauritius maintained their above-regional-average life expectancy rates at 71 and 68 years, respectively, whereas for countries like Botswana, plagued by the AIDS epidemic, the rates deteriorated sharply.

FIGURE A.1

Smoothed Average Life Expectancy at Birth

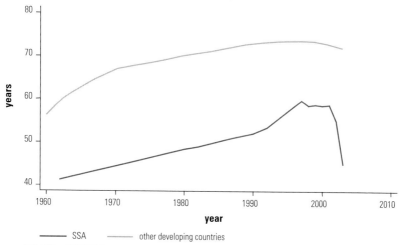

Sources: GDN 1998 and WDI 2006.

Age dependency. Rising dependency ratios dilute the contribution of any given real GDP growth per worker to real GDP growth per capita. Bloom and Williamson (1998) emphasize the *demographic dividend* that accrued to East Asian countries between 1960 and 2000 as a result of a falling ratio of dependents to workers. Bloom and Sachs (1998) emphasize additional adverse impacts operating through the discouraging effect of high dependency ratios on national saving and the quality of human capital formation. The ratio of population below age 15 or over age 65 (dependent population) to working-age population grew steadily. The fertility rate began to fall in Africa in the mid-1980s, suggesting entry into the final phase of the demographic transition but at a slower pace. This observation is further complicated by the huge impact of HIV/AIDS on life expectancies starting in the late 1980s.

Potential labor force growth rate is defined as the difference between the average growth rate of the population of labor force age 15 to 65 and the average growth rate of the total population over each five-year period. The rate shows persistent growth, but it has not been growing fast enough to overshadow the effects of high age-dependent populations. Figure A.2 shows that this disparity remains valid even when compared with all the other developing regions.

FIGURE A.2
Demographic Indicators

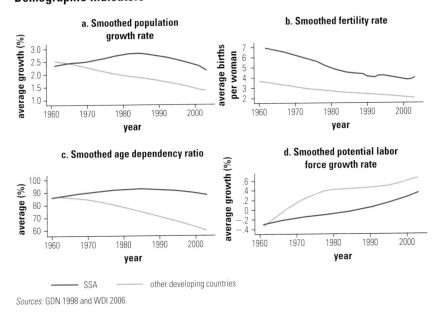

Sources: GDN 1998 and WDI 2006.

Exogenous Shocks

Three clusters of exogenous shocks are grouped under this caption—income effects of terms of trade, trading partner growth, and political instability.

Income effects of terms of trade (TOT) improvements is the half-decadal average income effect of the change in the terms of trade using the final year of the previous half-decade as base. Higher values represent more favorable terms-of-trade movements. The risk-related effects of income terms of trade are largely driven by the price volatility in the commodity market. Given the large share of primary commodities in income generation and export earnings in the majority of African countries, volatility in the prices of these commodities also translate into volatility of income growth. Although these shocks are reversible, where management of responses to such shocks is weak or not prudent, second-round effects may be triggered in the form of policy distortions, which tend to have more lasting effects on growth.

The variable is defined as the product of the share of exports in GDP pertaining to the initial year of the half-decade and the cumulative effect of the changes in terms of trade, which is then averaged over the five-year period. (Terms-of-trade data have been supplemented by data made available from the Collins-Bosworth growth accounting data set, updated through 2003.) For the half-decade starting in year H, this is calculated as:

$$ctot(H) = x(H) \times (1/5) \sum_{t=1}^{4} [\ln TOT(H+t) - \ln TOT(H-1)],$$

where TOT $(H-1)$ is the terms of trade prevailing in the final year of the half-decade immediately preceding the half-decade starting in year H, and $x(H)$ is the ratio of exports to GDP in the initial year of the half-decade: namely year H.

Trading partner growth. Ability to engage in international markets also has an indirect but positive impact on a country's performance. Generally, higher growth rates of the trading partners tend to enhance a country's potential benefits from cross-country productivity spillovers as well as from increased demand for the home country's exports. Thus, high growth rates of a trading partner are positively correlated with the growth of a country. Some of the effects of export expansion on growth may be coming from the demand side in the short run, as captured by the terms-of-trade variable. A long-run growth impact could also operate through either increased investment or learning-by-doing externalities from expanded export production. Trading-partner growth is the half-decadal average weighted growth rate of real GDP per capita for the country's trading partners, with weights defined as the partner's share in total imports plus exports. The trade weights were calculated from the exports–imports data in the IMF: Directions of Trade database.

Political instability is measured by the half-decadal period average number of assassinations, revolutions, and general strikes occurring in a year in a country. The data are available in the Arthur S. Banks Cross National Time-Series Data Archive (2004).

Political instability exerts an adverse effect on security of property and hence on investment and growth, primarily on account of the uncertainty associated with an unstable political environment (Barro 1991). We are aware of the reverse causality from growth to political stability discussed widely in the existing literature; for instance, poor economic performance may lead to government collapse and political unrest. However, our interest for now is the other direction of influence.

Policy

The government can affect the economic environment for growth in at least four major ways: by intervening in markets, by producing or distributing goods and services, by providing social overhead capital, and by defining and/or enforcing property rights. The first two categories constitute what is conventionally treated as economic policy in the growth econometrics literature. Policy failures are at the heart of a critique of African governance that began with Bates (1981) and the World Bank's Berg Report (1980) and converged in the early 1980s with the emergence of structural adjustment lending throughout Africa and Latin America (Ndulu and O'Connell 2006a).

The two standard indicators of the policy environment considered in this analysis are inflation indexes and black market premium rates.

Inflation. High inflation distorts the information content of price signals, generating large forecast errors and endangering efficiency of resource allocation. High and unpredictable inflation discourages investment and saving (Barro 1995), and through this channel adversely affects the growth of economic activity. Furthermore, risk or uncertainty associated with high and volatile inflation has adverse effects on the rate of return to capital and investment (Bruno 1993; Pindyck and Solimano 1993), accumulation of human capital and investment in innovations, and total factor productivity because of frequent changes in prices, which are costly to firms, and changes in the optimal level of cash holdings by consumers (Briault 1995). The annual inflation rate is calculated as $100*\ln(1 + \pi)$, where π is the consumer price index inflation rate. Data have been supplemented by the GDP deflator series wherever necessary.

Black market foreign exchange premium. Black markets for foreign exchange arise as a result of the imposition of exchange controls. Governments impose exchange controls to protect international reserves, which in turn create excess demand that needs to be satisfied at a premium in a parallel market, thus giving incentives for the emergence of a black market for foreign currency. Thus, a black market premium arises when there is a deep inconsistency between domestic aggregate demand policies and exchange rate policy, or when the government tries to maintain a low level of the exchange rate in order to counteract a balance-of-payments crisis (Ndulu and O'Connell 2006a). Therefore, the existence of sizable black market premiums over long periods of time reflects a wide range of policy failures, including unsustainable macroeconomic policy, inward-looking trade and exchange rate regimes, and patronage-driven governance structure (O'Connell and Ndulu 2000). Investment is encouraged if official exchange rates are stabilized, or if there is a gradual cessation of the parallel market and, hence, the elimination of black market exchange rate premiums.

The black market premium is the percentage excess of the annual average black market exchange rate over the annual average official exchange rate. Parallel market exchange rate data were obtained from the Easterly, Levine, and Roodman (2004) data set. For the years 2001–04, these data were obtained from the Monetary Research International publication *MRI Bankers' Guide to Foreign Currency*. For both inflation and the black market premium, we omit half-decadal observations where these take values above 500 percent.

Government current consumption. The ratio of real government current consumption (spending) to GDP is another policy indicator used in this analysis. Fiscal deficits often coexist with high government spending. These have implications for macroeconomic stability and funding with respect to the public investment necessary to raise the absorptive capacity of the economy and crowding-in of private investment. The ratio of real government current consumption (spending) to real GDP, both at constant international prices, has been obtained from PWT 6.1. Data beyond 2000 have been updated using the series: ratio of nominal government current spending to nominal GDP from the national accounts in the United Nations Common Database (UNCDB). Figure A.3 shows that substantial differences existed in the ratio of average government spending to GDP levels and black market exchange rates prevailing in the region over the entire period, in contrast to the other developing regions. All three policy variables followed the same pattern as the rest of the developing world, with average inflation rates almost identical and the black market premium converging around 2002. Government consumption is the only policy variable that did not bridge the gap between Africa and the rest of the developing world.

FIGURE A.3
Policy Variables over Time

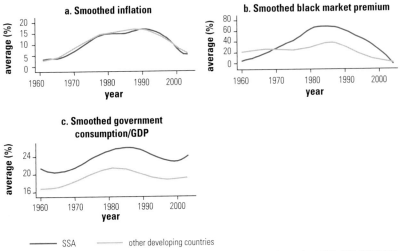

Sources: GDN 1998; WDI 2006; Easterly, Levine, and Roodman 2004; Monetary Research International 2001–2004; PWT 6.1 (Heston, Summers, and Aten 2002); UNCDB 2006.

Geography. Although there are important variations across countries in the region, for most African countries distance from their primary markets and the high transport intensities of their products (low value–high weight and sparsely produced) are major impediments to production and trade (Esfahani and Ramirez 2003). The measure of geographic isolation considered in the present analysis is the landlocked dummy variable, which takes on a value of one if the country has zero miles of coastal boundary, and zero if it has a positive number of coastal boundaries. Specifically, in developing countries, the attribute of being landlocked is detrimental to presenting positive opportunities for growth by discouraging investment in capital (by both foreign and domestic agents), because of the high transport costs together with the poor infrastructure services prevailing in these economies. Average growth rates of the landlocked economies in other developing regions, for example, were 1.0 to 2.5 percent lower than the coastal countries over the period from 1960 to 2004.

Infrastructure. Limao and Venables (2001) note that landlocked countries are able to offset a significant proportion of their disadvantages related to being landlocked and to sovereign fragmentation, through improvements in their own and their transit countries' infrastructure. Thus, *ceteris paribus,* a country that is landlocked would have to incur higher transport costs and suffer the consequences of barriers of transit countries to reach the world market. This is globally true for developing countries because a significantly higher proportion of the intercontinental and international commerce takes place using water and land (intracontinental trade) rather than the more costly air transportation.

Figure A.4 shows the significant differences prevailing in Africa and other developing regions and the diverging trends in the evolution of one such infrastructure stock index: telephone mainlines per 1,000 people, from 1975 to 2004.

Initial income. Initial income is incorporated to capture the effect of the conditional convergence paradigm; that is, countries that are poorer relative to their own country-specific steady states grow faster. Hence, we expect the sign of the coefficient to be negative, implying that the lower the level of initial income prevailing in a certain country in 1960, the higher the potential for growth in terms of a country converging toward its own steady state. Initial income is measured by the value of purchasing power parity adjusted, real GDP per capita at 1996 international prices, for the first year of each half-decade (PWT 6.1).

Table A.1 presents the pooled conditional regression results, including the institutions and infrastructure factors. The R-squared for the original model (1) is 0.35, implying that approximately 35 percent of the variability of real per capita growth rates is accounted for by the included variables

FIGURE A.4
Telephone Lines

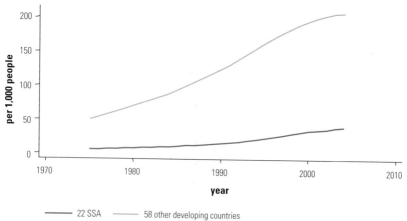

Source: WDI 2006.

in the model. The F statistics are reported below the R-squared. The F-test for the inclusion of all the right-hand-side variables is statistically significant for all three specifications, which means that the model's specification is overall significant. The p-value of the F-test also reveals that the overall model is significant in all three cases.

TABLE A.1
Regression Results

	Growth in real GDP per capita			
	(1)	(2)[a]	(3)	(4)
	Pooled conditional model	With country clusters	With institutional quality	With telephone lines per capita
ln (initial income)	−1.17	−1.17	−1.66	−1.47
	(−0.44)**	(−4.41)**	(−0.76)**	(−0.59)**
Life expectancy	0.06	0.06	0.02	0.04
	(0.25)**	(2.01)*	(0.08)	(0.19)+
Age dependency ratio	−0.04	−0.04	−0.07	−0.05
	(−0.29)**	(−3.85)**	(−0.51)**	(−0.36)**
Growth of potential	0.92	0.92	0.84	1.13
LF participation	(0.19)**	(3.27)**	(0.18)**	(0.24)**
Landlocked	−0.58	−0.58	−0.66	−0.30
	(−0.08)+	(−1.52)	(−0.09)	(−0.04)
Trading partner growth	0.38	0.38	0.42	0.62
	(0.15)*	(2.43)*	(0.12)+	(0.20)**
Income effect of terms-of-trade	0.04	0.04	0.04	0.05
changes	(0.09)**	(2.66)**	(0.12)*	(0.12)**
Political instability	−0.31	−0.31	−0.16	n.a.
	(−0.13)**	(−4.11)**	(−0.08)	n.a.
Inflation	−0.01	−0.01	−0.01	−0.01
	(−0.08)*	(−2.27)*	(−0.12)*	(−0.09)*
Black market	−0.01	−0.01	−0.00	−0.01
premium	(−0.14)**	(−3.79)**	(−0.08)	(−0.17)**
Government consumption/GDP	−0.03	−0.03	−0.02	−0.01
	(−0.11)**	(−2.24)*	(−0.08)	(−0.05)
African coastal economies	−0.87	−0.87	−1.90	−0.91
	(−0.12)**	(−2.09)*	(−0.29)**	(−0.13)*
International Country Risk Guide	n.a.	n.a.	0.18	n.a.
	n.a.	n.a.	(0.27)**	n.a.
Telephone lines per capita	n.a.	n.a.	n.a.	2.09
	n.a.	n.a.	n.a.	(0.15)+
Constant	10.91	10.91	17.41	13.25
	(3.88)**	(4.15)**	(7.04)**	(4.79)**
Observations	687	687	312	513
R-squared	0.35	0.35	0.35	0.31
F-stat	17.56	11.04	9.91	13.26
p-value (prob > F)	0.0000	0.0000	0.0000	0.0000

Source: Author calculations based on specific data in the appendix.

Note: n.a. = not applicable. Normalized beta coefficients in parentheses.

a. Robust t statistics in parentheses.

+ Significant at 10%; * significant at 5%; ** significant at 1.

Results

The estimated coefficients of the original model (1) are discussed in this section. The estimates of the other models in table A.1 have similar interpretations. All variables included in the regression have expected signs and are significant at least at the 10 percent level or less, with nine out of the 12 included variables (not including the half-decadal dummy variables) significant at 1 percent. What comes out quite strongly is the powerful influence of demographic and opportunity variables (location and trading partners' growth).

From the table, we can see that initial income affects the growth rate negatively as expected, consistent with the conditional convergence effect. For example, if other factors were constant and if the initial income level of a country was lower by $1 at international prices, its growth would rise by 1.2 percent.

Life expectancy has a significant positive effect. One more year of life expectancy achieved by a country would raise the growth rate by 0.06 percent. Both indicators of demography have the expected impact on growth, with highly significant coefficients. Age dependency has a negative impact of 0.05 percent, while growth of the potential labor force is expected to increase economic growth by 0.92 percent.

A rise in the trading partner growth rate is a positive shock to the economy. A 1 percent rise in the growth rate of a country's trading partner is associated with an increase in the country's growth rate by 0.4 percent. The result also supports the hypothesis that an outward-oriented economy can gain more by exploiting the potential gains from trade, especially in the form of technology transfers and specialization of inputs of production.

Income effects of terms of trade likewise have the expected effect on growth, though with a very small positive coefficient. The result confirms the importance of first-order effects of terms-of-trade changes, particularly for primary commodity-dependent economies. Finally, as expected, an increase in political instability reduces growth, with a negative coefficient of 0.3 percent.

All three macroeconomic indicators have their expected significant effects. A 1 percent rise in inflation or black market premium rate negatively affects growth by 0.01 percent, while a 1 percent increase in the ratio of government consumption to GDP is associated with a reduction in growth by 0.03 percent. The estimates confirm the expectations that high inflation indexes are related, with greater risk and hence uncertainty about investment decisions, while increasing government consumption has its implications for existence of commensurate fiscal instability.

As expected, being a landlocked country exerts a negative and significant influence on growth at the global level. *Ceteris paribus*, if there were a 1 percent greater chance of a country being landlocked, its growth rate would decline by 0.6 percent.

Finally, the negative coefficient for the dummy variable capturing the effect of being an African coastal economy represents a lost opportunity. African economies have been unsuccessful in exploiting their positive opportunities for growth; that is, countries that are endowed with greater proximity and accessibility to the world market for trade and commerce are unable to grow as fast as coastal economies in the rest of the world (Collier and O'Connell 2006).

The results of the pooled conditional model previously discussed give us an idea of how each factor affects growth. While it is clear that all the drivers have some part in explaining growth performance, we are also aware that some variables would be considerably more important than others, even though in the pooled conditional regression, the size of the estimates implies otherwise. Therefore, to better inform policy making, we need to know the strengths of these factors relative to all included variables. For this purpose, we use the beta coefficients reported in table A.1.[2] With beta coefficients, all the variables are standardized and the units of measurement are the same. Thus, the relative magnitudes of these coefficients have a meaningful interpretation, which allows us to make conclusions about which driver contributed the most to explaining the growth performance.

The strengths of individual factors for predicting growth range from as high as 0.44 percent to as low as 0.08 percent. It is apparent that, globally, initial income has the strongest explanatory power for predicted growth. This implies that the relatively low income status of many of the African countries potentially provides its most powerful motor for accelerating growth to the levels required to meet the Millennium Development Goals (MDGs). The estimated beta coefficients for the cluster of demographic variables follow next, at -0.29 percent for age dependency, followed by initial life expectancy at 0.25 percent and labor force participation at 0.19 percent. Trading partner growth, black market premium, political instability, and ratio of government consumption spending to GDP rank next in that order. The rest have beta coefficients of less than 10 percent.

In terms of clusters of the growth drivers, the three demographic variables—age dependency, life expectancy, and growth of labor force participation, have the strongest influence on growth. This calls for a particularly strong focus on the demographic transition in Africa. Risk and openness to trade are the next strongest cluster of drivers, but almost similar to the strength of the cluster of policy variables.

Models (3) and (4) look at two additional factors that have been known to drive growth in the positive direction in the existing literature, but we do not have data for those factors for the entire 45 years of the African growth experience. In column (3), growth model (1) is presented, along with an index of institutional quality, which incorporates perceptions of corruption, law and order, and quality of bureaucracy as indicators of the institutional environment prevailing in a country. Data on this index go back only until 1984. Higher values of this index are expected to exert a positive effect on growth rates, since the index not only favors accumulation of human and physical capital by attracting more private investment on account of a better investment climate, but it also improves productivity of labor and capital for both public and private investment through the synergistic effects of diffusion of technology and skills. Results in column (3) can be interpreted as an increase in this index by one unit, leading to a rise in predicted growth rates by 0.18 percent. Political instability and some of the policy variables are correlated with this institution's index, since they have an adverse effect on private property rights and are related to corruption and perceptions of rule of law, resulting in these variables falling out of significance.

In column (4) of table A.1, we consider another factor that has been known to be crucial in terms of driving growth in a favorable direction. Provision of social overhead capital, including public investments in transportation and communications infrastructure, primary education, and health, is a vital function of a growth-promoting government (Ndulu and O'Connell 2006a). Internal infrastructure stocks, such as telephone mainlines per capita and road density, are expected to improve growth performance because they serve to promote capital and labor accumulation by raising the standards of investment climate prevailing in a country at the same time as boosting productivity of factors of production. Data on telephone mainlines per capita are available from 1975 onward. In column (4), the variable's coefficient is interpreted as an increase in this communications infrastructure asset by one unit, leading to an increase of expected growth rates by 2.09 percent. The impact of a country being landlocked falls out of significance because of its correlation with this infrastructure variable.

Notes

1. Ndulu and O'Connell (2006a, 16) explain that the fundamental assumptions behind estimating a pooled, conditional model are that the observations for different countries and time periods are governed by the same joint distribution of variables and that OLS estimation provides a good approximation of the expected value of growth conditional on observed determinants (Wooldridge 2003).

2. The beta coefficients can be obtained by transforming the growth and all the included determinants, subtracting their respective means, dividing by the standard deviation, and then fitting the least squares regression on the transformed data.

Bibliography

Acemoglu, D., S. Johnson, and J. Robinson. 2001. "The Colonial Origins of Comparative Development: An Empirical Investigation." *American Economic Review* 91 (December): 1369–1401.

———. 2003. "An African Success Story: Botswana." In *Search of Prosperity: Analytic Narratives on Economic Growth*, ed. Dani Rodrik, 80–119. Princeton, NJ: Princeton University Press.

Adams, R., and J. Page. 2005. "The Impact of International Migration and Remittances on Poverty." *World Development* 33 (10): 1645–69.

AERC (African Economic Research Consortium). Forthcoming. *The Political Economy of Economic Growth in Africa, 1960–2000*, ed. Benno Ndulu, Stephen O'Connell, Robert Bates, Paul Collier, and Charles Soludo. Cambridge, UK: Cambridge University Press.

AfDB (African Development Bank). 1999. *African Development Report 1999*. Oxford, UK: Oxford University Press for the African Development Bank.

AfDB/OECD (Organisation for Economic Co-operation and Development). 2005. "African Economic Outlook." Development Centre, Paris. http://www.oecd.org/dataoecd/35/20/36739479.pdf.

Africa Partnership Forum. 2006. "Resources for Development in Africa." Paper prepared for the African Partnership Forum Meeting in Moscow, October 2006.

Agu, C. C. 2004. "Efficiency of Commercial Banking in the Gambia." In *African Review of Money Finance and Banking*, 2004 issue: 31–50.

Alawode, Abayomi A. 2003. "Analyzing Financial and Private Sector Linkages in Africa." Africa Region Working Paper 43, World Bank, Washington, DC.

Allen, Donald S., and Léone Ndikumana. 2000. "Financial Intermediation and Economic Growth in Southern Africa." *Journal of African Economies* 9 (2): 132–60.

Amjadi, Azida, and Alexander J. Yeats. 1995. "Have Transport Costs Contributed to the Relative Decline of Sub-Saharan African Exports? Some Preliminary Empirical Evidence." Policy Research Working Paper 1559, World Bank, Washington, DC.

Andersen, Thomas Barnebeck, and John Rand. 2005. "Mice Do Not Take Bribes." Discussion Paper, University of Copenhagen, Denmark.

Anoruo, Emmanuel, and Yusuf Ahmad. 2001. "Causal Relationship between Domestic Savings and Economic Growth: Evidence from Seven African Countries." African Development Bank.

Apraku, K. K. 1991. *African Emigres in the United States. A Missing Link in Africa's Social and Economic Development*. New York: Praeger.

Artadi, Elsa V., and Xavier Sala-i-Martin. 2003. "The Economic Tragedy of the XXth Century: Growth in Africa." Working Paper 9865, National Bureau of Economic Research, Cambridge, MA.

Aryeetey, Ernest. 2004. "Household Asset Choice among the Rural Poor in Ghana." Institute of Statistical, Social and Economic Research, University of Ghana.

Aryeetey, Ernest, and Lemma W. Senbet. 2004. "Essential Market Reforms in Africa." Technical Publication 63, Institute of Statistical, Social and Economic Research, University of Ghana.

Aryeetey, Ernest, and Christopher Udry. 1998. "Household Asset Choice in Ghana." Institute of Statistical, Social and Economic Research, University of Ghana.

———. 2000. "Saving in Sub-Saharan Africa." Working Paper 38, Center for International Development, Harvard University, Cambridge, MA.

Atieno, Rosemary. 2001. "Formal and Informal Institutions' Lending Policies and Access to Credit by Small-Scale Enterprises in Kenya: An Empirical Assessment." Research Paper 111, African Economic Research Consortium, Nairobi.

Azam, Jean-Paul. 1995. "How to Pay for the Peace? A Theoretical Framework with References to African Countries." Springer *Public Choice* 83(1–2) April: 173–84.

———. 2005. "Political Geography and Redistribution." Paper prepared for the African Economic Research Consortium/Harvard University workshop on Explaining African Economic Growth, 1960–2000, Weatherhead Center for International Affairs, March 18–19, 2005.

———. 2006. "Aid and the Delegated Fight against Terrorism." *Review of Development Economics* 10 (2) April: 330–44.

Barro, Robert J. 1991. "Economic Growth in a Cross-Section of Countries." *Quarterly Journal of Economics* 106 (2) May: 407–43.

———. 1995. *Determinants of Economic Growth*. London: The MIT Press.

————. 1999. "Notes on Growth Accounting." Springer *Journal of Economic Growth* 4 (2) June: 119–37.

Barro, Robert J., and Jong-Wha Lee. 1993. "International Comparisons of Educational Attainment." *Journal of Monetary Economics* 32 (3) December: 363–94.

Barro, Robert J., and Xavier Sala-i-Martin. 1995. *Economic Growth.* New York: McGraw-Hill.

Basu, A., R. Blavy, and M. Yulek. 2004. "Micro Finance in Africa: Experience and Lessons from Selected African Countries." Working Paper 04/174, International Monetary Fund, Washington, DC.

Bates, Robert H. 1981. *Markets and States in Tropical Africa: The Political Basis of Agricultural Policies.* Berkeley, CA: University of California Press.

————. 2006. "Institutions and Development." *Journal of African Economies* 15 (1): 10–61.

Beck, Thorsten, Asli Demirguc-Kunt, and Maria Soledad Martinez Peria. 2005. "Reaching Out: Access to and Use of Banking Services across Countries." Draft, World Bank, Washington, DC.

Berthelemy, Jean-Claude, and Ludvig Soderling. 2001. "The Role of Capital Accumulation, Adjustment and Structural Change for Economic Take-Off: Empirical Evidence from African Growth Episodes." World Development 29 (2): 323–43.

————. 2002. "Will There Be New Emerging-Market Economies in Africa by the Year 2020?" Working Paper 02/131, International Monetary Fund, Washington, DC.

Bhattacharya, Amar, Peter J. Montiel, and Sunil Sharma. 1997. "How Can Sub-Saharan Africa Attract More Private Capital Flows?" *Finance and Development* 34 (June): 3–6.

Biggs, Tyler, and Manju Shah. 2006. "African SMEs, Networks and Manufacturing Performance." *Journal of Banking and Finance* 30 (11): 3043–66.

Bigsten, Arne, and Måns Söderbom. 2005. "What Have We Learned from a Decade of Manufacturing Enterprise Surveys in Africa?" Policy Research Working Paper 3798, World Bank, Washington, DC.

————. 2006. "What Have We Learned frim a Decade of Manufacturing Enterprise Surveys in Africa?" *The World Bank Research Observer 2006* 21(2): 241–65.

Blattman, Christopher, Jason Hwang, and Jeffrey G. Williamson. 2004. "The Impact of the Terms of Trade on Economic Development in the Periphery, 1870–1939: Volatility and Secular Change." Working Paper 10600, National Bureau of Economic Research, Cambridge, MA.

Bloom David E., David Canning, and Jaypee Sevilla. 2001. "Economic Growth and the Demographic Transition." Working Paper 8685. National Bureau of Economic Research, Cambridge, MA.

Bloom, David, and Jeffrey D. Sachs. 1998. "Geography, Demography, and Economic Growth in Africa." *Brookings Papers on Economic Activity* 2: 207–73.

Bloom, David, and Jeffrey G. Williamson. 1998. "Demographic Transitions and Economic Miracles in Emerging Asia." *World Bank Economic Review* 12(3): 419–55.

Bollag, Burton. 2004. "Improving Tertiary Education in Sub-Saharan Africa: Things That Work." Africa Region Human Development Working Paper, World Bank, Washington, DC.

Bonaglia, Braga de Macedo, and Maurizio Bussolo. 2001. "How Globalization Improves Governance." Discussion Paper 2992, Center for Economic and Policy Research, London, UK.

Borensztein, E., J. De Gregorio, and J-W. Lee. 1998. "How Does Foreign Direct Investment Affect Economic Growth?" Elsevier *Journal of International Economics* 45 (1) June: 115–35.

Bosworth, Barry, and Susan Collins. 2003. "The Empirics of Growth: An Update." *Brookings Papers on Economic Activities* 2 (Sept. 22): 113–79.

Braga, Carlos A. Primo. 2006. "The Doha Development Agenda: An Update." Presentation for Vietnam: Trade Policy and World Trade Organization Accession, May 15, 2006.

Briault, C. 1995. "The Costs of Inflation." *Bank of England Quarterly Bulletin* February: 33–45.

Briceno, C., Antonio Estache, and Nemat Shafik. 2004. "Infrastructure Services in Developing Countries: Access, Quality, Costs, and Policy Reform." Policy Research Working Paper, World Bank, Washington, DC.

Bruno, Michael. 1993. "Inflation and Growth in an Integrated Approach." Working Paper 4422, National Bureau of Economic Research, Cambridge, MA.

Brynjolfsson, Erik, and Lorin M. Hitt. 2000. "Beyond Computation: Information Technology, Organizational Transformation and Business Performance." *Journal of Economic Perspectives* 14 (4): 23–48.

Bulatao, Rodolfo A. 1998. "The Value of Family Planning Programs in Developing Countries." Rand Corporation, Santa Monica, CA.

Burnside, Craig, and David Dollar. 2000. "Aid, Policies, and Growth." *American Economic Review*, American Economic Association 90 (4) September: 847–68.

Calderon, Cesar, and Luis Serven. 2004. "The Effects of Infrastructure Development on Growth and Income Distribution." Policy Research Working Paper 3400, World Bank, Washington, DC.

Carrington, W. J., and E. Detragiache. 1999. "How Extensive Is the Brain Drain?" *Finance and Development: A Quarterly Magazine of the IMF* 36 (2).

Carter, Gwendolen M., ed. 1962. *African One-Party States*. Ithaca, NY: Cornell University Press.

———., ed. 1963. *Five African States: Responses to Diversity*. Ithaca, NY: Cornell University Press.

———., ed. 1966. *National Unity and Regionalism in Eight African States*. Ithaca, NY: Cornell University Press.

Casterline, J., and S. Sinding. 2000. "Unmet Need for Family Planning in Developing Countries and Implications for Population Policy." Policy Research Division Working Paper 135, The Population Council, New York.

Chandra, Vandana, ed. 2006. *Technology, Adaptation and Exports—How Some Developing Countries Got It Right*. Washington, DC: World Bank.

Chandra, Vandana, and Shashi Kolavalli. 2006. "Technology, Adaptation, and Exports—How Some Developing Countries Got It Right." In *Technology, Adaptation and Exports—How Some Developing Countries Got It Right* ed. Vanadana Chandra, 1–48. Washington, DC: World Bank.

Chigumira, Gibson, and Nicolas Masiyandima. 2003. "Did Financial Sector Reform Result in Increased Savings and Lending for the SMEs and the Poor?" Research Paper 03–7, International Labour Organization.

Chirwa, Ephraim W., and Montfort Mlachila. 2004. "Financial Reforms and Interest Rate Spreads in the Commercial Banking System in Malawi." *IMF Staff Papers* 51 (1).

Cleaver, F. 2000 "Participatory Development at the World Bank: The Primacy of Process." In *Participation: the New Tyranny?* ed. B. Cooke and U. Kothari. London: Zed Books.

Coe, David T., Elhanan Helpman, and Alexander W. Hoffmaister. 1997. "North-South R&D Spillovers." *Economic Journal* 107 (440) January: 134–49.

Collier, Paul. 1991. "Africa's External Relations: 1960–1990." *African Affairs* 90: 339–56.

———. 1999. "On the Economic Consequences of Civil War." *Oxford Economic Papers* 51 (1): 168–183.

———. 2000. "Ethnicity, Politics and Economic Performance." *Economics and Politics* 12 (3) November: 225–45.

———. 2002. "Implications of Ethnic Diversity." Economic Policy 32 (April): 129–66.

Collier, Paul, and David Dollar. 2002. "Globalization, Growth, and Poverty: Building an Inclusive World Economy." World Bank and Oxford University Press, Washington, DC; London.

Collier, Paul, and Jan Willem Gunning. 1999. "Explaining African Economic Performance." *Journal of Economic Literature* 37 (March): 64–111.

Collier, Paul, and Anke Hoeffler. 2000. "Greed and Grievance in Civil War." Policy Research Working Paper 2355, World Bank, Washington, DC.

———. 2002. "On the Incidence of Civil War in Africa." *Journal of Conflict Resolution* 46 (1): 13–28.

————. 2004. "Greed and Grievance in Civil War." *Oxford Economic Papers* 56(4) October: 563–95.

————. 2006. "Military Expenditure in Post Conflict Societies." *Economics of Governance*, vol. 7, no. 1. 88–107.

Collier, Paul, Anke Hoeffler, and Catherine Pattillo. 1999. "Flight Capital as a Portfolio Choice." Policy Research Working Paper 2066, World Bank, Washington, DC. http://ssrn.com/abstract=569197.

Collier, Paul, and Stephen A. O'Connell. 2006. "Opportunities and Choices." Draft Chapter 2 of the synthesis volume of the African Economic Research Consortium's Explaining African Economic Growth project.

Collins, Susan M., and Barry P. Bosworth. 1996. "Economic Growth in East Asia: Accumulation versus Assimilation." *Brookings Papers on Economic Activity* 2: 135–203.

Cramer, Chris. 1999. "The Economics and Political Economy of Conflict in Sub-Saharan Africa." CDPR Discussion Paper 1099, School of Oriental and African Studies, University of London.

Daumont, Roland, Francoise Legall, and François Leroux. 2004. "Banking in Sub-Saharan Africa: What Went Wrong?" Working Paper 04/55, International Monetary Fund, Washington, DC.

Deaton, A. S. 1992. "Saving and Income Smoothing in Côte d'Ivoire." *Journal of African Economies* 1 (1): 1–24.

Dehn, Jan. 2000. "Commodity Price Uncertainty and Shocks: Implications for Investment and Growth." PhD dissertation, 232, Oxford University.

Devarajan, Shantayanan, Margaret J. Miller, and Eric V. Swanson. 2002. "Goals for Development: History, Prospects and Costs." Policy Research Working Paper 2819, World Bank, Washington, DC.

Dick, Astrid. 1999. "Banking Spreads in Central America: Evolution, Structure and Behavior." Development Discussion Paper 694, Harvard Institute for International Development, Cambridge, MA.

Easterly, William. 2001. Global Development Network Growth Database (GDN 1998). World Bank, Washington, DC.

Easterly, William, Michael Kremer, Lant Pritchett, and Lawrence Summers. 1993. "Good Policy or Good Luck?" *Journal of Monetary Economics* 32 (3): 459–83.

Easterly, W., and Ross Levine. 1997. "Africa's Growth Tragedy: Policies and Ethnic Divisions." *Quarterly Journal of Economics* 112 (4) November: 1203–50.

————. 1998. "Troubles with the Neighbours: Africa's Problem, Africa's Opportunity." *Journal of African Economies* 7 (1): 120–42.

————. 2003. "Tropics, Germs, and Crops: The Role of Endowments in Economic Development." *Journal of Monetary Economics* 50 (January): 1.

Easterly, William, Ross Levine,and David Roodman. 2004. "Aid, Policies, and

Growth: Comment," *American Economic Review*, American Economic Association, vol. 94(30):774-780, June.

Eatwell, J. 1996. *Global Unemployment Loss of Jobs in the 90s*. New York: M. E. Sharpe.

Economic Commission for Africa. 2000. "Finance and Development in Africa." Issues Paper for the Eighth Session of the ECA Conference of Ministers of Finance, Addis Ababa, November 21.

Edwards, Sebastian. 2001 "Information Technology and Economic Growth in the Emerging Economies." http://www.anderson.ucla.edu/faculty/sebastian .edwards/.

Edwards, S., and Henry Ford. 2001. "Information Technology and Economic Growth in the Emerging Economies." Unpublished manuscript.

Eifert, Benn, Alan Gelb, and Vijaya Ramachandran. 2005. "Business Environment and Comparative Advantage in Africa: Evidence from the Investment Climate Data." Working Paper 56, Center for Global Development, Washington, DC.

Elbadawi, Ibrahim, Taye Mengistae, and Albert Zeufack. 2002. "Geography, Supplier Access, Foreign Market Potential, and Manufacturing Exports in Developing Countries: An Analysis of Firm Level Data." Policy Research Working Paper, World Bank, Washington DC. http://www.csae.ox.ac.uk/conferences/ 2001NIRaFBiA/ PDFS/elbadawi_meg_zeu.pdf.

Elbadawi, Ibrahim, and F. Mwega. 2000. "Can Africa's Saving Collapse Be Reversed?" *World Bank Economic Review* 14 (3): 415–43.

Elbadawi, Ibrahim, and N. Sambanis. 2000. "Why Are There So Many Civil Wars in Africa?" *Journal of African Economies* 9 (3): 244–69.

Ersado, Lire, Jeffrey Alwang, and Harold Alderman. 2000. "Changes in Consumption and Saving Behavior Before and After Economic Shocks: Evidence from Zimbabwe." Paper Presented at the International Food and Agribusiness Management Association Conference, Chicago, IL, June 25.

Esfahani, Hadi Salehi, and Maria Teresa Ramirez. 2003. "Institutions, Infrastructure and Economic Growth." *Journal of Development Economics* 70 (2): 443–77.

Estache, Antonio. 2004. "Emerging Infrastructure Policy Issues in Developing Countries—A Survey of the Recent Economic Literature." Policy Research Working Paper 3442, World Bank, Washington, DC.

———. 2005. "PPI Partnerships vs. PPI Divorces in LDCs." Policy Research Working Paper 3470, World Bank, Washington, DC.

———. 2006. "Infrastructure: A Survey of Recent and Upcoming Issues." Paper presented to the ABCDE Conference, Tokyo, May 29.

Estache, Antonio, and Ana Goicoechea. 2005. "How Widespread Were Private Investment and Regulatory Reform in Infrastructure Utilities during the 1990s?" Policy Research Working Paper 3595, World Bank, Washington, DC.

Estache, Antonio, Ana Goicoechea, and Marco Manacorda. 2006. "Telecommunications Performance, Reforms, and Governance." Policy Research Working Paper 3822, World Bank, Washington, DC.

Estache, Antonio, and M. E. Pinglo. 2004. "Are Returns to Public-Private Infrastructure Partnerships in Developing Countries Consistent with Risks since the Asian Crisis?" Policy Research Working Paper 3373, World Bank, Washington, DC.

Faber, M. 1997. "Botswana's Somnolent Giant: The Public Debt Service Fund—Its Past, Present and Possible Future." In *Aspects of the Botswana Economy: Selected Papers*, ed. J. S. Salkin et al. Oxford, UK: James Curry.

Fafchamps, Marcel. 2004. *Market Institutions in Sub-Saharan Africa.* Cambridge, MA: MIT Press.

Fay, Marianne, and Tito Yepes. 2003. "Investing in Infrastructure: What Is Needed from 2000 to 2010?" Policy Research Working Paper 3102, World Bank, Washington, DC.

FinScope. 2005. "Botswana, Namibia, Lesotho, and Swaziland Pilots." www.finscope. co.za.

Fisman, Raymond J., and Roberta Gatti. 2000. "Decentralization and Corruption: Evidence across Countries." Policy Research Working Paper 2290, World Bank, Washington, DC. http://ssrn.com/abstract=629144.

Fjeldstad, Odd-Helge, and Lise Rakner. 2003. "Taxation and Tax Reforms in Developing Countries: Illustrations from Sub-Saharan Africa." Paper Presented at a seminar organized by the Norwegian Agency for Development Co-operation, Oslo, April 24, 2003.

Fofack, Hippolyte. 2005. "Nonperforming Loans in Sub-Saharan Africa: Causal Analysis and Macroeconomic Implications." Policy Research Working Paper 3769, World Bank, Washington, DC.

Foroutan, Faezeh, and Lant Pritchett. 1993. "Intra-Sub-Saharan African Trade: Is It Too Little?" *Journal of African Economies* 2 (1) May: 74–105.

Frankel, Jeffrey A., and David Romer. 1999. "Does Trade Cause Growth?" *American Economic Review* 89 (3) June: 379–99.

Fraser, Ashley, Russell Green, and Megan Dunbar. 2002. "Costing Cairo: An Annotated Bibliography of the Cost Literature on ICPD Programme of Action Components in Sub-Saharan Africa." Bay Area International Group, University of California, Berkeley, CA.

Freeman, C. 1991. "Networks of Innovators: A Synthesis of Research Issues." *Research Policy* 20: 499–514.

Gallup, John Luke, Jeffrey D. Sachs, and Andrew Mellinger. 1999. "Geography and Economic Development." In *Annual World Bank Conference on Development Economics 1998*, ed. Boris Plescovic and Joseph E. Stiglitz. Washington, DC: World Bank.

Gatti, Roberta. 1999. "Corruption and Trade Tariffs, or a Case for Uniform Tariffs." Unpublished manuscript.

Gelb, Alan. 2000. *Can Africa Claim the 21st Century?* Washington, DC: World Bank.

————. 2006. "Costs and Competitiveness in Africa." PSD Forum June 2006, World Bank, Washington, DC. http://rru.worldbank.org/Documents/ PSDForum/2006/alan_gelb.pdf.

Gelb, Alan, et al. 2007. "What Matters to African Firms? Evidence from the Investment Climate Surveys." Unpublished manuscript.

Glaeser, E, R. La Porta, F. Lopez-de-Silanes, and A. Shleifer. 2004. "Explaining Growth: Institutions, Human Capital, and Leaders." Paper presented at the Brookings Panel, March 2004.

Gleditsch, Nils Petter, Peter Wallensteen, Mikael Eriksson, Margareta Sollenberg, and Håvard Strand. 2002. "Armed Conflict 1946–2001: A New Dataset." *Journal of Peace Research* 39 (5): 615–37.

Government of Zambia. 2006. "Public Financial Management Performance Report and Performance Indicators." Lusaka, Zambia.

Guillaumont, Patrick, Sylviane Guillaumont Jeanneney, and Jean-Francois Brun. 1999. "How Instability Lowers African Growth." *Journal of African Economies* 8(1) March: 87–107.

Gupta, Sanjeev, Robert Powell, and Yongzheng Yang. 2005. "The Macroeconomic Challenges of Scaling Up Aid to Africa." Working Paper 054/179, International Monetary Fund, Washington, DC.

Haddad, Lawrence James, Harold Alderman, Simon Appleton, Lina Song, and Yisehac Yohannes. 2002. "Reducing Child Undernutrition: How Far Does Income Growth Take Us?" FCND Discussion Paper 137, International Food Policy Research Institute, Washington, DC.

Hall, Robert J., and Robert Jones. 1999. "Why Do Some Countries Produce So Much More Output Than Others?" *Quarterly Journal of Economics* 114 (1): 83–116.

Hamdok, A. 2002. "Governance and Policy in Africa: Recent Experiences." In *Reforming Africa's Institutions: Ownership, Incentives and Capabilities*, ed. Steve Kayizi-Mugerwa. Tokyo, Japan: United Nations University Press.

Hanushek, Eric A., and Dongwook Kim. 1995. "Schooling, Labor Force Quality, and Economic Growth." Working Paper 5399, National Bureau of Economic Research, Cambridge, MA.

Haque, Nadeem Ul, and M. Ali Khan. 1997. "Institutional Development: Skill Transference through a Reversal of 'Human Capital Flight' or Technical Assistance." Working Paper 97/89, International Monetary Fund, Washington, DC.

Haque, Ul. N., and J. Aziz. 1998. "The Quality of Governance: 'Second–Generation' Civil Service Reform in Africa." Working Paper 164, International Monetary Fund, Washington, DC.

Hejazi, W., and E. Safarian. 1999. "Trade, Foreign Direct Investment, and R&D Spillovers." *Journal of International Business Studies* 30: 491–511.

Heston, Alan, Robert Summers, and Bettina Aten. 2002. "Penn World Table Version 6.1." Center for International Comparisons at the University of Pennsylvania (CICUP).

Ho, Kong Weng, and Hian Teck Hoon. 2006. "Growth Accounting for a Follower-Economy in World Ideas: The Example of Singapore." Working Paper 15-2006, Singapore Management University, Singapore.

Hoeffler, A. 1999/2000. "The Augmented Solow Model and the African Growth Debate." Centre for the Study of African Economies, University of Oxford. Background paper, revised April 2000.

Honohan, Patrick, and Thorsten Beck. 2006. *Making Finance Work for Africa.* Washington, DC: World Bank.

Iimi, Atsushi. 2006. "Did Botswana Escape from the Resource Curse?" Working Paper 06/138, International Monetary Fund, Washington, DC.

Ikhide, S. 1996. "Commercial Bank Offices and the Mobilization of Private Savings in Selected Sub-Saharan African Countries." *Journal of Development Studies* 33 (1).

IMF. 2005. Economic Data Sharing System (EDSS). International Monetary Fund, Washington, DC.

Inter Press News Agency. September 19, 2006. "Health Africa: There Hasn't Been Adequate Emphasis on Family Planning." Inter Press News Agency. http://ipsnews.net.

Ishikawa, S. 2006. "Comments on the World Bank's New Growth Strategies for Sub-Saharan Africa." Professor Emeritus, Hitotsubashi University, Tokyo.

Jones, B. F., and B. A. Olken. 2004. "Do Leaders Matter? National Leadership and Growth since World War II." Working Paper, Harvard University, Cambridge, MA.

Jorgenson, Dale W. 2001. "Information Technology and the U.S. Economy." *American Economic Review* 91 (1) March: 1–32.

Jorgenson, Dale W., and Kevin Stiroh. 1999. "Information Technology and Growth." *American Economic Review* 89 (2): 109–115.

Juma, Calestous. 2006. "Reinventing Growth." In *Going for Growth: Science, Technology and Innovation in Africa,* ed. Calestous Juma. London: The Smith Institute.

Kahn, Qaiser, Yaniv Stopnitzky, and Syed Rashed El Zayed. 2006. "Reaping the benefits of Girls' Secondary Education in Bangladesh—Impact on Fertility and Malnutrition." Presentation at the World Bank, Washington, DC, July.

Kelly, Roger, and George Mavrotas. 2003. "Savings and Financial Sector Development: Panel Cointegration Evidence from Africa." Discussion Paper 2003/12, World Institute for Economics Development Research, Helsinki.

Kirsten, M. 2006. "Policy Initiatives to Expand Financial Outreach in South Africa." Paper Prepared for the World Bank/Brookings Institute Conference, Washington, DC, May 30–31.

Knack, Stephen, and Philip Keefer. 1995. "Institutions and Economic Performance: Cross-Country Tests Using Alternative Institutional Measures." *Economics and Politics* 7 (3): 207–28.

Knippenberg, Rudolf, Fatoumata Traore Nafo, Raimi Osseni, Yero Boye Camara, Abdelwahid El Abassi, and Agnes Soucat. 2003. "Increasing Clients' Power to Scale Up Health Services for the Poor: The Bamako Initiative in West Africa." Background paper to the *World Development Report*, World Bank, Washington, DC.

Lacina, B., and N. P. Gleditsch. 2005. "Monitoring Trends in Global Combat: A New Dataset of Battle Deaths." *European Journal of Population* 21: 145–66.

Lall, S. 2000. "Technological Change and Industrialization in the Asian Newly Industrializing Economies: Achievements and Challenges." In *Technology, Learning and Innovation. Experiences of Newly Industrializing Economies*, ed. L. Kim and R. R. Nelson. Cambridge, UK: Cambridge University Press.

Lawson, A., P. de Renzio, and Mariam Umarji. 2006. "Final Report on the Current Status of PFM Systems and Processes, Overview of Reforms and Perspectives for 2006." ODI and SAL Consultoria e Investimentos Lda., London and Maputo.

Levine, Ross, and David Renelt. (1993). "A Sensitivity Analysis of Cross-Country Growth Regressions." *American Economic Review* 82 (4): 942–63.

Levy, Brian, and Sahr Kpundeh. 2004. *Building State Capacity in Africa: New Approaches, Emerging Lessons*. Washington, DC: World Bank.

Limao, Nuno, and Anthony J. Venables. 2001. "Infrastructure, Geographical Disadvantage and Transport Costs and Trade." *World Bank Economic Review* 15: 451–79.

Lindbaek, J. 1997. "Emerging Economies: How Long Will the Low-Wage Advantage Last?" Background paper for a speech by IFC Executive Vice President at the APPI Meeting, Helsinki, Finland, October.

Loayza, Norman, Klaus Schmidt-Hebbel, and Luis Serven. 2000. "What Drives Private Savings across the World?" *Review of Economics and Statistics* 82 (2) May: 165–81.

Lopez, Humberto, and Quentin Wodon. 2005. "The Economic Impact of Armed Conflict in Rwanda." *Journal of African Economies* 14 (4): 586–602.

Lorrain, D. 1999. "Ten Years of Public Utility Reforms: 7 Lessons from Privatization to Public-Private Partnership." In *Financing of Major Infrastructure and Public Service Projects*, ed. J. Y. Perrot and G. Chatelus, 31–40.

Lucas, Jr., Robert E. 2003. "The Industrial Revolution: Past and Future." In *Federal Reserve Bank of Minneapolis, Annual Report*. Minneapolis, MN.

Luckham, Robin, et al. 2001. "Conflict and Poverty in Sub-Saharan Africa: An Assessment of the Issues and Evidence." Working Paper 128, Institute of Development Studies, Brighton, UK.

Lumbila, K. N. 2005. "What Makes DFI Work? A Panel Analysis of the Growth Effects of FDI in Africa." African Region Working Paper 80, World Bank, Washington, DC.

Maddison, Angus. 2001. *The World Economy: Historical Statistics*. Paris: Organisation for Economic Co-operation and Development.

Maimbo, S. M., and George Mavrotas. 2003. "Financial Sector Reforms and Savings Mobilization in Zambia." Discussion Paper 2003/13, World Institute for Economics Development Research, Helsinki.

Maipose, Gervase S., and Thalepo C. Matsheka. 2006. "The Indigenous Developmental State and Growth in Botswana." Draft Chapter 15 of the synthesis volume 2 of the African Economic Research Consortium's Explaining African Economic Growth project.

Mansuri, G., and V. Rao. 2003 "Evaluating Community Driven Development: A Review of the Evidence." Policy Research Working Paper 3209, World Bank, Washington, DC.

Masters, William, and Margaret S. McMillan. 2001. "Climate, Scale and Economic Growth." *Journal of Economic Growth* 6 (3).

Mauro, P. 1995. "Corruption and Growth." *Quarterly Journal of Economics* 110 (3): 681–712.

Mengistae, Taye. 2001. "Indigenous Ethnicity and Entrepreneurial Success in Africa: Some Evidence from Ethiopia." Policy Research Working Paper 2534, World Bank, Washington, DC.

Mengistae, Taye, and Catherine Pattillo. 2004. "Export Orientation and Productivity in Sub-Saharan Africa." *IMF Staff Papers* 51 (2): 6.

Messick, Richard. 2004. "Judicial Reform and Economic Growth: What a Decade of Experience Teaches." Presented at "A Liberal Agenda for the New Century: A Global Perspective," a conference cosponsored by the Cato Institute, the Institute of Economic Analysis, and the Russian Union of Industrialists and Entrepreneurs, Moscow, April 8–9.

Miguel, E. 2004. "Tribe or Nation? Nation-Building and Public Goods in Kenya versus Tanzania." *World Politics* 56 April: 327–62.

Milanovic, Branko. 2005. "Why Did the Poorest Countries Fail to Catch Up?" Carnegie Paper 62, Carnegie Endowment for International Peace, Washington, DC.

Mkandawire, T., and C. C. Soludo. 1999. *Our Continent, Our Future: African Perspectives on Structural Adjustment*. Trenton, NJ: Africa World Press.

Monetary Research International. 2001-04. *MRI Bankers' Guide to Foreign Currency.* Houston: Monetary Research International.

Mwanawina, Inyambo, and James Mukungushi. 2006. "Zambia." Draft Chapter 27 of the synthesis volume 2 of the African Economic Research Consortium's Explaining African Economic Growth project.

Mwega, F. 1997. "Saving in Sub-Saharan Africa: A Comparative Analysis." *Journal of African Economies* 6 (3) Supplement: 199–228.

Ndulu, Benno J. 2006a. "The Evolution of Global Development Paradigms and Their Influence on African Economic Growth." Draft Chapter 9 of the synthesis volume of the African Economic Research Consortium's Explaining African Economic Growth project.

———. 2006b. "Infrastructure, Regional Integration and Growth in Sub-Saharan Africa: Dealing with the Disadvantages of Geography and Sovereign Fragmentation." *Journal of African Economies* 15 December: 212–44.

Ndulu, Benno J., and Stephen A. O'Connell. 2003. "Revised Collins/Bosworth Growth Accounting Decompositions." Explaining African Economic Growth project, African Economic Research Consortium, Nairobi, Kenya.

———. 2006a. "Policy Plus: African Growth Performance 1960–2000." Draft Chapter 1 of the synthesis volume of the African Economic Research Consortium's Explaining African Economic Growth project.

———. 2006b. "The African Development Challenge from a Global Perspective." Draft.

Ndung'u, Njuguna S., and Rose W. Ngugi. 2000. "Banking Sector Interest Rate Spread in Kenya." Discussion Paper 5, Kenya Institute for Public Policy Research and Analysis, Nairobi.

Nordhaus, William D. 2001. "New Data and Output Concepts for Understanding Productivity Trends." Working Papers 8097, National Bureau of Economic Research, Cambridge, MA.

O'Connell, Stephen A., and Benno J. Ndulu. 2000. "Explaining African Economic Growth: A Focus on Sources of Growth." Working Paper Series, African Economic Research Consortium, Nairobi.

Pindyck, Robert S., and Andres Solimano. 1993. "Economic Instability and Aggregate Investment." Working Paper W4380, National Bureau of Economic Research, Cambridge, MA.

Porter, Michael E. 1990. *The Competitiveness of Nations*. New York: Free Press.

Porter, Michael E., Klaus Schwab, and Augusto Lopez-Claros, eds. 2006. *The Global Competitiveness Report 2006–2007*. New York: PalgraveMacmillan.

Pritchett, Lant. 1994. "Desired Fertility and the Impact of Population Policies." *Population and Development Review* 20 (1).

———. 1998. "Patterns of Economic Growth: Hills, Plateaus, Mountains, and Plains." Policy Research Working Paper 1947, World Bank, Washington, DC.

Pritchett, Lant, and Michael Woolcock. 2002. "Solutions When *the* Solution Is the Problem: Arraying the Disarray in Development." Paper presented at Kennedy School of Government, Harvard University, Cambridge, MA, April 1.

Quartey, P. 2006. "Shared Growth in Ghana: Do Migrant Remittances Have a Role?" Paper prepared for the Cornell/ISSER/World Bank International Conference on Shared Growth in Africa, Accra, July 21–22, 2005.

Ramachandran, Vijaya, and Manju Kedia Shah. 2006. "Why Are There So Few Black-Owned Businesses in Africa?" Unpublished manuscript.

Ramachandran, Vijaya, Gaiv Tata, and Manju Kedia Shah. 2006. "The Challenge of Growth in the African Private Sector." Manuscript.

Rau, Neren. 2004. "Financial Intermediation and Access to Finance in African Countries South of the Sahara." Africa Development and Poverty Reduction Forum Paper, Cornell University, Ithaca, NY.

Ravallion, Martin. 2001. "Growth, Inequality, and Poverty: Looking Beyond Averages." *World Development* 29 (11): 1803–15.

Reinikka, Ritva, and Paul Collier, eds. 2001. *Uganda's Recovery: The Role of Farms, Firms, and Government.* Washington, DC: World Bank.

Rodrik, Dani. 1998a. "Globalisation, Social Conflict and Economic Growth." *World Economy* 21 (2): 143.

———. 1998b. "Where Did All the Growth Go? External Shocks, Social Conflict, and Growth Collapses." Draft, John F. Kennedy School of Government, Harvard University, Cambridge, MA, August.

———, ed. 2003. *In Search of Prosperity: Analytic Narratives on Economic Growth.* Princeton, NJ: Princeton University Press.

———. 2004. "Industrial Policy for the Twenty-First Century." Discussion Paper 4767, Center for Economic and Policy Research, London, UK.

Rodrik, Dani, and Arvind Subramanian. 2004. "From 'Hindu Growth' to Productivity Surge: The Mystery of the Indian Growth Transition." CEPR Discussion Paper 4371, Center for Economic and Policy Research, London, UK.

Rojas-Suarez, and Steven R. Weisbrod. 1996. "Financial Markets and the Behavior of Private Savings in Latin America." Paper presented at the International Development Bank–Organisation for Economic Co-operation and Development Conference on Promoting Savings in Latin America, Paris, November 7–8.

Roy, Amit. 2006. "Africa Fertilizer Crisis: Summit Background and Process." Presented at the Technical Session: High-Level Dialogue, Africa Fertilizer Summit, Abuja, Nigeria, June 9.

Ruttan, Vernon W. 2001. *Technology, Growth, and Development.* New York: Oxford University Press.

Sacerdoti, Emilio. 2005. "Access to Bank Credit in Sub-Saharan Africa: Key Issues and Reform Strategies." Working Paper 05/166, International Monetary Fund, Washington, DC.

Sachs, Jeffrey D., John W. McArthur, Guido Schmidt-Traub, Margaret Kruk, Chandrika Bahadur, Michael Faye, and Gordon McCord. 2004. "Ending Africa's Poverty Trap." *Brookings Papers on Economic Activity* 1: 117–216.

Sachs, Jeffrey D., and Andrew Warner. 1995. "Economic Reform and the Process of Global Integration." *Brookings Papers on Economic Activity* 1: 1–95.

———. 1997. "Sources of Slow Growth in African Economies." *Journal of African Economies* 6 (3): 335–76.

———. 2001. "The Curse of Natural Resources." *European Economic Review* 45 (4–6): 827–38.

Sala-i-Martin, Xavier, Gernot Doppelhofer, and Ronald I. Miller. 2004. "Determinants of Long-Term Growth: A Bayesian Averaging of Classical Estimates (BACE) Approach." *American Economic Review* 94 (4): 813–35.

Solo, Tova Maria, and Astrid Manroth. 2006. "Access to Financial Services in Colombia: The Unbanked in Bogota." Policy Research Working Paper 3834, World Bank, Washington, DC.

Stotsky, J. G., and Asegedech WoldeMariam. 1997. "Tax Effort in Sub-Saharan Africa." Working Paper 97/107, International Monetary Fund, Washington, DC.

Subramanian, Arvind. 2001. "Mauritius: A Case Study." *Finance and Development* 38 (4).

Syrquin, M., and H. Chenery. 1989. "Three Decades of Industrialization." *World Bank Economic Review* 3: 145–81.

Tangri, Roger. 1999. *The Politics of Patronage in Africa*. Trenton, NJ: Africa World Press.

Tanzi, Vito, and Howell Zee. 2001. "Tax Policy for Developing Countries." *IMF Economic Issues* 27, International Monetary Fund, Washington, DC.

Temple, Jonathan. 1999. "The New Growth Evidence." *Journal of Economic Literature* 37 (1): 112–156.

Timmer, C. Peter. 2003. "Food Security and Rice Price Policy in Indonesia: The Economics and Politics of the Food Price Dilemma." In *Rice Science: Innovations and Impact for Livelihood*, ed. T. W. Mew, D. S. Brar, S. Peng, D. Dawe, and B. Hardy. Proceedings of the International Rice Research Conference, Beijing, September 16–19, 2002.

UNAIDS (Joint United Nations Programme on HIV/AIDS). 2006. *Report on the Global Aids Epidemic*. New York: UNAIDS.

UNCTAD (United Nations Conference on Trade and Development). 2000. "Capital Flows and Growth in Africa." UNCTAD, Geneva.

United Nations Statistical Division. 2006. United Nations Common Database (UNCDB). United Nations, New York.

Utz, Anuja. 2006. "Fostering Innovation, Productivity and Technological Change: Tanzania in the Knowledge Economy." Discussion Paper, World Bank Institute, Washington, DC.

Valverde, S., R Lopez del Paso, and F. Fernandez. 2004. "Banks, Financial Regional Growth." Unpublished manuscript. Department of Economics, University of Granada, Spain.

Van Biesebroeck, Johannes. 2005. "Firm Size Matters: Growth and Productivity in African Manufacturing." *Economic Development and Cultural Change* 53:545–83.

Versi, Anver. 2006. "Fertilizers—Food for a Hungry Earth, Africa Launches Green Revolution." *African Business* December: 18.

Vishny, R., and A. Shleifer. 1993. "Corruption." *Quarterly Journal of Economics* 108 (3): 599–617.

Wade, James. 1993. "Dynamics of Organizational Communities and Technological Bandwagons: An Empirical Investigation of Community Evolution in the Microprocessor Market." Proceedings of the Eighth Annual Texas Organizations Conference, University of Texas at Austin, April 1993, 124–28.

Washington Post. October 3, 2006. "New Conductors Speed Global Flows of Money." The *Washington Post,* Washington, DC.

WEF (World Economic Forum). 2006. *Global Competitiveness Report, 2005–2006.* New York: Oxford University Press.

Wellenius, Bjorn, Vivien Foster, and Christina Malmberg-Calvo. 2004. "Private Provision of Rural Infrastructure Services—Competing for Subsidies." Policy Research Working Paper 3365, World Bank, Washington, DC.

Westoff, C., and A. Bankole. 2000. "Trends in the Demand for Family Limitation in Developing Countries." *International Family Planning Perspectives* 26 (2).

Wooldridge, Jeffrey M. 2003. *Introductory Econometrics: A Modern Approach.* Mason, OH: Thompson South-Western.

World Bank. 1981. *Accelerated Development in Sub-Saharan Africa: An Agenda for Action.* Washington, DC: World Bank.

————. 2000a. *Can Africa Claim the Twenty-First Century?* Washington, DC: World Bank.

————. 2000b. *World Development Report.* Washington, DC: World Bank.

————. 2001. *Global Economic Prospects, 2001.* Washington, DC: World Bank.

————. 2003. "Project Overview, Southern Africa Regional Gas Project (SASOL)." World Bank, Washington, DC.

————. 2004a. *Investment Climate Assessment: Improving Enterprise Performance and Growth in Tanzania.* Washington, DC: World Bank.

————. 2004b. *World Development Report.* Washington, DC: World Bank.

————. 2005a. "Building Effective States, Forging Engaged Societies." Report of the World Bank Task Force on Capacity Development in Africa, World Bank, Washington, DC.

————. 2005b. "Capacity Building in Africa." An Operations Evaluation Department Evaluation of World Bank Support, World Bank, Washington, DC.

————. 2005c. *Doing Business in 2006.* Washington, DC: World Bank.

————. 2005d. *Economic Growth in the 1990s: Learning from a Decade of Reform.* Washington, DC: World Bank.

————. 2005e. "Meeting the Challenges of Africa's Development: A World Bank Group Action Plan." Africa Region, World Bank, Washington, DC.

————. 2005f. *World Development Report.* Washington, DC: World Bank.

————. 2006a. "Capturing the Demographic Bonus in Ethiopia: The Role of Gender Equitable Development and Demographic Actions." Country Department for Ethiopia, World Bank, Washington, DC.

————. 2006b. *Doing Business in 2007: How to Reform.* Washington, DC: World Bank.

————. 2006c. World Development Indicators. World Bank, Washington, DC.

————. 2006d. *World Development Report.* Washington, DC: World Bank.

————. 2007. Private Particpation in Infrastructure Database. World Bank, Washington, DC.

Wormser, Michel. 2004. "FPSI's Role in Alleviating Poverty and Promoting Growth in Africa." Draft.

Yeats, Alexander, and Francis Ng. 1997. "Open Economies Work Better! Did Africa's Protectionist Policies Cause Its Marginalization in World Trade?" *World Development* 25 (6).

Yusuf, Shahid. 2003. *Innovative East Asia: The Future of Growth.* Washington, DC: World Bank.

Zagha, Roberto. 2005. "Economic Growth in the 1990s: Learning from a Decade of Reform." World Bank, Washington, DC. http://www1.worldbank.org/prem/lessons1990s/.

Zeleza, P. T. 1998. *African Labor and Intellectual Migrations to the North: Building New Transatlantic Bridges.* Urbana, IL: Center for the Studies of African Studies, University of Illinois at Urbana-Champaign.

Index

ECO-AUDIT
Environmental Benefits Statement

The World Bank is committed to preserving endangered forests and natural resources. The Office of the Publisher has chosen to print *Challenges of African Growth* on 50% recycled paper including 30% post-consumer recycled fiber in accordance with the recommended standards for paper usage set by the Green Press Initiative, a nonprofit program supporting publishers in using fiber that is not sourced from endangered forests. For more information, visit www.greenpressinitiative.org.

Saved:

- 4 trees
- 396 lbs. of solid waste
- 786 gallons of water
- 632 lbs. of net greenhouse gases
- 5 million BTUs of total energy